Praise for books by Graham

Great Australian Journeys

'Readers familiar with Gra ... ne finds and writes ripper, fair-dinku ... ussie yarns. His books are great reads and do a lot for ensuring cultural stories are not lost. His new book, *Great Australian Journeys*, is no exception.' —*The Weekly Times*

'Epic tales of exploration, survival, tragedy, romance, mystery, discovery and loss come together in this intriguing collection of some of Australia's most dramatic journeys from the 19th and early 20th century.'—*Vacations and Travel*

Great Australian Stories

'The pleasure of this book is in its ability to give a fair dinkum insight into the richness of Australian story telling.'—*The Weekly Times*

'. . . a treasure trove of material from our nation's historical past . . . you don't have to be Australian to enjoy it, but it helps.' —*Courier Mail*

'This book is a little island of Aussie culture—one to enjoy.' —*Sunshine Coast Sunday*

The Savage Shore

'A fascinating, entertainingly written, voyage on what have often been rough and murky seas'—*Daily Telegraph*

'Colourful stories about the spirit of navigation and exploration, and of courageous and miserable adventures at sea.'—*National Geographic*

'. . . a gripping account of danger at sea, dramatic shipwrecks, courageous castaways, murder, much missing gold, and terrible loss of life'—*Queensland Times*

'Collected tales of exploration, epic journeys, shipwrecks, conflict and amazing survival'—*Sydney Morning Herald*

Larrikins, Bush Tales and Other Great Australian Stories

'. . . another collection of yarns, tall tales, bush legends and colourful characters . . . from one of our master storytellers' —*Queensland Times*

Great Anzac Stories

'. . . allows you to feel as if you are there in the trenches with them.'—*The Weekly Times*

'They are pithy short pieces, absolutely ideal for reading when you are pushed for time, but they are stories you will remember for much longer than you would expect.'—*Ballarat Courier*

GREAT *Australian* JOURNEYS

Gripping stories of intrepid explorers, dramatic escapes and foolhardy adventures

GRAHAM SEAL

This edition published 2018
First published in 2016

Allen & Unwin
83 Alexander Street
Crows Nest NSW 2065
Australia
Phone: (61 2) 8425 0100
Email: info@allenandunwin.com
Web: www.allenandunwin.com

Cataloguing-in-Publication details are available
from the National Library of Australia
www.trove.nla.gov.au

ISBN 978 1 76063 097 3

Set in Sabon by Midland Typesetters, Australia
Printed and bound in Australia by SOS Print + Media Group

10 9 8 7 6 5 4 3 2 1

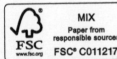

The paper in this book is FSC® certified. FSC® promotes environmentally responsible, socially beneficial and economically viable management of the world's forests.

CONTENTS

FOREWORD

Graham Seal's book of Australian journeys covers a lot of ground. One minute the reader is travelling in a convict ship with Christopher Tomlinson, a mere strip of a lad sentenced to fourteen years' transportation to Botany Bay, and then, a hundred or so years later, aboard the *Dunera* with 2500 refugees escaping Hitler's Nazis. Graham has set out to explore how we have travelled down through the years, how Australians have journeyed.

Much of the Australian treasury of storytelling is bound by tales of great exploration—and it's about time they were placed in the one travel bag. Some journeys, like those of Burke and Wills, Lasseter's First Find, and the razing of the riverboat *Rodney*, are relatively well known. Others, mostly unknown, are tales of bravado, determination and, sometimes, sheer madness. In a land as challenging and wide as Australia it is inevitable that journeying captures much of our imagination and should be the making of great yarns. Graham Seal has the knack of the storyteller and this collection adds another dimension to our endless search for signposts to our national identity.

Warren Fahey AM
Cultural historian

INTRODUCTION

A NOMAD NATION

Australia has long been a land of arrivals and departures. The first peoples travelled constantly around their country, following the movements of game and the seasons. Their stories are full of journeys through the landscape by creation beings that form the land and its natural features.

When others began to arrive here they braved dangerous journeys, whether they were fishermen in search of trepang or abalone from the area we now know as Malaysia, or the first Europeans to journey here from Holland. They were followed by the British and French and perhaps by the Portuguese, to judge by the many legends about wrecks of Portuguese ships along our coasts.

The first Europeans to arrive here braved vast distances in frail craft. A few were cast away on these shores long before the arrival of convicts and their jailers in 1788. They were followed by more transports, then by free migrants, in a long chain of travel that has continued today with the arrival of boat people, refugees and asylum seekers.

Once settlement began, people soon journeyed inland to discover the nature and extent of the continent's interior. Exploration, pioneering and land occupation gradually and unevenly followed and what had once been an unknown southland began to reveal its secrets and its terrors. Was there a vast inland sea? Could the arid land be crossed and conquered? The great journeys of land exploration are a vital part of the modern Australian experience, complemented by equally astonishing journeys of maritime exploration as the shape and size of this vast continent—and that it was, in fact, an island—was gradually confirmed.

Throughout the nineteenth century, people kept arriving in increasing numbers, journeying from all parts of the globe. The largest groups were from Britain, but from the very beginning new arrivals came from many countries, as well as religions, classes and occupations: they were convicts, farmers, merchants, gold diggers, administrators, soldiers, tradespeople and shopkeepers, often arriving with their entire families. Once they landed, many had further journeys to make 'up the country'—to the diggings or even further out. These men and women were often in search of better lives than those they had left behind.

As European settlement spread, the great distances to be covered created a characteristically Australian nonchalance about the time and difficulty often involved in undertaking even relatively short journeys. It was frighteningly easy to perish along dusty tracks, in thick scrub or arid wilderness. Accidents in rivers and creeks, on mountains and at sea, were the frequent end of everyday journeys. But the risks had to be accepted, or perhaps just ignored: the country was wide and people needed to get around it.

And exploration did not stop here. Some sought to found a new Australia in South America. A handful of intrepid Australians journeyed further southwards to the icy unknown of Antarctica and continue to do so today.

Within, around and between all these journeys are woven epic adventures, terrifying ordeals and more than the odd mystery—journeys of the heart, the track, of arrival and departure, of survival, danger and sometimes of tragedy. Together they add up to a picture of a restless nation, a travelling community always ready to move on, move out or take a trip to somewhere else.

•

1

ARRIVING

> So us here is off to New Holland if God will spear our lifes
> All with littel families, hower sweethearts and hower wifes.
>
> Migration song of the Henty family and workers, 1829

THE FIRST JOURNEY

Australia's first journeyers came from the north. They were the descendants of the populations that moved out of Africa perhaps 70,000 years ago. But instead of going north to Europe they went south and lived in Asia, before working further south into Borneo, Java and Papua New Guinea.

Some of those people found their way across the islands, and the seas between, onto the Australian mainland more than fifty thousand years ago. The descendants of these first peoples are now known as Aborigines. They established and evolved a culture rich in mythology, spirituality and creativity that thrived until European settlement, and continues in communities across Australia to this day.

The only way to tell the story of this first journey is to imagine how it might have happened. First people made their way from Asia to islands further south. As they reached one and found it hospitable, they settled. Then, after perhaps a few or many generations, the younger men and women began to look with interest at another island, far away but still tantalisingly visible. What was that yonder island like? If there were people on it, were they like themselves? Perhaps they were dangerous. What about the animals? Could they be hunted for food? Perhaps there were bad spirits of some kind.

The questions must have mounted until some brave souls, probably both men and women, were curious enough—or perhaps desperate enough—to put to sea in whatever craft they had and strike out for the unknown. This final trip across the sea may have been undertaken by many groups over time, from many islands, either by design or perhaps cast away by storms. If they survived the currents and winds, they landed. If they then survived whatever dangers awaited them in that new place, they settled—living, hunting, gathering and having children.

Eventually, this same urge to go beyond spurred a group into a final dangerous sea journey to a very large and very distant island. These travellers landed on the northern shore of what we now call Australia.

Upon arriving they probably followed rivers inland where they would have found plants and animals mostly unlike any they had seen before. These groups eventually split, evolving their own variations on language, customs and beliefs.

We will probably never know exactly who the first Australians were, or exactly where they came from or why. We do know that they came as part of the great waves of humanity that rolled out of Africa time and time again. If these first Australians were indeed descended from the people who first left Africa they would be the oldest humankind outside of Africa itself. And they would have been living, hunting, building, singing, dancing and surviving in Australia millennia before other African groups reached Europe.

They are still here.

FIRST ENCOUNTERS

The first known European visitor arrived on the Cape York Peninsula early in 1606. His name was Willem Jansz, master of the small Dutch East India Company sailing ship *Duyfken*, or Little Dove. The *Duyfken* was a fast and nimble craft, at 110 tons and about twenty metres long and six metres broad. She was lightly armed with eight cannon and probably crewed by fewer than twenty sailors.

The *Duyfken* had sailed from Batavia, now Jakarta, along the coast of New Guinea and then to the unknown southland. Jansz was an experienced Dutch East India Company skipper, probably in his mid thirties. His orders were to search for trading possibilities in New Guinea and any other lands to the east and south. It did not go well.

The log of this voyage has been lost and so what happened is based only on word-of-mouth accounts. These tell us that there was at least one violent encounter between the sailors and the Aborigines. When the *Duyfken* made a landing, probably on the Wenlock River, the crew was attacked by Aborigines and one sailor was speared to death. Jansz may have already, by this time, lost up to half his crew through fights with either Australians or New Guineans.

It is possible that the oral traditions of the Wik people of Cape York Peninsula also hold a clue to what happened in one of these encounters. As the inherited story goes, the devils, as the Dutch sailors are called in these stories, landed and began to dig on the beach. The Aborigines were curious and through sign language discovered that the sailors were digging for water. The Wik people were recruited as labourers to dig wells and also taught to smoke tobacco, bake damper and make tea. But the Wik eventually decided that the Dutch were a nuisance, and probably evil as well. There was a fight during which both Wik people and sailors died, then the Dutch sailed away.

With a severely weakened complement, Jansz got the *Duyfken* back to Batavia. His voyage had been a failure as far as the notoriously hard-to-please masters of the Dutch East India Company were concerned. However, Jansz was the first to chart a section of the Australian coast and so to begin the long process of revealing the southland previously unknown to Europeans.

A BOY TRANSPORTED

When possibly just a ten-year-old boy, Christopher Tomlinson stole a pair of shoes in Preston in 1830. The year before he had received four months' imprisonment and a whipping for a minor offence. But this time he was arrested, tried at the Lancaster Quarter Sessions and given a sentence of fourteen years' transportation to Botany Bay.

Christopher was moved south to foggy London and probably held in one of the rotting ships known as 'hulks' that dotted the Thames. These unpleasant dwellings housed many convicts awaiting transport to Australia. In March 1831, he sailed aboard the *Camden* along with 197 other male convicts. They were guarded by 29 men of the 11th Light Dragoons. A few army officers and their families were also aboard as passengers, bound for service in the colony of New South Wales.

Built in 1799, the *Camden* was a reasonably seaworthy vessel of over 400 tonnes with an experienced master, and a competent surgeon named David Boyter. A few of the prisoners from the hulks had not been fit enough to make the arduous voyage and were left behind as the ship departed. Many of the convicts suffered from leg ulcers from the work they had been made to do in chains on the London docks. Those who left on the *Camden* were mostly young and reasonably fit. At least until the ship reached the open sea—then the surgeon was busy treating his charges for seasickness.

We do not know if Christopher Tomlinson suffered from seasickness or ulcers. Perhaps his youth and diminutive stature might have saved him from hard labour on the wharves, sparing him the ulcers. But we do know that like everyone else aboard the *Camden* he had to cope with life on a cramped transportation ship and the extreme climates through which they passed on their 119-day voyage to the other end of the earth.

As they sailed south the temperature increased far above any experienced in Britain. By the time they neared Tenerife the soldiers were lying out on the deck complaining of headaches, although Boyter suspected that might have more to do with the spirits they were allowed to consume.

After four or so weeks in the warmer latitudes the temperatures began to ease as they continued southwards. Sore throats and coughs featured in Boyter's sick list but no more serious complaints were recorded until about a week out from their destination when the diet of salted meat began to take its toll in the form of scurvy. Fortunately, the *Camden* anchored at Port Jackson on 25 July 1831 with only six of her complement requiring hospitalisation. This, the surgeon's second voyage on a transport, had been mostly untroubled.

Christopher did not appear in Boyter's clinical records or in his list of those injured. His voyage was seemingly uneventful, perhaps even enjoyable. But its aftermath would be very different.

After landing, Christopher was taken to the Hyde Park Barracks along with his fellow prisoners and later transferred to a special program for young offenders at Carters' Barracks. Like most such institutions at the time the authorities tried to instil a firm religious belief in their charges along with basic education and skills in a trade.

This regime was not to Christopher's liking. He tried to run away and received a flogging of 24 lashes. A subsequent attempt to escape with some other boys was again unsuccessful. This time he suffered 36 lashes.

In April 1833, Christopher was arrested for a second time, this time for theft. Between 1837 and 1839 he was imprisoned at Parramatta Gaol. The gaol records describe him as 5 foot 4 and a half inches tall (about 1.6 metres), with a fair and freckled complexion, hazel eyes and a cut on his left arm. After these gaol records, he disappears from colonial history.

What happened to him we do not know. Perhaps, like many other transports he found a good lodging as an assigned servant, worked hard and served his time. He may have joined the thousands of other emancipists who contributed to the foundation of modern Australia. Of course, he may not have been so lucky. Many others met sad or violent ends on the colonial frontier, their deaths unrecorded and mostly unmourned.

ALL HIS JOIFUL CREW

The surprise intersection of two journeys lies behind the foundation of what is now the state of Victoria. In March 1836, the surveyor-general of New South Wales, Major Thomas Mitchell, was intent on following the course of the Murray River from its junction with the Darling. Once he reached this fork, he struck out along the previously uncharted Murray River, moving his large expedition south into what is now known as the Wimmera. He wrote, 'Of this Eden I was the first European to explore its mountains and streams—to behold its scenery—to investigate its geological character . . .'

With five drays, over fifty bullocks, herds of sheep, oxen and horses, and a cart carrying a boat, Mitchell's convoy left such a scar on the land over which it passed that Mitchell's Line was still visible in the ground into the twentieth century. It also left its mark on the indigenous people when the expeditioners killed seven Aborigines at Mount Dispersion.

Towards the end of the year Mitchell and his lumbering troupe reached the coast at Portland Bay, where he believed he was the first European to tread..He was more than surprised when the Aboriginal guide—Tommy Came-last, as he was known—brought him shards of bottle and tobacco pipes. At first he thought they must have been left by passing whalers, but continuing round the bay he saw a brig anchored there and some deserted sealer sheds. Mitchell heard two shots, as he wrote in his journal:

> I then became somewhat apprehensive that the parties might either be, or suppose us to be, bushrangers and, to prevent if possible some such awkward mistake, I ordered a man to fire a gun and the bugle to be sounded; but on reaching the higher ground we discovered not only a beaten path but the track of two carts, and while we were following the latter a man came towards us from the face of the cliffs. He informed me in answer to my questions that the vessel at anchor was the Elizabeth of Launceston; and that just round the point there was a considerable

> farming establishment belonging to Messrs. Henty, who were then at the house.

The Henty family and workers were carrying on a brisk trade in whale oil, livestock imports and selling their abundant farm produce to the whaling ships that frequented the bay. How did an English family come to be farming and whaling on the shores of this unmapped land?

The long journey of the Henty family began in Sussex seven years earlier, in 1829, when Thomas Henty's eldest son, James, and two brothers, their farm workers and a load of livestock, sailed from England for the Swan River aboard the chartered ship *Caroline*. They set out with great optimism. Even their servants were hopeful of a better life. One composed a song for the occasion and wrote it down with some inventive spelling and punctuation that reflected the Sussex accent:

> Come all you English lads that have a mind to go
> Into some foring Conterey I would have you for to know
> Come join along with Henty and all his joiful crew
> For a Set of better fellows in this world you never knew
>
> Coris
> So us here is off to New Holland if God will spear our lifes
> All with littel families, hower sweethearts and hower wifes.

The rest of the song provides the reason for the migration journey: 'Now England [had] got very bad' and food was very expensive. If someone went to their parish for poor relief, as welfare was called in those days, they would be badly treated 'as if [they] weare a thif'. Australia—or New Holland as it was still then known by some—was a promised land, as the final verse explains:

> Now when we come to New Holland, I hope that soon will be
> All will send home to England and how happy there wee be

> With plenty of provishons, boys, and plenty for to do
> So hear is health to Henty and all his joiful crew.

The Hentys and their workers had a massive grant of land waiting for them in the Swan River colony, over thirty-four thousand hectares. But two poor seasons convinced James to transfer to Van Diemen's Land where the rest of the large Henty family, but for one son, had landed in 1832.

Unfortunately, the British government decided that no further grants were to be made in Van Diemen's Land. The Hentys had spent much of their capital in the failed Swan River venture and so were unable to buy land. They looked across the Bass Strait to the virgin coast of what was to become Victoria. After extensive investigation of the area, and in defiance of an official ban on settlement, Edward, the fourth-born of Thomas Henty's sons, sailed with a small party across the strait and simply squatted at Portland Bay in November 1834. Soon after, the Hentys shipped the first Merino sheep from the future colony of Victoria across Bass Strait.

Mitchell found them two years later. The Hentys provided the explorer and his men with flour and 'as many vegetables as the men could carry away on their horses'. Mitchell returned to Sydney covered in glory as the discoverer of an extensive fertile region he called Australia Felix, the fortunate Australia, a name that has not survived in official use. He was able to claim this triumph over the Hentys because he explored the unknown interior while they settled on its edge.

But the travelling Sussex family have the rightful claim to be the first known European settlers in what we now call Victoria. As Edward Henty would recall:

> I stuck a plough into the ground, struck a she-oak root, and broke the point; cleaned my gun, shot a kangaroo, mended the bellows, blew the forge fire, straightened the plough, and turned the first sod in Victoria.

The Henty family at Portland Bay continued to prosper, despite difficulties with the New South Wales government over their title to the land they occupied. By the mid 1840s the Hentys had claimed around 280 square kilometres (70,000 acres) and were breeding Merino sheep, as they had back in England. The difficulties with the government were more or less resolved in 1846 and the Hentys went on to play many significant roles in farming, government and the financial development of the Australian colonies.

ABOUT 600,000 ACRES, MORE OR LESS

The year after the Hentys made their voyage, another pioneer opportunist crossed the Bass Strait from Van Diemen's Land. John Batman's journey ended in the purchase of a large swathe of Wurundjeri country. On this land one of Australia's greatest cities would one day grow.

Batman sailed with his party in late May. After some difficulty, they navigated through the heads of Port Phillip Bay and landed on 29 May.

> We got well into the port about ten o'clock, where the water is very smooth and one of the finest basins of water I ever saw and most extensive. I would not recommend any one to come in until the tide was running in, when the surf is smooth at the mouth. As we were sailing up the port heard a dog on the shore howling; cannot think what brought it there. Just called upon deck to see about 100 geese flying near the vessel; they seemed very large, and flew up the port before us. We anchored in a small bay about 12 miles up the port and went on shore.
>
> Before we got into the boat we saw a dog on the shore. We pulled off and came up to the dog, which proved to be a native dog of N. H., [New Holland] which had surely left the natives within a day or so, as he came quite close to my natives and did not appear at all afraid, but would not allow them to take hold of him. Our dogs, after some time, took after him, and ran him into

> the water, where we shot him. He was a large dog, and much the same I have seen in New South Wales.
>
> We fell in with the tracks of natives which were only a day or two old, also huts on the bay, where they had been eating mussels. It cannot be more than two days back. We then went in the boat about 4 miles, and then passed over some beautiful land and all good sheep country, rather sandy, but the sand black and rich, covered with kangaroo grass about 10 inches high, and as green as a field of wheat. We then went in another direction for about 4 or 5 miles over good sheep land, gentle rises, with wattle and oak with stunted gum. None or very little of this timber would split.

In his journal, Batman continued to extol the beauty and plenty of the country—its forests, plains and wildlife. 'I never saw anything equal to the land in my life,' he noted many times. These features were what Batman hoped to find but he was also searching for the land's people. He found recently occupied huts and the day afterward he sighted smoke from far-off fires. 'I intend to go off to them early in the morning, and get, if possible, on a friendly footing with them, in order to purchase land from them.'

His account continues:

> At daylight this morning we landed to endeavor to meet the natives. We had not proceeded more than 14 miles when we saw the smoke at seven large huts. My natives stripped off and went up to them quite naked. When they got to the huts found that they had left this morning. Then with the natives went round and found their track and the direction they went in. We followed on the track for 10 miles or nearly, when one of my natives saw a black at the distance of a mile. We were at this time spread along. He made a sign to us, and all made in the same direction.
>
> He came up to the person (an old woman), quite a cripple; she had no toes on one foot. We then saw the remainder of the tribe about a mile further on. We made towards them, and got up to them about ten o'clock p.m. They seemed quite pleased with my natives, who could partially understand them. They sang and

danced for them. I found them to be only women and children, 20 of the former and 21 of the latter. The women were all of a small size, and every woman had a child at her back except one who was quite a young woman and very good looking. We understood that the men went up the river. They had four native dogs, and every woman had a load of 60 lb. to 70 lb. on her back, of one thing or another. Each had two or three baskets, net bags, native tomahawks, bones, &c. I found in one of the net bags a part of a strake of a cart wheel, which had two nail holes in. They had ground it down to a sharp edge and put it in a stick to cut with as a tomahawk. They had also several pieces of iron hoop ground sharp to cut with, several wooden buckets to carry water in. They had some water with them which was very bad.

They came back with us where I had some blankets, looking glasses, beads, handkerchiefs, sugar. I gave them 5 pairs of blankets, 30 handkerchiefs, 1 tomahawk, 18 necklaces of beads, 6 lb. of sugar, 12 looking glasses, a quantity of apples, which they seemed well pleased with; they then went off again. I promised to see them again to-morrow. The young woman who I have spoken of before gave me a very handsome basket of her own make, other women gave me two others . . .

The children were good looking, and of a healthy appearance. They were greatly affrighted by the discharge of a gun, and all of them dropped down immediately. I think they never heard the report or saw a man before.

Over the next six days, Batman and his party traversed the new land using their ship as a base. At every turn Batman found something new to praise—the bird life, the soil, the views. He busied himself naming mountains and other natural features after acquaintances, his wife and himself. He also found elaborate stone fish traps in the river as well as the remains of a large unknown creature.

On 6 June, they had another encounter with the local people.

We walked about 8 miles, when we fell in with the tracks of the natives, and shortly after came up with a family—one chief, his wife and three children. I gave him a pair of blankets, handkerchiefs, beads and three knives. He then went on with us and crossed a fresh water creek, the land on each side excellent. He took us on saying he would take us to the tribe, and mentioned the names of chiefs.

We walked about 8 miles, when, to our great surprise, we heard several voices calling after us. On looking back we saw six men all armed with spears, &c. When we stopped they throw aside their weapons, and came very friendly up to us. After shaking hands, and my giving them tomahawks, knives, &c., they took us with them about a mile back, where we found huts, women and children.

After some time, and full explanation, I found eight chiefs amongst them, who possessed the whole of the country near Port Phillip. Three brothers, all of the same name, are the principal chiefs, and two of them, men of 6 feet high and very good looking; the other not so tall but stouter. The other five chiefs were fine men, and after a full explanation of what my object was, I purchased two large tracts of land from them, about 600,000 acres, more or less, and delivered over to them blankets, knives, looking glasses, tomahawks, scissors, flour, &c., as payment for the land, and also agreed to give them a tribute or rent yearly.

The parchment the eight chiefs signed this afternoon, delivering to me some of the soil, each of them, as giving me full possession of the tracts of land. This took place alongside of a beautiful stream of water, and from whence my land commences, and where a tree is marked four ways to know the corner boundary.

The country about here exceeds any thing I ever saw both for grass and richness of soil, the timber light and consists of sheoak and small gum, with a few wattle. My natives gave the chiefs and their tribe a grand coroborrow to night. They seemed quite delighted with it. Each of the principal chiefs has two wives and several children each. In all, the tribe consists of 45 men, women and children.

The next day, he writes:

> Detained this morning some time drawing up triplicates of the deeds of the land I purchased and delivering over to them more property on the banks of the creek, which I have named Batman's Creek after my good self.
>
> Just before leaving the two principal chiefs came and brought their two cloaks or royal mantles and laid [them] at my feet wishing to accept the same. On my consenting to take them they placed them round my neck and over my shoulders, and seemed quite pleased to see me walk about with them on. I asked them to accompany me to the vessel. They very properly pointed to the number of young children then at their feet, meaning that they could not walk, but said they would come down in a few days.

Not only did Batman steal the land of these trusting people, he also learned their lore.

> I had no trouble to find out their sacred Matke. One of my natives, Bungett, went to a tree out of sight of the women, and made the Sydney natives' mark. After this was done I took with two or three of my natives the principal chief, and showed the mark on the tree. This he knew immediately, and pointed to the knocking out of the teeth. This mark is always made when the ceremony of knocking out the tooth in the front. However, after this I desired, through my natives, for him to make his mark, which, after looking about for some time and hesitating some few minutes, he took the tomahawk and cut out in the bark of the tree his mark, which is attached to the deed, and is the signature of their country and tribe.

On 8 June, Batman found a well-watered spot along the river now known as the Yarra and decided that, 'This will be the place for a village.' He departed a few days later, having left some of his party behind with three months' supplies and a 'written authority to put off any person or persons that might trespass on the land I have purchased from the natives'. Batman's ship made a good run on 10 June and was through Georgetown heads by early the next morning, then back in Launceston on the tide.

The land upon which Melbourne now stands had been purchased.

GYPSY JOURNEYS

Among the world's great travellers are the Romani people, more usually known in Britain and Australia as Gypsies. With their own language and culture, the nomadic Romani lifestyle has always marked them out for prejudicial treatment and when some Romani journeyed to Australia in the nineteenth century there was no exception.

Individual Romani were among those transported to New South Wales, Van Diemen's Land and Western Australia but the earliest account of a Romani group comes from the 1860s. In mid 1866 a local newspaper reported a number of Romani passing through Orange on their way to Mudgee. According to the paper, they had been in Australia for a couple of years already and they 'bear about them all the marks of the Gypsy'. The article continued:

> The women stick to the old dress, and are still as anxious as ever to tell fortunes; but they say that this game does not pay in Australia, as the people are not so credulous here as they are at home. Old Brown Joe is a native of Northumberland, and has made a good deal of money even during his short sojourn here. They do not offer themselves generally as fortune-tellers, but, if required and paid, they will at once 'read your palm'. At present they obtain a livelihood by tinkering and making sealing-wax. Their time during the last week has been principally taken up in hunting out bees' nests, which are very profitable, as they not only sell the honey, but, after purifying and refining the wax, manufacture it into beautiful toys, so rich in colour and transparency that it would be almost impossible to guess the material.

No more was heard of this group but in 1898, 23 Romani arrived in Adelaide. They claimed to be from Greece, although they are thought today to have actually hailed from the Balkans. The group camped at the booming town of Largs Bay, 15 kilometres north-west of Adelaide, where a journalist tracked them down and asked questions. Were they Greeks, possibly refugees from the conflict between Turkey and Greece? Or were they Gypsies who happened to depart from Greece? How would they support themselves in Australia? The answer was 'Oh, any way. We will go from town to town.'

The Greek Gypsies, as they became known, were clearly in dire straits and there was an initial flow of charity from local people. This soon turned into a desire to assist them to leave the colony. Apparently the Romani had originally paid their fare for a longer journey but had for unknown reasons disembarked at Adelaide with the intention of walking overland to their original destination. They clearly had little understanding of the distances and hardships involved. Nevertheless they were moved on from Largs Bay by the police.

Their journey took them through the Adelaide suburbs, then to Gawler, Williamstown, Mannum and Murray Bridge. The men walked while the women and children travelled in a dray. Wherever they camped a local subscription was taken up to help them along their way.

When they finally reached Victoria the then-small Greek population of Melbourne was quick to disassociate itself from the new arrivals. According to a letter to the editor published in *The Argus*, the Romani were not Greek nationals, even if they held Greek passports. Two days later the leader of the group replied in the same publication:

> The Greek people of Melbourne, according to your paper, say we are not Greek subjects. Well, we hold our passports from Greece and we speak their language. We make no claims to be Greeks. We are a distinct people, known as gipsies the world over, and claim our descent from Abraham and Hagar: something before the Greeks were heard of. Those people who doubt our words can examine our passports at the Victoria Hall, Burke Street, during the coming week.

Their presence in Melbourne sparked a debate in the Legislative Assembly. The Romani were described as 'vagrants' and legal grounds to move them on were sought, eventually resulting in legislation banning 'any person being a pauper or likely to become a public charge' from entering the colony.

By December, and now joined by another nomadic group, the Romani were camped at St Kilda and making a living by performing to noisy crowds, upsetting local residents. Efforts were made to have them removed but it seems that they moved on of their own accord. One group made for Sydney, though when they reached the border at Albury around mid January 1899, they were refused entry into the colony of New South Wales. Some later left Australia to continue their travels in America, New Zealand and Canada, but many remained, finding work in travelling shows and circuses. Their descendants still live in New South Wales, Victoria and Queensland today.

TO AUSTRALIA BY SUBMARINE

In March 1919 six British submarines (*J 1, 2, 3, 4, 5* and *7*), valued at around 1.5 million pounds and known as J-boats, were commissioned into the Royal Australian Navy. Although both the Royal Navy and the Royal Australian Navy were short on men, preparations began to ready the submarines and volunteer submariners from both navies for the long journey to Australia. The plan was for the J-boats to arrive in Australia in time for the Peace Day celebrations scheduled for July 1919.

The history of the J-boats during the war had not been a happy one. As well as technical problems and collisions, *J6* was lost towards the end of the war when it became the victim of a mistaken attack by a Royal Navy decoy ship. She was sunk with the loss of sixteen crewmembers on 15 October 1917.

Life aboard a J-boat was a cramped and dangerous affair. Leading Torpedo-man Tom 'Taff' Jones had been among the landing boat crews at Gallipoli. Jones subsequently served aboard *J2* and in 1935 published a rare account of the experience. After some brief but intense training, including just one practice dive, he was posted to the submarine. It was crewed by five officers and 40 men. Jones described the inside of *J2* and the living and working conditions as they were in 1916:

> it is divided into eight compartments separated by means of strong bulkheads with watertight doors. The first compartment, as we come from the bows, is the torpedo room, or 'Fort End', as we call it. In it are four torpedo-tubes, each containing a torpedo; and on each side of us there are two more spare torpedoes, in all eight 'tin fish'. All round us are dozens of pipes and valves, polished to perfection. The valves are for flooding the tubes and the hundred and one controls for operating the torpedo-tubes. At the back of the tubes are four tanks containing the air-charge for firing the 'fish'. Leaving Fort End we step through a bulkhead door to the ward-room. The captain and officers feed and sleep in the ward-room. Here again, we find all valves and pipes polished. On one side are the officers' bunks; on the other the wireless cabinet. At the after end of this compartment is a tiny officers' pantry.

Jones goes on to describe the operating hub of the control room, crammed with pipes, levers and gauges. 'Just abaft the control room are two beam or broadside torpedo-tubes, with two spare fish on top ready for loading.' The diesel engines made a 'terrific din' and air compression equipment was just as noisy.

The final compartment was the crew space 'where we ate, slept and played patience'. Half the crew would eat their meals here at any one time, 'otherwise the other half would have had to stand on their eyebrows as we termed it'. On deck was a three-inch recessing gun and a telescopic wireless mast. The J-boats were notorious for rolling and pitching, with seasickness afflicting even the hardiest submariners. It was not considered good form to show that you were seasick and so Jones, like many others, suffered silently.

In these confined quarters, the submariners worked, ate, slept and socialised as best they could. Some played cards, some read, some talked about their girlfriends or wives. 'The air seems thick, even in the morning,' Jones wrote. 'After a very long day of diving, about eighteen hours, breathing becomes very hard, and a sort of mist can be seen over the deck-boards, indicating that the fresh air is diminishing fast.' Smoking was officially banned but officers and men secretly smoked pipes and cigarettes, no doubt contributing to the breathing difficulties. Jones says that the only air supplies on board were used for the operation of the submarine, although he did see engineers occasionally open the airlines to 'put a little kick in the stale air'. Apart from this occasional assistance, the only pleasure was the daily ration of rum, in the tradition of the British navy.

It was not until early April 1919 that the six submarines and their crews, including seven Australian sub-lieutenants, were able to leave Portsmouth, escorted by the light cruiser HMAS *Sydney* and depot ship HMAS *Platypus*. They were followed by three more support craft, an oiler *Kurumba*, the battle cruiser HMAS *Australia* and another light cruiser, HMAS *Brisbane*. As with the earlier voyage of *AE1* and *AE2* from Britain to Australia, the J class boats suffered breakdowns and other disasters. In poor visibility, *J5* collided with a French sailing ship; the ship later sank as a result. As one experienced submarine captain put it, 'If you could drive a J-boat you could drive a bath.' The submarines were frequently under tow. One of *J2*'s engines failed as soon as she left Gibraltar and the submarine had to be towed by HMAS *Sydney*. The tow wire broke twice over the next few days before they were able to repair the submarine's engine and continue their slow passage to Malta. The other submarines suffered engine problems on this voyage as well; *J7* was also towed for some days by HMAS *Australia* between Aden and Colombo.

The flotilla limped on through the Suez Canal and reached Colombo, Sri Lanka, by mid May. The heat and cramped conditions were causing the crews great distress and there they paused for a much-needed few days of rest, including leave. From Colombo, the fleet split into smaller groups and sailed at various times for Singapore, which was 'another very welcome port', as

Torpedo-man Jones recalled. Again they rested and obtained vital supplies of fresh food. The submarines had all left Singapore for Thursday Island by 18 June.

During this final stage of the voyage tragedy again struck the J-boats. Due to the oppressive heat of the tropics, the crews had taken to sleeping on the casing. But on the morning of 20 June, the men of *J2* discovered the empty blankets of Sub-Lieutenant Larkins. All the submarines immediately conducted a search of the area until late in the afternoon, but without success. *J2*'s captain held a burial service with all the crew mustered. 'They were a band of downcast men who stood there bareheaded,' Jones wrote.

On reaching Thursday Island on 28 June, their luck did not improve. There was already dissatisfaction among the crews about the quality and quantity of the food supplied by the 'tin pot', as they called the poorly prepared HMAS *Platypus*, and rations were no better at Thursday Island—'a few tins of corn dog and a few old biscuits'. But soon after reaching the island the crews were also exposed to the pandemic scourging the postwar world, Spanish Flu, which would ultimately kill more people than the war itself. All the submarines were quickly quarantined, but the influenza claimed Stoker Henry Haggis of *J7*, who was buried on the island.

The flotilla sailed for Moreton Bay on 5 July, where they again rested for three days. However, when they were denied leave to go ashore, even though they were keen to spend their 'tons of spondulix', *J2*'s crew 'voiced our protest by staging a mild mutiny'. Their officers talked the crew around, however, holding up a vision of the tumultuous welcome they would receive when they reached Sydney. 'This made us quite a band of good boys again,' wrote Jones.

Most of the submarines finally arrived in Sydney on 15 July 1919. *J5*, still under tow, had already arrived in June. They were welcomed by the governor-general and a huge crowd as well. As Jones remembered the scene, 'We received a great welcome: hundreds of boats met us; the ferry steamers cock-a-doodle-dood themselves hoarse.'

The 19 July Peace Day celebrations had been planned as a day of national large-scale thanksgiving to mark the end of hostilities. Among the events that day, there was a march through Sydney's streets by the sailors of the warships anchored in the harbour, the crews of the J-boats among them. Jones wrote: 'After the impressive march, we returned to our ship, where we "spliced the main brace"' (they were given an extra ration of rum).

The J-boats and their crews enjoyed the peaceful postwar years conducting exercises and taking part in ceremonial duties, including the visit of the Prince of Wales in mid June 1920 and the Hobart Regatta of 1921. The submarines were enormously popular with the public. As a reporter for the Hobart *Mercury* wrote: 'Interest in the submarines, novel to the Hobart populace, is widespread and many people made their way to the wharf yesterday and indulged in respectful and fascinated inspection from the wharfside.' Large numbers clamoured to go abroad the submarines when they were opened to the public a few days later.

But the rising costs of maintaining the submarines and continuing navigation accidents led to their gradual mothballing. By 1930 they were all out of commission. HMAS *J1*, HMAS *J2*, HMAS *J4* and HMAS *J5* are now recreational training sites for divers in the ship's graveyard, as the area off Port Phillip Bay is known. HMAS *J4*'s conning tower was placed on St Kilda Pier and used as a starting tower for the local boat club until the demolition of the pier in 1956. HMAS *J3* was scuttled as a breakwater off Swan Island in Port Phillip Bay in 1926. The upper deck and superstructure of the submerged hulk are visible from the sea at low tide, and the location was marked by a plaque onshore erected in the 1980s. Finally, HMAS *J7*'s hull also appears above the water at low tide near the Sandringham Yacht Club, a ghostly reminder of an almost forgotten voyage.

S.Y.AURORA

2

SURVIVING

'Who in the name of wonder are you?'

Edwin Welch to lone survivor John King, 1861

WITHIN A FEW HOURS OF ETERNITY

Even before convicts arrived at Port Jackson they began to fantasise about escape. Folk beliefs circulated aboard transport ships and, wild though they seem to us, in those days these myths were believed by many.

One belief was that China was just across the Blue Mountains and convicts who managed to find their way there would be free. Another was that a colony of white people lived somewhere to the south of Port Jackson. Here, too, successful absconders would be liberated from their bondage. Many attempted these hopeless journeys, sometimes carrying magical 'compasses' scribbled on scraps of paper that would supposedly show the way to liberty. Most of those who made these desperate attempts either died, or limped back to the settlement starving and exhausted.

In May 1803, the English convict John Place, together with fellow convicts John Cox, William Knight and John Phillips, decided to act on the rumour of nearby China they had first heard while aboard their transport ship the previous year. Two of the men were married and were anxious to return to their families.

The small band set out from Castle Hill to the Hawkesbury area, and then, on 7 May, set out with one weeks' rations to cross the not-yet-traversed Blue Mountains. After seventeen days lost in the wilderness, their food was gone and they were forced to turn back:

> After they had eaten their provisions they found nothing to subsist on but wild currants [and] sweet-tea leaves, and had been oppressed with hunger for twelve days. Before they set off to return, John Phillips left them to gather some berries and they saw him no more; they heard him call several times, but could render him no assistance, they being so reduced by hunger and concluded he perished.
>
> . . . they travelled the whole of the seventeen days with the sun on their right shoulder, and found great difficulty in ascending some of the Mountains, and also attempted to return by the direction of the sun. After travelling for upwards of Twenty-days, all (except Phillips) reached within five miles of Richmond Hill, when William Knight, unable to proceed any further, lay down, where Place says he must have died. On the same day Place and Cox made the river above Richmond Hill, and in attempting to cross the Fall the current carried them down. One was carried to one side of the river, and the other to the opposite side, with difficulty [they] pulled themselves ashore by the branches of the trees. Cox had only his shirt and shoes on. Place saw him lain along the bank, where, being very weak, and the night extremely cold, he supposes he died. Place also lay down, despairing of life, and was found on the day following by a man, who, with some of the natives, was in quest of kangaroos: he was then too weak to walk alone, but was led by the natives to the nearest hut, where he remained all night; in the morning he was taken to Hawkesbury, and from thence sent to the Hospital at Parramatta.

Governor Hunter was concerned to stop convicts trying to escape in search of mythical freedom. The experience of Place and his companions was held up as an object lesson in the colony's only newspaper:

> None can read the above account without pitying the ignorance, and commiserating the sufferings of these deluded prisoners; and it is fervently to be hoped, that the inconceivable hardships they have endured from hunger and cold, with the almost constant prospect of death before their eyes, will deter all other prisoners from either advising any of their companions or from making a similar attempt themselves. It is well known, that those are not the only unfortunate men who have perished in this wild attempt, many others have never returned to relate the hardships they underwent, and must therefore have perished under every accumulation of misery by their rashness and folly. Place, who appears to be the only survivor, resigned himself to despair and death, and was found within a few hours of eternity. He seems to have been preserved by a particular providence, to give the above awful admonition to all others who now do or shall in future, entertain any idea of regaining their liberty by a similar act, in which nothing but inevitable death must be the final event.

Place recovered from his ordeal but five months later made another escape bid with two other convicts. A month later, one of his fellow escapees had died and Place and the other survivor returned to the settlement. For this second breakout, Place was sentenced to 500 lashes. This harsh punishment probably spurred him on to join a group of mainly Irish convicts in the disastrous Vinegar Hill uprising the following year. John Place's date with eternity came soon after it was suppressed. He was hanged at Parramatta on 8 March 1804.

UP, UP AND AWAY!

A very short but intrepid journey was taken over Sydney by an early 'aeronaut', Mr C.H. Brown. On the night of 17 January 1859, assisted by his partner Mr Dean, the aeronaut boarded his gas-powered balloon in the Domain and cast off 'with about twenty-eight pounds weight of fireworks attached my car'. The fireworks—perhaps ill-advised for a contrivance powered by combustible hydrogen—were for a publicity stunt promoting the delights of ballooning. Mr Brown's troubles began almost immediately, when he found the balloon had 'but little ascension power': it would not rise. He quickly threw the anchor overboard, and then a bag of ballast. Still dangerously low, he threw a second bag of ballast overboard while above Hyde Park, 'by which means [he] ascended gently to a height of about a mile as [he] judged from the expansion of the balloon'. Hopefully there was nobody taking the evening air in Hyde Park at that moment.

Despite these early troubles, Brown flew on and discharged the fireworks, at which 'deafening shouts reached [his] ears from the thousands of people assembled in the Domain and Hyde Park':

> I hailed the crowd in Hyde Park, some of whom inform me that my shouts were heard by them. I heard distinctly the sounds of a band of music at the Rotunda, Woolloomooloo, over which I passed. From the time of my leaving the Domain, until my descent, the shouts of the people and the barking of dogs did not become inaudible.

But now Mother Nature added to his own firework show: he flew high into the centre of an electrical storm, writing that 'at times the lightning appeared to form a complete and immense circle around me'. Despite this he reported feeling 'quite secure' and enjoyed the view of city of Sydney at night, 'with its thousands of lights present[ing] a beautiful sight'.

Once the fireworks, which had been smouldering on the ground for ten minutes, seemed to be extinguished, he began his descent. But now the daring young man in his flying machine really got into trouble. A sudden gust of wind sent him off-course towards Randwick but he didn't notice in time. Instead he descended more quickly, and then 'passing over the Orphan Asylum, at Randwick, came down with great violence in a garden, a few hundred yards further'. He writes, 'My first impression was, that my neck was broken, but a second or two afterwards, finding myself unhurt, I prepared for another shock, which I expected would be more violent than the first.' The balloon, after violently colliding with the ground, had lifted again and he now prepared for a second crash-landing:

> I twisted one leg around a rope, held one of the car-ropes with my left hand, and the string of the valve with my right. Down I came again with a frightful shock, and the balloon dragged me at a terrific rate through the scrub, the car cutting through the bushes like a knife. I expected every moment would be my last, but endeavoured to keep cool, and determined to endeavour to save myself by dropping over the side of the car, and setting the balloon free.
>
> After having been dragged along in this manner for at least a mile, expecting every moment to plunge into the bay, I put my legs over the side of the car and waited a favourable opportunity to get completely out. At last I sprang from the car, and was thrown violently on my hands and face into a bush. I soon got on my feet, and followed the balloon at least three quarters of a mile, when I lost sight of it.

Poor Mr Brown's wandering balloon was found near Botany Bay, four or five kilometres from where he had 'first struck the earth', as he put it. He had been in the air for just twenty minutes. Brown and Dean soon left for Melbourne for further ballooning antics. As the reporter of this aerial farce wrote, tongue in cheek: 'Monday's ascent concluding, for the present, aeronautic expeditions in New South Wales.'

AFTER BURKE AND WILLS

The doomed explorers Burke and Wills left Melbourne in August 1860 at the head of an elaborate exploration party. Bound for the Gulf of Carpentaria, their poorly defined and planned quest aimed to be the first to cross the continent from south to north. While officially called the Victorian Exploring Expedition and sponsored by the Royal Society of Victoria, the enterprise was known almost from the start, and ever since, as the Burke and Wills expedition.

Robert O'Hara Burke, a 39-year-old policeman, was the leader, and 26-year-old William John Wills was the surveyor and astronomer. Wills also became second in command following the resignation of the original number two partway through the journey. After ten months of hardship, misadventure and incompetence, Burke and Wills and their men were all dead, but for one survivor. He was being cared for by the Yandruwandha people of the desolate 'corner country' at the intersection of New South Wales, Queensland and South Australia. The fortunate man's name was John King.

King was a young Irishman who had joined the expedition as interpreter for the Afghans handling the expedition's camels, which had been shipped to Australia from Karachi, India. Eventually he became the chief camel handler for the expedition. And so it was that he was the fourth in the party of Burke, Wills and Charlie Gray that left the struggling main expedition at a camp at Cooper's Creek, in order to make a final desperate dash to the gulf. The return journey cost the three others their lives.

When there had been no news of Burke and Wills back at the Royal Society in Melbourne, a rescue party under the command of A.W. Howitt was despatched to find them. Second in command was Edwin Welch, a 24-year-old surveyor and photographer. The relief party reached the vicinity of the last known campsite of the Burke and Wills expedition only to find it deserted. They followed many tracks but found little to solve the mystery.

But early one Sunday morning, 15 September, many days after they had arrived at the abandoned campsite, Welch left and rode along Cooper's Creek, as it was then called by the Europeans. After a few hours he came across a group of Aboriginal people who shouted to him and pointed further along the creek. Welch rode on for a little distance and then:

> I was startled at observing what appeared to be a white man come from amongst them, although had it not been for the hat, it might still have been mistaken for an aboriginal as many of them had obtained old clothes at the depot. The hat convinced me it was a white man, and giving my horse his head I dashed down the bank towards him, where he fell on his knees on the sand for a few moments in the attitude of prayer. On arising I hardly asked 'who in the name of wonder are you?' and received the reply 'I am King, sir, the last man of the exploring expedition.'

King explained that Burke, Wills and himself had made it back to the expedition's last campsite only to find the depot party had left. Wills became too ill to move, and King pushed on with Burke to seek help. On 29 June Burke died. King, subsisting on nardoo (an aquatic fern) and a crow he had managed to shoot, struggled back to where he had left Wills. Four days later he arrived to find Wills dead. Alone, King remained with the body for several weeks then went again in search of help from the Yandruwandha people. He followed them around until he became a tolerated addition to the number of mouths to be fed, contributing to the common store by shooting birds. 'Living in this state, we found him, more like an animated skeleton than anything else, and a complete black fellow in almost everything but the colour', Welch wrote.

King now directed the relief party to Burke's body. They wrapped the skeletal remains in a Union Jack and buried him as Howitt read a chapter from the gospel of St Joan. The people who had kept King alive were given gifts: 'tomahawks, knives, looking glasses, beads, handkerchiefs, coloured ribbons', as well as flour and sugar. The relief party and the recovering survivor moved on the following day. The journey back was a dry and uncomfortable ride, made more miserable by sickness and large scorpions.

When they reached the boundaries of European settlement the rescuers were feted. King in particular was treated as a hero. Unfortunately, his experiences had made him shy of civilisation and he found the parties and public receptions given enthusiastically in his honour at each settlement they passed through to be very trying.

At Bendigo they were greeted by crowds of diggers 'blowing horns, firing guns and pistols, cheering and waving flags &c.- &c.- as much as if it were a triumphal entry of blood royal'. Flags were flying and they were greeted by a theatrical troupe and a brass band playing 'See, the Conquering Hero Comes'. King was put on stage but was unable to speak. Welch tried but was himself too ill to do the honours and so a local resident spoke to the crowd. He went on for so long that Welch was obliged to drag King away, fearful that it would all be too much for him. The crowd hissed, groaned and cursed. Photographers vied for permission to snap King. At one point Welch left King in his hotel room while he went for a smoke and returned to find the room full of the women of Bendigo, who 'under other circumstances would have shuddered at the idea of being in the next room to a strange man'.

On the train journey from Bendigo to Melbourne, Welch had to rescue King from the hero worshippers at Woodend station by barricading themselves in the station master's house. At every stop along the line crowds greeted them and at North Melbourne Welch had to fight to keep possession of the bewildered survivor.

When they reached Melbourne 'the crowd was terrific'. They barely escaped in a cab to Government House, where yet another mob barred their way. Welch and King pushed their way up to the executive council chambers. Here King was reunited with his sister and had a brief word with the governor and one or two other dignitaries. To appease the waiting crowd outside, Welch and King had to be shown from a balcony, before Welch could finally hand over his charge to the officers of the exploration committee who had sponsored the expedition and Howitt's rescue party.

John King was given a gold watch and a pension in the form of an investment that returned the tidy sum of 180 pounds per annum. However, physically and psychologically, he never recovered from his ordeals. In 1871 he married, but only five months later died of tuberculosis.

Edwin Welch went on to a varied career as surveyor, public

servant and journalist. He was a noted raconteur and wrote fiction and non-fiction under various pen names. He was also one of the most prolific collectors of pioneer and Aboriginal artefacts.

Burke and Wills' disastrous expedition was controversial immediately upon its dreadful end, and has since become a byword for futile action. The often-ambiguous details have been ground over and over again by historians, lawyers and the many others fascinated by the tale and its folklore. There is even a persistent story that King shot Burke dead, though little evidence supports it. Like many other Australian journeys, its history has fallen into myth.

A DANGEROUS VISIT

Australia's only royal assassination attempt took place the first time a British royal ever set foot on the colonies, during the reign of Queen Victoria. The target was her second son, Prince Alfred Earnest Albert, a navy officer and the Duke of Edinburgh, among other grand titles, who visited Australia in 1868 as part of a year-long world voyage during his command of the steam frigate HMS *Galatea*. The prince went firstly to South Australia, then Victoria, Tasmania, Sydney and Brisbane, before returning to Sydney where he was to attend a charity picnic for the Sydney Sailors' Home at Clontarf on 12 March.

There was great excitement and enthusiasm for the royal visit but it was also a time of high tension between Irish Catholics and the Protestant establishment in Britain and Australia. Supporters of Irish independence were known as Fenians and some were prepared to inflict violence on the symbols of the Crown. During Alfred's stay in Melbourne there had already been trouble between Catholic supporters of Ireland and Protestants loyal to the British monarch. In this atmosphere there were fears of an attack on the prince.

At the Clontarf picnic these fears were realised. Straight after lunch, as the prince handed over a no-doubt substantial cheque towards the Sailors' Home, Henry James O'Farrell walked up to within a metre or so of the noble and fired a shot from his revolver directly into Alfred's back. The prince fell forward, crying, 'Good God, my back is broken.' As O'Farrell was tackled by a couple of the dignitaries, he fired one more shot into another man's foot. Then they managed to pin the assassin's arms and the attack was over.

The prince was carried carefully away for medical attention.

> The dress of his Royal Highness was removed, and upon an examination of the wound it was found that the bullet had penetrated the back, near the middle, and about two inches from the right side of the lower part of the spine, traversing the course of the ribs, round by the right to the abdomen, where it lodged immediately below the surface. No vital organ, fortunately, appeared to be injured, the course of the bullet being, to all appearance, quite superficial.

In the meantime, elsewhere in the picnic grounds there was pandemonium:

> The people shouted 'lynch him', 'hang him', 'string him up', and so on, and there was a general rush to get at him. The police, headed by Superintendent Orridge, got hold of the assassin, and they had the greatest difficulty in preventing the infuriated people from tearing him limb from limb.

The police just managed to get O'Farrell onto the steamer at the nearby wharf:

> By that time all the clothing from the upper part of his body was torn off, his eyes, face, and body were much bruised, and blood was flowing from various wounds; and when he was dragged on to the deck of the *Paterson*, he appeared to be utterly unconscious.

But even aboard the steamer the sailors threatened to string up the bruised and beaten O'Farrell. Meanwhile, on shore the crowd convened a hasty meeting and decided to drag the would-be assassin off the steamer. They rushed for the boat as it drew away, demanding the captain return to shore. For a moment the captain looked as if he would comply, but a gentleman on the bridge ordered him to haul off.

> The effect of this dastardly attempt at assassinating the Prince, among the immense number of persons congregated at Clontarf, may be more easily imagined than described. A large number of ladies fainted, others were seized with hysterics, and the whole multitude was convulsed. Suddenly a joyous throng had been converted into a mass of excited people, in whose breasts sympathy for the Royal sufferer, and indignation for his murderous assailant, alternately prevailed; while pallid faces and tearful eyes told of the deep anxiety that was felt in reference to the extent of the injuries which his Royal Highness had sustained.

Hundreds crowded anxiously around the tent where the Prince lay. He remained conscious, saying, 'Tell the people I am not much hurt, I shall be better presently.' He was taken back to Sydney for further medical attention, where it was confirmed that the prince had luckily suffered only a relatively minor wound.

O'Farrell was taken to gaol. There, he was described as of fair complexion, just under 6 foot, with a beard, moustache and 'military air'. When questioned he provided only flippant answers, leading many to suspect he was mentally deficient. But he was definitely Irish and feelings against the Irish in the colony became hysterical. The government made it an offence not to drink the queen's health and tried hard to paint the affair as an act of organised terror. Although he provided a deathbed confession insisting he was not connected with any nationalist movement, O'Farrell was condemned as a Fenian and hastily hanged at Darlinghurst Gaol on 21 April.

The prince made an excellent recovery and, before his attacker was executed, continued his journey back to England.

There were some positive results of the affair. The people of New South Wales subscribed a great deal of money for a memorial to the recovery of the prince. These funds took the practical form of Sydney's much-loved Prince Alfred Hospital, later known as the Royal Prince Alfred, or just RPA. Melbourne's Alfred Hospital came from the same patriotic outpouring of money.

HARRY STOCKDALE'S LONG RIDE

The Stockdale expedition left Sydney on the steamer *Whampoa* on 26 August 1884. There were seven men in the group, along with 25 horses and provisions for a year. Harry Stockdale, a man of many parts and talents, had financed the venture himself. He had contracted with a number of parties to carry out a rapid survey of their unseen holdings throughout the north-west of the country. He was to report back by 14 January the following year, an agreement he would come to regret.

They landed in Cambridge Gulf, at the very top of Australia near the border of the present-day Western Australia and the Northern Territory, and on 19 September began trekking inland.

The seven men passed through terrain unknown to European settlers. It was rich with birds, animals and plant life, much of it new to the explorers. Despite temperatures of 106 degrees Fahrenheit in the shade, rising up to 115 degrees later in the journey, the expedition made good progress. Nevertheless the first of their horses died after only three weeks.

On 21 October, Stockdale left two men, Mulcahy and Ashton, at a depot on Leopold Downs. Stockdale pushed on with his surveyor Ricketson, blacksmith Carl Pottmer, and two other men, Pitt and McIllery, into country that 'only wants to be seen to be believed in; all my party agreeing that they had never seen anything much superior to it, either in N.S.Wales or Queensland, and nothing to approach it for permanent water.'

Twelve days later the explorers encountered a group of Aboriginal people:

> . . . came suddenly upon a camp of natives. The women and children remained quiet, but the men were bold and aggressive, and poised their spears, the one nearest me, about 25 yards off, was in the act of throwing when a [I] fired close past him. They all turned for the moment, but turned & faced me again. By this time all the party had their firearms in readiness (I had waited till the rest came up, having come upon some ducks, and wanting a gun, having only a rifle with

> me) and though we hoped they would not compel us to do them violence, we were sure the victory would be with us, though one of us at so close a range might have been speared, but after the firing of the shot, they pointed in the direction we had come from, gesticulating wildly, shaking their spears, and talking loudly what seemed to us to sound so like our 'Go away'. There were only 7 men—fine stalwart fellows they were, perfectly naked, well made, tall and strong looking. Each had a bundle of spears and a boomerang. We made several attempts to parley with them in a friendly way, but it was evident they wished us to go on, and we did so.

There was another encounter a few days later, but this group was friendly and on 6 November, Stockdale came across some Aboriginal rock art:

> Came upon a native art gallery in the cliffs, with drawing by natives of Emu, Kangaroo, Opossums, frogs, platypus, and a really fine, spirited, but rather crude drawing a black fellow doing the corrobboree, the bust of a gin or native black woman, and a drawing almost the facsimile of a monkey. They were done in different colours, and shewed some artistic taste. The emu was shown as feeding, and the attitude was really good. I suppose in all there some 30 sketches in some 2 or 3 of the one kind. [Note: These drawings were shaded or filled in, not merely outlines]. I remember Captain, now Sir George, Grey, mentioning that he had discovered traces of something similar on the Western coast, but I never thought it would fall to my lot to decipher discover [sic] such a grand display of native talent. I intend to publish with my diary a facsimile drawing of some of those we saw today.

Stockdale left Ricketson, Pitt and McIllree to form another depot on 8 November and pushed on with Carl. They became worn down and separated. Stockdale returned to the depot, hoping to find the missing man there. But despite Stockdale's frantic efforts to find him, the blacksmith did not turn up for some days. Stockdale, who had been 'half out of my mind' with worry, was elated when the smith reappeared. But his relief was soon tempered when he discovered that the three men left at the depot had not been looking after the horses: 'a serious blow to the success of the expedition—in fact almost jeopardising its safety'.

On 23 November, the party returned to their first depot and were reunited with their three comrades. These three had been troubled with lack of food but, unlike the men at the second depot, they had looked after their horses, so the animals were fresh and ready to work:

> I immediately set to work, and within ½ an hour they were all hard at it on a good sized doughboy [a lump of boiled dough] each, the sweetest, they say they ever ate, and full of hopes, and talking about home and friends, and how long it would take to reach them once again. What a weight of anxiety is now off my mind, and how light hearted I feel to see us all together once again, and everyone safe and right. I feel like a new man altogether, for no pen can tell how anxious I have been about the 3 boys left with so little, and for so long a time.

This relief was short-lived. Bad feeling soon set in between some of the party, with rations mysteriously disappearing and mutterings about Stockdale's leadership. They were facing a 500-mile (800 kilometre) trek, leading their remaining packhorses, and most of the men were now without shoes, their boots having worn away. They soon lost two more horses to the unrelenting heat. Stockdale was now bitterly regretting the tight deadline he had contracted for his expedition:

> had I not been bound by time, I could have saved all my horses, and had much easier times now. I am up early and late, and harassed out of my life, but I am going to get the report through at all hazards if my health is spared me . . .

This low point eased and soon they were moving along moderately well and managing to live off the land. But by early December a new challenge arose: they were running out of nails for the horses' shoes, due to an oversight in the original provisioning. They had to improvise nails from copper rivets. Stockdale complained that this, together with ill treatment of the horses by two of the party, had forced him to add 400 miles (650 kilometres) to his expedition, as they were unable to cross stony ranges with unshod mounts.

On 9 December, they encountered a small group of Aboriginal people who seemed panicked by the presence of the explorers and climbed a steep hill to get away. A few days later they were again forced to keep the horses shod with improvised nails. There was still tension in the group: Mulcahy was malingering and dosing himself with opium. But even in the midst of this, the artistic Stockdale had time to appreciate the beauty around him: 'Our friends the chattering birds gave us quite a rondelay last night. The bush is full of birds of exquisite note, and as whistlers not to be surpassed.'

Within a few days Mulcahy was acting very oddly: in a delusional state, he disappeared from camp and had to be retrieved. Stockdale resolved to take his drugs away. At this, Mulcahy admitted having stolen scarce supplies and said he was not worthy to be among them. Stockdale wrote that, 'We all forgave him the wrong he had done us freely and truly,' but the next morning the opium eater and Ashton, who seems to have been suffering a chronic complaint of some kind, asked to be left at the camp with supplies until a rescue party could be sent back for them. Stockdale was stunned by this collapse of the two largest and strongest of their group, but knew he could not show it for fear of dispiriting the other men.

So the group split again on 22 December, leaving only Stockdale and Ricketson to push on towards the Ord River. By Christmas Day they were still short of their destination. Stockdale wrote:

> Our Christmas dinner consisted of doughboys, Johnny cakes and gooseberry jam, and very well it went. We know there are some very anxious thoughts about us this Christmas tide, and [many] eaters of good dinners are wishing all sorts of good luck to us, and the knowledge we are so cared for is cheering in our solitude today.

A few days later they realised they must have unwittingly crossed the upper reaches of the Ord River and were running very low on food. Fortunately they were now in range of Panton and Osmond's cattle station and shot a stray bull.

> We soon had his tongue, heart, kidneys and about 30 lbs of rump and loin cut off, and hide to mend our boots, and, our horses let go, camped and spelled for the remainder of the day, feeling all the better for our grilled steak, which was as tender as chicken. This is our first piece of cattle duffing.

By now they were far into the Northern Territory with 'no food, no pack horses, no maps, no direction, no certain knowledge, only that we must now travel NE and strike the telegraph, if Providence aids us in keeping up our strength'. They did not know how long it would take them to reach the relative safety of the Overland Telegraph Line and although they were free of scurvy they were weak from lack of food.

On 31 December, they came upon an Aboriginal camp, shared some of their bush tucker and were lucky enough to find a few stray horses in good condition. On New Year's Day in 1885 they reached Victoria River Station around 500 kilometres south of Darwin: 'How our hearts jumped! New Years day and New Years fare!' Stockdale was greatly relieved, not only to be saved but also because 'we may consider our troubles are more or less over, and fair sailing all the way; and if my health holds out my report will be in time, and I shall be able to send relief to those behind, and all my engagements will have been kept, and a rest fairly earned'.

They were unable to immediately organise a rescue party for the two men left behind but pushed on in high spirits through good country. Both men and horses grew fat and they travelled at a good speed. The expedition reached Spring Vale Station on 11 January and the next day the two exhausted explorers sent telegrams from the nearby Katherine telegraph station.

Stockdale's journal ends abruptly at this point but the story continues. Searchers sent to rescue the three left at the first depot eventually reached the camp. But McIllree had died before they arrived and Pitt was demented. Carl, a good bushman, seems to have been in reasonable shape. The other two men left much further out at the second depot were never found.

Despite some controversy in the press about the deaths of nearly half of the expedition, Stockdale was generally hailed as another intrepid explorer. He returned to the area the following year and went on to a career as a bushman and sometime artist, as well as collector and dealer in Aboriginal artefacts, including skulls, of the Ngarrindjeri people from South Australia. These ended up in the Pitt Rivers Museum in Oxford, where they controversially remain today. He was also a showman, exhibiting the items collected on his many travels in his Australian Curios display in 1901. Four years later Stockdale was reported to be broke and ill, with a large family to support. He died in 1919.

ACROSS THE ICE

'Deeply regret delay only just managed to reach hut.' With these words Douglas Mawson telegraphed his survival to his fiancée Paquita Delprat. This message is one of history's great understatements. Mawson endured a punishing and tragic journey from the relative safety of his base camp to the frozen eastern wastes of Antarctica and back again.

The young Mawson was a geologist and lecturer at the University of Adelaide when he first became interested in Antarctic exploration. In 1907, he joined Earnest Shackleton's two-year attempt on the geographic South Pole, proving himself an outstanding leader, physically tough and mentally resilient. After successfully raising funds for his own polar investigations, in December 1911 Mawson led the Australasian Antarctic Expedition southwards for what would be more than two years in the home of the blizzard.

After almost a year on the ice, in company with British army officer Belgrave Ninnis and Swiss lawyer and champion skier Xavier Mertz, the 30-year-old Mawson set out on a scientific survey of the almost unknown far eastern glaciers. They left their base at Cape Denison on 10 November 1912. The first five hundred or so kilometres went reasonably well. But then things began to go wrong. There were accidents, minor but irritating ailments and some unsettling incidents. A petrel smashed into the side of one of the sleds. How a seabird came to fly this far into the frozen inland was deeply puzzling. One of the huskies gave birth and devoured its offspring. Not unusual behaviour in the extreme conditions but troubling, especially as they began to hear the ominous sounds of ice cracking deep beneath them.

Around 1 p.m. on 14 December, Ninnis vanished down a 45-metre crevasse that his companions had just safely crossed. Peering into the gloom they could just make out one dead and one dying husky on a ledge. There was no sign of Ninnis and the vital supplies that Mawson had commanded, unwisely as it now turned out, be loaded onto the one sled. They did not have enough rope to descend and so could only call out to their lost companion for five despairing hours. There was only silence from the frigid depths.

Now endangered by the loss of their supplies, including the shelter for that night, the two survivors decided to head back along their trail to Cape Denison. They reached their previous night's camp where they had left a sled. Mawson used the runners and some canvas to make a temporary tent. They had little food so killed and ate their weakest dog, including the liver. After a few more days' travel Mawson went snow blind. A whiteout slowed them further as did Mertz's deteriorating health, probably due to the toxicity of the husky livers they were consuming, as well as hunger and exhaustion. By 5 January, Mertz was losing the skin from his legs and struggling to find the will to continue. The next day he developed diarrhoea and began convulsing.

They travelled unsteadily on for another day with Mawson dragging his disabled companion on the sled. But Mertz's condition worsened and they had to camp. He began to rave and thrash about, breaking a tent pole. Eventually Mawson could only hold him down. Mertz became calmer but died in the early hours of 8 January.

So heavy were the winds that it was two days before Mawson could get out of the tent to bury the body. Despite his own fading physical condition and feeling 'utterly overwhelmed by an urge to give in' he prepared his remaining equipment for a last desperate trek.

Before he had staggered far though, he discovered that the skin was separating from the soles of his feet. He smeared lanoline on the raw new skin and bandaged the bottom of his feet together, all covered with six pairs of woollen socks. Then he took most of his clothes off. The polar sun bathed his decaying body: 'A tingling sensation seemed to spread throughout my whole body, and I felt stronger and better.' Despite this, he wrote in his diary that night, 'My whole body is apparently rotting from want of proper nourishment.'

He rested for 24 hours or so then managed to push slowly on. Nine days after Mertz's death and still far from base, it almost ceased to matter when Mawson fell through the lid of a crevasse. Fortunately, his cut-down sled became jammed in the gap of the crevasse, leaving him to dangle 4 metres below the surface, spinning slowly at the end of a rope. He managed to drag himself back up but as he was climbing out the snow gave way and he plunged back into the crevasse once more, his fall again arrested by the rope tied between himself and the sled.

Miraculously, the sled remained wedged into the ice above. With bare hands, exhausted, and dangling over a black abyss, he was tempted to slip his harness and end the pain. Instead, he hauled himself up the rope with 'one last tremendous effort'. This time, the snow at the lip of the newly opened crevasse held and he was able to pull himself onto it. He lay there for an hour, unable to move.

In his tent that night he made a rope ladder he thought would help if he fell into any more crevasses. The next day he did and the crudely fashioned rope ladder saved him from a dark death.

After a bad night of troubled sleep, Mawson resolved to push on and 'leave the rest to Providence'. He marched doggedly on through a blizzard. Ill and with his hair falling out, he was now

65 kilometres from base and still about 50 kilometres from a cache of food. He came across some emergency supplies left by another party of expeditioners that gave him enough strength to reach the food store—aptly named Aladdin's Cave—on 1 February. He was snowed in there for five days. When the blizzard cleared he made a last push for the base camp, arriving just as the expedition's ship, *Aurora*, sailed away. A small party had been left behind but Mawson would have to wait until the following year before he could be taken home.

Nursed slowly back to relative health Mawson now had to contend with the madness of one of his companions, even while fearing for his own sanity. As the days of their enforced solitude passed slowly by in the howling Antarctic winter, Sidney Jeffryes, the radio operator, became paranoid and aggressive. He was particularly obsessed with Mawson who, as leader, had the unenviable task of managing a delusional companion. Jeffryes would be hospitalised on his return to Australia.

Mawson finally arrived back home in Adelaide at the end of February 1914. On 31 March 1914, Douglas Mawson and Paquita Delprat were married.

Mawson's 1911–14 expedition was the first to use radio communication from the Antarctic. Valuable contributions to scientific knowledge were made in their exploration of around 6500 icy kilometres. They found new species and collected meteorological and geomagnetic data.

Mawson was knighted and showered with many other scientific honours from around the world. He served in munitions management during World War I and was admitted as an OBE in 1920. Between 1929 and 1931 Mawson returned to the ice. Among other advances, this expedition mapped much of the Antarctic coastline, establishing the extent of the Australian Antarctic Territory. He died in 1958 and has at various times been featured on Australian postage stamps and the hundred-dollar note. His dreadful journey across the ice, not only to save himself but also to tell the fate of his companions, is widely considered to be the greatest epic of polar exploration and survival.

LIFEBOAT NO. 7

The voyage of Lifeboat No. 7 is a tale of mariner skills and perseverance across more than 2000 kilometres of unforgiving South Atlantic Ocean. The hero of the story was a young naval officer from Victoria's Western District.

Sub-Lieutenant Ian McIntosh was a passenger aboard the merchant ship *Britannia* out of Liverpool during World War II, in March 1941. Off the west African coast the ship was attacked by the German raider *Thor*. Outgunned, the *Britannia's* captain gave the order to abandon ship and McIntosh found himself and many others desperately launching Lifeboat No. 7 beneath the starboard side of their sinking ship. McIntosh organised some of the men already in the boat to push it off with oars while the European, Goenkar [from Goa], Sikh, Lascar and Madrassa traders making up most of the ship's complement clambered aboard.

They cleared the sinking ship but with over eighty souls aboard were well over the lifeboat's limit. They soon discovered that there were more shrapnel holes in the hull than they originally thought and the wooden boat was taking water badly. But with frantic bailing the lifeboat remained afloat as they watched their ship disappear, beneath the waves: 'Soon *Britannia*'s forward hold filled, her bows went down and, with her stem vertical, she finally slid under with a great bubble and swirl of water and the last of the steam blowing off with much loose wreckage shooting to the surface . . .'

Lifeboat No. 7 now gathered other survivors and set a sea anchor to keep their damaged craft near the other lifeboats from the lost *Britannia*. But despite this they soon they drifted apart and were faced with some life or death decisions.

As a child, Ian McIntosh had been fascinated with tales of the sea, particularly the voyage of Captain William Bligh, cast adrift by the *Bounty* mutineers in 1789. He read all he could about navigation and dreamed of joining the Royal Australian Navy. At that time and at the age of thirteen, the only way of enlisting was as a cadet. But McIntosh missed the deadline for applications and so remained at Geelong Grammar School until he was 18 when he won a Commonwealth scholarship for the Royal Navy, in England, in 1938. His boyhood reading and subsequent naval training gave him a set of skills and knowledge which complemented his determined nature. This would determine the fate of Lifeboat No. 7 and those aboard.

McIntosh and a small group of others, mostly with naval experience, soon took control of the lifeboat. According to his account, many of the 82 aboard were apathetic and reluctant to assist with their own survival. Although McIntosh did not say how, these men were organised into groups for bailing and other tasks vital to keep the 28-foot vessel afloat.

They had little equipment and less food. There was a small axe, scissors in an inadequate first-aid kit and some blankets. There were 48 tins of condensed milk and some ship's biscuit but hardly any water. The men in Lifeboat No. 7 were rationed to just one biscuit, a smear of condensed milk on the palm of their hands and an eggcup full of water twice a day.

In the frantic time before launching the lifeboat, they had filled the few shrapnel holes in the hull with cloths. But there was still too much water pouring in and they soon discovered several more serious holes. McIntosh fashioned a number of makeshift patches from empty condensed-milk tins. They still needed to bail but nowhere near as much as before.

The challenge now was to make for the nearest land. Or was it? They were around a thousand kilometres off west Africa but the prevailing winds meant that the waterlogged and over burdened lifeboat would take a long time to get there, if it ever did. McIntosh's navigational knowledge, together with that of a retired sea captain Bill Lyons among the survivors, now came into play. They realised that the trade winds and sea currents meant that they should steer for South America. That continent was at least 2500 kilometres away. McIntosh calculated it would take them 24 days. Recalling the logs of old sailing ships that he had read and taking account of wind and current, McIntosh found a few scraps of paper and set a westerly course to 33 degrees, at which point he would change to a south-west course to catch the south-east trade winds to the isolated coast of Brazil.

As they steered slowly towards their longed-for destination there were repeated attempts by some of the passengers to claim more than their meagre rations. Men soon began to die. The first drank seawater and threw himself into the dark sea one night.

McIntosh did most of the sailing and also acted as a religious minister, focusing a mixture of religious beliefs into a form of Anglican service, complete with some hymns. One night he got the Sikhs to sing. The sound was 'soothingly beautiful'.

Dodging whales, cold at night, hot and parched during the day, the passengers aboard Lifeboat No. 7 sailed on. Snuffling seawater through the nose and spitting it out helped McIntosh relieve the dreadful thirst, as did sucking on a button. Fortunately, a couple of squalls brought rain which they captured for drinking water and, as the death toll mounted, there were more rations to share among the survivors.

At dawn on the twenty-second day the dark blue water beneath their boat turned green. They saw plants floating in the sea and the number of birds increased. They were close to land. But as they neared the coast they could spy nowhere safe to land through the shoals and breaking waves. They lost sight of the land, and Captain Bill Lyons died that night. But by noon the next day they saw the coast again and found a sheltered bay to come ashore. The place they landed was amazingly close to where they had navigated towards from the other side of the Atlantic.

The wallowing lifeboat ground into sand about 300 yards off the beach. Some of the passengers were unwilling to get into the water but McIntosh threw them overboard. Those first ashore found fresh water and the 38 survivors made a fire and cooked up some of the berries growing there. They relaxed around the fire, stretching out horizontal for the first time in 23 days and hardly noticing the saltwater boils covering their bodies. But they were not safe yet. There was fresh water but little else. They could see no signs of human habitation.

But suddenly two native boys appeared and led the group to their fishing village a kilometre or so along the coast. The villagers fed and cared for the survivors of Lifeboat No. 7 from their own meagre resources and were able to get a message to the authorities. Travelling a network of creeks and waterways in a flotilla of dugout canoes, the survivors were eventually transferred to trucks and taken to São Luíz, where they received hospital treatment. The poor fisher people, who had almost certainly saved their lives, trekked all the way to the capital from their village to bring them fruit. All the survivors recovered and were transported by luxury liner to Trinidad. McIntosh took a passage to Bermuda and went on to a stellar naval career. For his exploits in Lifeboat No. 7 he was awarded the honour of Member of the British Empire. He subsequently won many more decorations in the Royal Navy, retiring as a vice admiral in 1980. After a busy and productive retirement, Sir Ian McIntosh KBE CB DSO DSC MBE died in England in 2003.

DUNERA BOYS

They had no idea where they were going. They only hoped that it would be safer than where they had come from. On 10 July 1940, the hired military transport ship *Dunera* left Liverpool docks with around 2500 souls aboard, bound for somewhere else.

In the first fearful months of World War II the British government became concerned that refugees who had flooded to their shores seeking sanctuary from Hitler's Nazis might be enemy spies. In what Winston Churchill later admitted was 'a deplorable and regrettable mistake', the British government decided to deport these people. Around two thousand male German refugees, mostly Jewish, were placed aboard the *Dunera*, along with several hundred Italian prisoners of war and over two hundred Nazis. They were guarded by over three hundred army troops. Together with the ship's crew, those aboard added up to around twice the carrying capacity of the *Dunera*. The scene was set for disaster.

At first the *Dunera* passengers were told they were bound for Canada. But one man found an atlas, and with the aid of a sextant and some trigonometry, worked out that they were actually sailing to Australia.

The men on the overcrowded vessel were mainly aged between eighteen and 45. Space was so limited that they slept wherever they could. Held below decks for most of the day and night, apart from 30 minutes of exercise per day, sickness was inevitable. Many suffered from diarrhoea and the ten toilets available were strictly policed to control their use. One man was bayoneted as he tried to reach the toilet after dark when access had been forbidden. Someone whimsically calculated that over the length of the 57-day voyage, each of them had just seven minutes use of a toilet a day. Raw sewage often flooded the decks.

Those troops assigned to guard the passengers behaved appallingly, abusing, robbing and beating them, and destroying medicine and religious items. Water was in short supply and razors confiscated, increasing the misery throughout the poorly ventilated ship.

When the *Dunera* reached Australia, the prisoners of war, the Nazis and some internees were put ashore in Melbourne. Most of the Dunera boys, as they would come to be known, continued to Sydney. There, an Australian medical officer, Alan Frost, boarded the ship and was shocked by what he saw. The passengers were dirty, unkempt and poorly dressed. It was soon clear that a serious wrong had been done. Frost wrote a scathing report that eventually led to questions being asked in the British Parliament. The commanding officer aboard the *Dunera* was severely reprimanded and a regimental sergeant major in charge of the army guards was broken to the ranks, imprisoned and then dishonourably discharged. Several other guards were also penalised for their actions during the voyage.

The Dunera boys were transferred by train to an internment camp in Hay in New South Wales where they received much better treatment. Some would tell a story of a casual Australian guard asking an internee to hold his rifle while he rolled a smoke. Later the internees were moved to Tatura in Victoria. In both places they continued the cultural and educational activities established on the *Dunera*, with a camp 'university' and musical groups. They even developed their own currency for use in the camp, a denomination known as a goodonya, after the continual use of the term by their friendly Australian guards.

When the mistake made by the British government was realised and accepted, the Dunera boys were reclassified as friendly aliens and gradually released from internment. Some returned to enlist in British forces or joined the Australian forces. Many received compensation for the loss of their belongings.

After the war, a notable number of the 900 Dunera boys who remained here went on to make valued contributions to Australian education, science and business. Of those who had returned to Britain, many also contributed there, one even becoming a lord.

ARATHO

3

DANGEROUS JOURNEYS

> He did not seem a bit afraid of the police, but, on the contrary, laughed at them and at their efforts to capture him and his mates.
>
> Robert Scott, manager of the Euroa Bank, on Ned Kelly in 1878

VOYAGE TO FREEDOM

James Martin stole some scrap metal belonging to Lord Courtney of Powderham Castle in Exeter. He was arrested, tried, found guilty and transported for seven years to Botany Bay with the First Fleet in 1787. Three years later, on the night of 28 March 1791 Martin joined William and Mary Bryant, their children Charlotte and Emanuel, and six other men in a small leaky boat stocked with food, water and weapons. They rowed the governor's cutter straight through Sydney Heads and set a course north to freedom.

William Bryant's Cornish sailing and fishing skills would be invaluable during the ordeals to come. Some of the other men also had some experience with navigation and handling boats. But nothing they had seen could have prepared them for this daring voyage that would take them along dangerous coasts and through some of the world's least-known waters.

In his surviving account of the voyage, Martin says that after two days they found a creek where they camped for two nights and where 'The Natives came down to whom we gave some Cloaths and other articles, and they went away very well satisfied.' After a couple more days of sailing they landed in 'a very fine harbour' to repair their boat but 'were drove off by the Natives, which meant to destroy us'. Escaping downstream they found another place to land but 'the Natives came in great numbers armed with Spears and Shields &c. we form'd ourselves in parts, one party of us made towards them to pacify them by signes, but they took not the least notice accordingly we fired a Musket thinking to affright them but they paid no attention to it'.

The escapees fled and continued their voyage along the unknown north coast, suffering from exposure, lack of food and dangerous storms. They again attempted to frighten off groups of Aboriginal people by firing over their heads. They were buffeted by howling winds and deluged by rain. During one terrifying storm they were forced to throw their clothes into the sea to avoid sinking. Martin wrote: 'I will leave you to consider what distress we must be in the Woman and the two little babies were in a bad Condition every thing being so wet that we could by no means light a fire we had nothing to eat except a little raw Rice at night.'

By now it was mid May. After about six weeks they had reached the Great Barrier Reef and were surviving mainly on fish and turtle they caught, and rain water. They made land again at the Gulf of Carpentaria where they encountered more 'Natives', probably Torres Strait Islanders, who attacked them with bows and arrows when they again fired their muskets. Later, another group of Islanders chased the escapees into the gulf on sail-rigged canoes. The band outran their pursuers and made a fast three-day passage across the gulf to Arnhem Land where they found fresh water that enabled them to reach the island of Timor, then held by the Dutch.

When they reached Timor, it was 5 June 1791 and the small group of escapees had been at sea for sixty-nine days and sailed 5000 kilometres from Port Jackson. Passing themselves off as survivors of a sunken whaling ship, the group remained on Timor for two months, enjoying the governor's excellent hospitality. Unfortunately, according to Martin's account at least, Mary Bryant and her husband 'had words with [the governor's] wife [and] went and Informed against himself wife & children and all of us which we was immediately taken Prisoners and confined in the Castle'. After some months' confinement they were taken to Batavia, now Jakarta, in chains. Three weeks after their arrival the twenty-month-old Emanuel Bryant died. Three weeks later fever also took his father, the leader of the group.

From there the survivors were taken to Cape Town on separate ships, though three of the remaining men died on the way. The survivors assembled in Cape Town in March 1792. Martin wrote that despite their recapture the fugitives were relieved not to have perished. In April, they left for England aboard HMS *Gorgon.* Sailing through the tropical heat, some of the children of the soldiers aboard began to die. On 6 May, young Charlotte Bryant died and was buried in the sea on which she had lived much of her brief life. The five surviving escapees landed back in England on 18 June 1792. They were conveyed to Newgate prison to await their uncertain futures, quite possibly a sentence of death.

But public interest in the plight of the prisoners, and their astounding escape story, worked in their favour. At their trial before the Old Bailey Bar on 7 July, a sympathetic magistrate decreed that they would only have to serve out the reminder of their existing sentences. Mary Bryant was released in May 1793. The four men, including Martin, were discharged by proclamation in November that year.

What did they do with their hard-won freedom? Although historians have speculated on the subsequent life of Mary Bryant aka Broad, nothing definite is known. The men mostly faded into the shadows of history. James Martin had a wife and son in Exeter and was thought to be willing to return to his trade in Ireland or London. Two of the other men had a brief association with the philosopher and reformist Jeremy Bentham, who took up their case as part of his campaign against transportation.

Wherever they all went and whatever they did, their extraordinary journey to Botany Bay and back and their ultimate path to freedom had cost them five years of their lives.

NED KELLY'S POOR DRIVING

Robert Scott was manager of the National Bank at Euroa. Just before 4 p.m. on 10 December 1878, he received a visit from Ned Kelly and his gang, wishing to make a large but unauthorised withdrawal. Ned pointed a large revolver at the manager and told him to 'bail up'. Steve Hart then joined them, carrying two revolvers.

'I did not bail up at first and they called again upon me to do so,' Scott later stated. 'I had a revolver, but it was lying on the opposite side of the table from me, and I could not reach it without placing myself in the certain danger of being immediately shot.'

The bushrangers again demanded that Scott surrender. Wisely, he decided that although he was armed he had no chance of reaching the weapon before being shot. 'On their again ordering me to throw up my arms I said, "It is all right", and raised my hands to the armpits of my vest.' Ned Kelly then ransacked the bank, taking between three and four hundred pounds worth of gold, silver and banknotes while Hart guarded the helpless bank manager.

In those days, bank managers and their families lived on the premises. Kelly went towards the living quarters and Scott spoke up again: 'Fearing that he would do them harm I said to him "Kelly, if you go there I'll strike you, whatever the consequences may be." Thereupon Hart presented his revolvers at my head, and Kelly passed through.'

To Scott's surprise, his wife, family and servants took the sudden appearance of an armed bushranger very calmly. They were not harmed, but Ned returned to the front of the bank saying he knew there was more money. Scott refused to give him any more, but Ned forced the bank's teller to hand over more gold, sovereigns and cash. The bushrangers had now seized up to the value of 1500 pounds, an enormous amount of money at the time. Ned also broke into the bank vaults but left the share certificates and other securities untouched.

Now the bank manager's slightly surreal journey with Australia's most feared outlaws began. The gang had obtained a hawker's wagon and a small cart. Kelly ordered Scott to also harness his own horse and buggy but Scott refused, saying 'Do it for yourself.' Surprisingly, Kelly agreed mildly and harnessed the horse.

Adding to the carnival atmosphere developing around the convoy of carts and horses, Scott offered the bushrangers a drink. They accepted, although they were careful to watch him drink first. However, Scott's further attempts to slow the procession down come to nothing, and they set out on the five kilometre trek to Younghusband's Station, a property already taken over by the bushrangers in preparation for what was to follow. The brave bank manager described the journey thus:

> Every person about the bank was taken. There was myself, my wife and her mother, my seven children—four boys and three girls the eldest being a boy 13 years of age—the accountant, clerk and two servants. The hawker's van was placed in front, then followed my buggy, which Mrs Scott was driving. The spring cart, driven by Ned Kelly, came next, and Stephen Hart brought up the rear on horseback. I may say here that when the bank was stuck up my wife and family were all in one room, preparing to go out for a walk, and was making ready to attend a funeral. Our arrangements were, however, rudely upset and it appeared for the time that my own funeral would be the next. The distance between Euroa and Younghusband's station is about three miles and a half.

As the slow journey proceeded, Scott opened up a conversation with Kelly. 'I asked him, "What would that fellow Hart have done if I had struck you when you were going into my private house?" He replied, "He would have shot you dead on the spot."'

Kelly let on that the bushrangers had done their background research on the bank manager.

> He further said that he had heard a good deal about me, and had been told that he would find me a difficult person to deal with, and that whilst the hawker he bailed up had been bad, I had been worse, and was, in fact, the worst and most obstinate fellow he had ever met with. The hawker, I believe, was very impertinent to him. He also said, 'I have seen the police often, and have heard them often.' He did not seem a bit afraid of the police, but, on the contrary, laughed at them and at their efforts to capture him and his mates.
>
> The other ruffians appeared to have as little dread of their pursuers. I asked Hart which way he was going when he left the station, and Kelly answered carelessly, 'Oh, the country belongs to us. We can go any where we like.' He said, however, that he was getting sick of bushranging life. In reply to a question as to how Constable M'Intyre behaved when his comrades were murdered, he simply said that that officer made no resistance. He would not say where he and his gang had been concealing themselves, nor what they as outlaws wanted with the money he had stolen. I presume, however, that they intend the money for their relatives.

Kelly was driving the cart badly. Scott asked to take the reins as he knew the road, but Kelly refused. It wasn't long before the bushranger ran the conveyance into a bank and turned it over.

> We were nearly all thrown out. I jumped out, and got hold of the horse, and Kelly lifted out the servant. He then got the horse released, harnessed it again, and we started afresh. After driving a little he said, 'You drive very well, you had better go on.' I was then proceeding to take a short cut to Younghusband's station—for we had been informed that it was our destination when Kelly, suspecting that I was misleading him, said, 'If you play me any pranks, I will make it hot for you.' I told him that the others had taken the wrong road—or rather a longer one—and he allowed me to proceed. The notes stolen from the bank were lying beside me, and I felt sorely tempted to regain them, but restrained myself.

Ned Kelly's convoy reached Younghusband's to find the remainder of his gang had already captured a group of local workers.

> They were standing beside the hut, and the fourth man of the gang, who is named Byrne, was marching in front of them with two guns and his belt stuck full of revolvers. Ned Kelly had previously threatened to roast them alive and to do all sorts of things to them. There were 22 men in all bailed up here. I now learned that the ruffians had arrived at the station about mid day on Monday, and that they had stayed there all night, and the men they had secured were bailed up all the time. The station was a handy place for making a descent from upon the bank.

While the captured men looked a little cowed, the bushrangers and their horses were in fine condition. The horses were rested and well fed, although a little overburdened by the stolen gold and silver. And Scott noted that the bushrangers 'had evidently been feeding well':

> they were rigged out in the new clothes they had obtained from the hawkers van. They were also fully equipped with arms, and had plenty of ammunition. Daniel Kelly exactly like the picture of him in the papers. Ned is a good looking man, with reddish whiskers.

Ned Kelly's 37 'guests' were given supper and treated to a display of horsemanship by Dan Kelly and Steve Hart. Ned made his usual speech about the persecution suffered by himself and his family. In her account of the incident, Mrs Scott famously declared that 'Ned Kelly was a gentleman.'

About 7.30 that evening the prisoners were gathered into a hut and told to stay there for three hours. According to Scott:

> I looked at my watch and said, 'Then we will leave at 11 o'clock.' Ned Kelly replied, 'No, not until half past 11. You must stop here for three hours, and if any of you leave before then we will find you out and make it hot for you.'

> Just before they left, the man Byrne returned to the door of the hut, and said, 'I want to see Mr Scott. Give me your watch.' I said 'No, I won't. You can take it if you like,' and he accordingly un-hooked it from my vest and carried it away.

The outlaws rode away towards Violet Town and the prisoners waited until 11 p.m., as commanded. Mrs Scott drove the family home in the buggy. Robert Scott, minus his watch, walked behind. When they reached Euroa they discovered that no one in the town had suspected anything until they found the Scotts' living quarters deserted at 9 p.m. The town's only policeman was nowhere to be found and it wasn't until 4 a.m. the next morning that a party of police and a backtracker arrived from Benalla. As usual, the Kellys and the loot were long gone.

THE CAMELEER FACTOR

Albert Calvert was a man of many parts and many interests. Some of them included mining, exploration, and making—and losing—money in rather large quantities. He was known in England as 'the prophet of the west', due to his fascination with the mineral wealth in that large part of Australia. In 1896, barely in his mid twenties, Calvert offered funds to the South Australian Royal Geographic Society for an expedition to gather scientific evidence, search for the missing explorer Ludwig Leichhardt and pioneer a stock route from the Northern Territory to the western goldfields. Of course, the unspoken main purpose of the enterprise was to search for mineral wealth.

The expedition was led by Lawrence 'Larry' Wells, with his twenty-year-old cousin Charles as second in command, as well as six other men, including two experienced Afghan cameleers, Bejah Dervish and Said Ameer. Camels became popular on exploration treks from the 1840s onwards for their stamina, carrying capacity and comparative cheapness. Wells wisely took twenty with him.

Wells's party set off north from Mullewa in June 1896. By

August they were moving into the Great Sandy Desert. Water was scarce there and the camels were falling sick from eating poisonous weeds. Charles Wells and the expedition's photographer, mineralogist George Jones, made a separate exploration north-west in October. They planned to rejoin the main party the following month. Anxiety began to mount when their return date came and went. Several attempts were made to find them, effectively turning the expedition intended to 'fill in the blank spaces on the map' into a desperate rescue bid. It was not until May the next year that their remains were found, as described by Wells:

> we travelled to Ngoaaddapa and Kullga Agunum to a point about fourteen miles north-north-east of Johanna Springs. On May 24th we sent Bejah and a tracker along the pad to Johanna. Ord, Nicholson and myself, with the other tracker, pushed on in the direction of smoke seen the previous day, and after going fourteen miles we ran some natives down in their camp. Here we found a large piece of the iron bow of a camel riding saddle. The natives said it was taken from dead white men, and added that the sun had killed them. The natives were bold, and refused to go with us until the handcuffs were used. They tried many devices to avoid going to Johanna Springs, Ord and Nicholson having to drive them.
>
> After that we spelled a day at Johanna, and tried to induce the natives to point out the direction of the dead men, but without success. The following day we travelled the pad, going westerly twelve miles, when we reached a high point from which we obtained a good view of the surrounding country. Here again we tried the natives, but they would eagerly point in any direction except that in which they knew the dead men to be. It was found necessary to resort to stronger measures, and they then took us south-east for five miles, and south-west for two miles, to the spot for which we had so long been seeking.

It was only 10 kilometres from the spot they had searched the month before. Wells wrote:

> I at once recognised Charles by his beard and features, the skin having dried on his face and body. He lay under a desert gum tree, where he had been erecting a fly for a shade. On the top of a sand ridge, about one chain westerly, the remains of George Jones were found. The body had evidently been covered with sand by Charles, who had then gone to the other tree to wait death itself. The natives had carried off everything of any use to themselves. The woodwork of both kegs, portions of the camel pack-saddle and one riding saddle, one leather pack-bag, a leather satchel, Jones's compass, a Prayer Book, a leather pouch, a tin box with medicines, a journal, and a note to his parents were close by him. We could find no plan or any letter left by Charles. All the firearms had been carried off by the natives.

From the journal Jones left, Wells worked out the course the unfortunate men had taken. One camel died in the intense heat and the remaining two had wandered off into the desert. The men were too weak to chase them. They were down to two quarts of water and did not expect to live much longer. Wells was also able to deduce how they had perished.

> There was no date to this letter, but from his statement they must have left Separation Well on October 23rd. They probably travelled by night and lost my track. Allowing fifteen days, they would have reached the spot where we found them about November 8th. From what we saw of the spot where the equipment was, it would appear that my cousin's riding camel had died, and that they had left his saddle, bringing everything else on. The remains are sewn up in canvas and will be placed in coffins here, ready for removal to Adelaide by the next boat.

The dead men were given a state funeral in Adelaide. But Calvert, an inveterate mining speculator, had lost his money in the meantime and was unable to provide the funds he had promised. The leader of the expedition came in for a good deal of criticism, though he was later exonerated by a Parliamentary Select Committee.

As Larry Wells freely acknowledged, the rest of the expedition probably escaped death in the extreme conditions through Bejah's amazing ability to keep many of the camels going:

> Anyone who has read the plain, unvarnished tale of that terrible and fateful Calvert expedition as told in the diary of Mr. Wells understands why the humble camel driver in Marree has so many friends and admirers. A more devoted colleague no leader of an expedition could have had. Mr. Wells describes him as 'one of Nature's gentlemen', and says that his word is his bond.

The flamboyant Albert Calvert continued his volatile careers in mining and speculation, as well as writing and publishing many books. In 1923, he was at the centre of a scandal involving royal Russian jewellery and was lucky to escape criminal proceedings. He died in London in 1946.

WHEELS ACROSS THE WILDERNESS

The bicycle in its modern form arrived in Australia in the late 1860s. It soon became wildly popular, with bicycle races and bicycle clubs springing up around the country. It was not long before intrepid types began to push the limits of man and machine (it was long considered unladylike for women to ride bicycles). Transcontinental rides were attempted by many, particularly from the 1890s when Albert MacDonald of Orroroo rode over 3300 kilometres from Port Darwin to Adelaide in just under 27 days.

But the man destined to become one of the most famous long-distance cyclists (and later, motor car adventurers) was Victorian man Francis Birtles. At the age of 25 in 1906, he announced his intention to cross the continent from the west coast to the east coast. When interviewed by a journalist, the 'calm-eyed, wiry-looking Australian' summed up his motivations and his strategy:

> I have been a wanderer for ten years since I left my native State, Victoria. For the last five-years I have been in South Africa, and

> have travelled all over that country with the mobile columns of the constabulary, from Capetown to Koomati Poort, and from the Orange River to the Limpopo. As a cyclist, I have done a deal of racing on the Transvaal roads, and have crossed the Karoo and Kalahari deserts. Now I want to ride from the Indian to the Pacific Oceans.
>
> Next Wednesday I shall mount my machine at Fremantle, and will call at the Exhibition at Hay-street East for a final send-off at 4 p.m. From Perth I shall ride to Laverton, and will then strike north-easterly to cross the border into South Australia. I want to go through country which has not yet been traversed, and if I get through all right will come out near Alice Springs, on the overland telegraph line. The ride to Adelaide will be comparatively easy, and then I shall cross to Ballarat, Melbourne and Sydney.

Birtles thought he 'might have trouble with the natives' but would 'watch them' as he traversed the arid country on a spring-frame machine BSA roadster with a freewheel back-pedal brake and Dunlop bushman's tyres. 'With ordinary luck, I'll get through,' he manfully declared. Asked why he was making the ride at all, he replied:

> Oh . . . I fancy the trip. It will fill in time and will satisfy my passion for wandering. I'm only 25 years of age, and I've travelled a bit. No, I don't expect to make much money out of it, seeing that I'm paying all my expenses. I shall write all about it. You may have seen my articles, 'An Australian Trooper in Zululand', in 'Life'. I expect to be about two months on the journey, and, as I say, I have only myself to look after.

On Boxing Day 1906, a mass of Perth cyclists gave Birtles a hearty send-off. He carried two waterbags and concentrated food weighing 40 pounds. By 4 January, he had reached Coolgardie feeling 'well and confident'. Four days later he wrote from Kalgoorlie:

> I am travelling along quietly through the various inland towns; I will not be leaving Laverton before the end of this month. I want to catch the rains which generally fall in the beginning of the year. The people have treated me well on the 'run up' here. From Grass Valley, to Kalgoorlie the pipe tracks are good travelling. As for the main road it is best left alone. The roads over the ranges are very gravelly, the wheels skidding all the way. A man could make a hundred miles a day here. As for myself, I pedal along four or five hours a day on an average. There are so many people to see; that one loses a lot of time. But I do not mind: I am in no hurry. I feel in splendid going order now. I have had two water-tanks fitted to my 'bike'. They will have to carry me through the dry country. The holding capacity of the two is five gallons. Pretty weighty, certainly, but I shall want it. In conclusion, I wish to thank you and all brother cyclists for your hearty send-off and good wishes.

At this time his route was through almost unexplored and untracked country. By early February he was beginning to find water scarce. He could carry about 22 litres of water but he was struggling through dense mulga:

> Twenty six miles must now be made before I can reach the next waterhole, it is eight days since I saw the last one. Waterhole to waterhole is about 180 to 200 miles apart. Am utilising at the rate of two quarts of water a day, and my supply lasts 10 days. When I get further south, I am told, there is no scarcity of water, and as the tracks will then be better, I hope to be able to make more satisfactory progress.

But by March Birtles had run into trouble, as he wrote to a friend:

> I have made my second attempt to cross the desert, and have failed. On this occasion I got out 120 miles into the desert, which is in a terrible condition, owing to the last two dry seasons. On Sunday (February 10) I was forced back, and had to retreat for lack of water. The following day I had nothing to drink. I was in a horrible

> condition, legs cut and swollen, and a bad head, some insect had bitten me while sleeping. Add to this that I had to push my bike nearly all the way sometimes in sand nearly up to the hubs of the wheels. You will readily understand my plight when I tell you that the temptation to leave my machine and take my clothes off was well nigh unconquerable, but I knew that I would be finished if I did so. During the 240 miles I travelled in the desert country, I only found water twice. In one instance the rock-hole was full of dead rabbits. Even the dingoes are lying dead round empty holes.
>
> On my retreat from the desert I had a terrible time. Luckily I happened to know of a soak some 60 miles away, and about 40 miles out of Kurnalpi, and to this I managed to struggle. On the way to the soak I began to get so bad that I could continuously see water alongside of me, whilst every time I took a rest I saw a dingo slinking around in the scrub. He followed me for 60 miles to the soak. Here I got a couple of quarts of water, and waited a day, then I got two more, which carried me back to Kurnalpi.
>
> You can imagine what I had to go through when I mention the fact that the temperature at Kurnalpi when I got back was 110 degrees in the shade, so you can form an idea of what it was like pushing a cycle and luggage weighing close on 120lb through the desert.

He had covered over 2000 kilometres by then, 800 of them through 'trackless country'. His bike and tyres had held up well but he had 'come to the conclusion that it is absolutely impossible to negotiate the desert in its present state, so I intend crossing to Adelaide, Melbourne, and Sydney, via the coastal route'.

Birtles did succeed in his aim by taking the coastal route. He was in Adelaide by late April and rode into Melbourne on 29 April. He wheeled into Sydney on 8 May 1907, having been 113 days on the road and cycling over seven thousand kilometres from the Indian to the Pacific oceans. A 'host of cyclists' greeted him, along with his mother and brother. His achievement was applauded 'as one of the most important that had been performed anywhere'. Birtles recounted his arduous journey and then cycled to Bondi to complete it. He said 'he would not like to do it again—for some time, at any rate'.

But it was not long before the persistent pedaller was back on the road. By 1912 he had twice cycled round the continent and crossed it seven times. And then he started doing it all again in motorcars, but that is another story.

MRS BELL'S OLDSMOBILE

'The wanderlust was on her and just HAD to be satisfied!' At least that was how it was put in the advertisement celebrating Mrs Marion Bell's 1925–26 round-Australia drive in her Oldsmobile Six. The advertising copywriters and the press made much of the fact that the 29-year-old Mrs Bell had done it all without the help of a man and 'against the advice of the car agents, members of Parliament and police'.

This 'brave little woman of the west' was born in New Zealand. She was an outstanding runner, horsewoman and rifle shot and 'ha[d] tried her hand at all classes of sport indulged in by man'. By the time she set out on her epic journey she and her husband were running a garage in Fremantle. Marion Bell became the first woman to drive a motor car around Australia.

She did not travel alone; her eleven-year-old daughter, also named Marion, came along for the ride. They left Perth on 12 October 1925 and headed north through Marble Bar, Broome, Derby, then into the Northern Territory via Katherine and Victoria Downs. Then it was on through Cloncurry, Longreach, Roma and Toowoomba to Brisbane, then Murwillumbah and Bangalow. They reached Lismore on 16 December.

By now Mrs Bell and her daughter had experienced adventure and adversity aplenty. Somewhere in the west dingoes attacked them. Mrs Bell drew her revolver and dropped one. She then chased the rest of the pack down until one of the dingoes dropped dead in front of her car.

Near Marble Bar Mrs Bell's daughter fell ill. Burning with fever, she was barely able to stand and her lips bled from sunburn.

Her mother administered quinine but she came close to death. The younger Marion recovered, allowing the journey to continue. At one point the Oldsmobile lost its brakes and they drove for 1000 miles of rough country with no means of stopping other than gearing down.

There were other encounters with mortality along the way. In the Territory they came across a wanderer on an isolated track. He was near death already and there was little they could do other than ease his passing. A few hours later the Oldsmobile's radiator ran dry and they now faced the prospect of a lingering death themselves from lack of water. Fortunately, a few days later came the first rain in a year and they were able to catch enough in a tarpaulin to get them and their car to the next settlement, almost 300 kilometres away.

At one point Mrs Bell managed to stop a tribal conflict between warring Aboriginal groups.

> Hundreds of stark naked natives were hurling spears and boomerangs at one another. Short stone knives rattled on the hardened shields carried by the warriors, while there were some who fell never to rise again. Mr Wilson, manager of the station, advised me not to go near the natives, but nevertheless, I drove my car as close as possible and went up amongst them. They stopped fighting immediately and crowded round. Beads and sweets put them in a good humor and the result was that they parted with some of their weapons as a keepsake.

As she motored across the continent, Mrs Bell was tracked by the press and celebrated by advertisements by the agents for Oldsmobile. Some called her the wonder woman. It was a great story of woman and machine pitted against the forbidding might of the great Australian continent.

In Adelaide the local press reported that hundreds had inspected Mrs Marion Bell's Oldsmobile: 'It speaks highly for Mrs Bell's driving ability that no dent is to be found on the car. The duco finish has withstood the sand, mud and heat remarkably well, and the engine ticks over like a clock.' The journalist wound up the report by writing, 'Keenly interested in motors and imbued with the sympathy between car and driver that should exist, she has come "smiling through" one of the most, if not the most strenuous trial a car and a woman have ever attempted.'

Marion and her daughter returned to the west and made their grand entrance at Sawyer's Valley in April 1926:

> Smartly clad in riding breeches, with a leather motor-coat and cap, and with a happy smile on her face, Mrs Bell, who had just completed a circuit of Australia by motor-car—a distance of 12,000 miles—stepped out of her car, and remarked, smilingly, 'It is a warm day.' On the front seat of the car was her little daughter, Marion, who accompanied her throughout the trip.

Mrs Bell gave an account of her trip to the press:

> 'I started on my trip on October 14 last,' said Mrs Bell to a Press representative, 'and no hand but mine has touched the wheel of the car since we left home. Even from the worst of bogs, I extricated the car myself. For many days the temperature was 123deg. in the shade. My little girl contracted fever, and I had to nurse her in the car, and drive on, day after day. At times the journey seemed fearfully monotonous; for days on end the scenery was unchanging, and we appeared to get no further ahead. We had no trouble with the natives—indeed, they treated me everywhere as if I were a little god. By some means they seemed to be apprised that I was coming, and I was told that some of them with their piccaninies had camped on the road for a fortnight waiting for me to pass. I wish especially to pay a tribute to dwellers in the Northern Territory, and throughout the route for the manner in which they treated me. They could not do enough for us. The police also were excellent. They offered us hospitality at the stations, and waited on us hand and foot. Although we left Perth with only 11lb. of groceries, we had no difficulty in getting further provisions; we lived on tinned meat and biscuits, chiefly.'

Then a procession of fifteen or so cars escorted the Bells the forty or so kilometres to Perth where an enthusiastic crowd cheered their achievement. The president of the Royal Automobile Club of Western Australia gave a speech emphasising the uniqueness of Mrs Bell's journey. 'I assure you that it is jolly nice to be back again,' Mrs Bell replied. The news was reported throughout the country and the lady motorist from the west became a celebrity.

But the celebrations were hardly over before the trouble began. Circumnavigating the continent in motor cars of all kinds was a positive mania in the 1920s. Two other expeditions had left Perth the same year as Mrs Bell. One of these was Joshua Warner in a four-cylinder Citroen. Warner claimed that he had to help Marion out with petrol and other necessities because of her lack of preparation and incompetence. He said that he towed her out of trouble on more than one occasion. Mrs Bell retorted that this was not true. On the contrary, Warner did not even know how to change the tyres on his car and she had to provide him with oil from her own supplies.

Worse followed. Scandal-sheet *The Mirror* in Perth reported that the Oldsmobile in which Mrs Bell had left Perth was not the Oldsmobile that had returned. According to the newspaper, the original car broke down at Fitzroy Crossing where it was abandoned. Another was obtained locally in which she completed her famous journey.

And so the dispute went on. The local Oldsmobile agents in Perth tried unconvincingly to disown their connection with the drive, admitting in the process that, contrary to some reported statements by Mrs Bell, that she had changed cars.

Mrs Bell replied through another newspaper:

> 'Some people are trying their best to give me a rough spin', she complained. 'What it is all about, or what is the motive behind it, may not be so clear to the public as it is to me . . . My domestic concerns and my business affairs are being dragged in, and I think it is very unfair. After all is said and done, I did motor around Australia. I have newspaper extracts to show the different towns,

> large and small, at which I was interviewed on arrival, and my daughter can support my statement, that no one but I handled the wheel of the car from the time we left Fremantle in October last until we returned a fortnight ago.'

She went on to say that she thought the public was not 'at all interested to know whether I helped Mr. Warner or Mr. Warner helped me':

> but in view of what has been said and printed on that aspect, all I want to say now is that I rendered quite a lot of service to Mr. Warner in critical circumstances. But I did only what any motorist would do for a fellow motorist in difficulties. I hope I will be pardoned for suggesting that, even, though it was true that Mr. Warner did for me all that he claims to have done, a spirit of chivalry—to say nothing of the Freemasonry of the motor car—would have urged him to do no less, and should have restrained from criticism said to have been uttered by him concerning me—a woman who at least had the pluck to undertake a journey of that kind.
>
> That's all I want to say.'

Others wanted to say more but the controversy soon faded from the press. The book of her exploits promised by Mrs Bell never appeared. But the Oldsmobile company did not mind at all. Mrs Marion Bell and her daughter had provided them with months of priceless copy and public relations imagery for the virtues of their product.

In November 1928 the list of motor vehicle registrations for Western Australia showed Mrs Marion Bell of 130 Queen Victoria Street, Fremantle, had a new car—a Hudson.

THE SECRET ORDER OF THE DOUBLE SUNRISE

The outbreak of the Pacific war in 1941 dealt an almost fatal blow to Australia's fledgling airline, Qantas. The company's business—then known as Qantas Empire Airways—was based largely on flights between Britain and Australia, and from February 1942 it was no longer possible for civilian aircraft to fly that route.

After a lot of investigation and negotiation the managing director of Qantas, Hudson Fysh, convinced the British government to lend his company five Royal Navy flying boats, which were already travelling on an established route from Ceylon (now Sri Lanka) to Perth. In June 1943, Qantas crew began operating the Cats, as the Catalinas were affectionately known. They flew from their base on the Swan River to Exmouth then directly to Lake Koggala in Sri Lanka where it was safe to connect with British military transport.

The covert journey took between 28 and 33 hours nonstop. As they were timed to ensure they flew only at night across Japanese-occupied areas, each flight saw two sunrises. Almost total radio silence was observed and although the planes were not fitted with guns they usually carried military documents. The top-secret character of the route meant that the six-man crews did not wear uniforms. If intercepted the crews and their passengers would almost certainly have been executed as spies.

Those who flew as passengers were issued with a special certificate stating that they had become members of the Secret Order of the Double Sunrise. In the two or so years of its operation, the double-sunrise flight transported around eight-hundred passengers. They included Rupert Murdoch's father, Keith, and a British minister of parliament, as well as others travelling mainly on official business related to the war effort.

Conditions for the passengers were far worse than even the most cramped cattle-class accommodation of today's passenger flights. There were a couple of bunks intended for the crew and three chairs. The rear wall of the plane featured a small toilet—just the toilet. The need to keep the Cats as light as possible meant they were fitted only with vital equipment; there was no allowance for privacy. Temperatures inside the fuselage could fall as low as minus 14 degrees Celsius. Skin was easily burned off if it touched the metal body of the plane. Four or five meals were served during the long flight.

One of the first to fly the usually overloaded Cats was Rex Senior. He was first officer and navigator on the initial flight and eventually completed many flights on the route. He later recalled a shopkeeper telling him to join up and was once given a white feather, the symbol of cowardice.

When the Japanese advance in the Pacific was rolled back in August 1944, Hudson Fysh spoke publicly about the Double Sunrise route. He revealed that the Japanese had once attacked a flying boat and there had been the occasional problem with fuel supplies. In one incident, a plane flew the last 400 kilometres or so of the flight on just one engine. He called the operation 'one of the epic transport feats of the war' and pointed out:

> It is an enormous flight non-stop. Payload is limited, and it is essentially a war-time service. A civil air route could not be economically operated over so wide an expanse of ocean.

It is said that the Double Sunrise Cats still hold the world record for the longest continuous flight of 33 hours.

The Cats were no longer needed after the war. Four were towed to sea and sunk by machine gun fire near Rottnest Island off the coast of Western Australia. The fifth was eventually sunk outside Sydney Heads.

In 2009, a surviving plane of the same type was located in Spain. Qantas purchased the relic and restored it at great cost, and it can now be seen in the Qantas Founders Museum in Longreach.

THE REAL GREAT ESCAPE

Stalag Luft III is best known as the Nazi prison camp from which the Great Escape took place in March 1944, an event immortalised but also mythologised in the Hollywood movie of the same name. But the Australian dimension to the story and its aftermath is less well known.

Paul Royle was one of a number of Australians who joined the Royal Air Force before the outbreak of World War II. He was shot down during a reconnaissance flight in 1940. After crashlanding in a field near the northern French town of Cambrai, the injured Royle and his crew managed to seek medical attention in a nearby village. Royle went back to destroy the Blenheim but later passed out from loss of blood. He was soon taken prisoner.

After spending time in and attempting to escape from one prisoner-of-war camp, Royle was transferred to Stalag Luft III in 1942. Here, almost 200 kilometres south-east of Berlin, in what is now Poland, he was imprisoned with other pilot officers, many of whom were intent on leaving as soon as possible. Royle became involved with a British tunnelling plot known as X Organisation.

The camp had been carefully designed to prevent escapes. Microphones were buried under the wire fences to detect any tunnelling sounds and there was a trip wire at knee height all round the inside of the camp's fence. Officers were not made to work in prison camps and the monotony of the everyday routine sharpened their sense of duty to plot an escape, as well as find infinite ways to disguise the necessary preparations and practise the necessary deceptions.

Three tunnels were started. One was discovered and closed and one abandoned. But escape preparations continued in the tunnel codenamed Harry. The prisoners were ingenious in discreetely disposing of the soil they laboriously scooped out almost 10 metres underground. Paul Royle was one of the 'penguins' that carried earth held in their trousers. When they found a suitable spot to dump it, they pulled a string sewn into their cuffs allowing the soil to trickle unseen onto the ground as they strolled along. While carrying out this important task, Royle was also a lookout.

The tunnel itself was so cramped and airless that a ventilation device had to be built of old tin cans. A miniature wooden railway carried the workers backwards and forwards on a tiny trolley as they toiled and sweated through their dangerous digging shifts. The unstable walls and ceilings were shored up with wood taken from the wall lining and bunks in prison huts. But at least the diggers had light, courtesy of some cabling stolen from their captors and powered through an illicit connection to the camp's electrical circuit.

Clothes, rations, maps and forged German papers were produced for the 200 men the escapers planned to push through the 100-metre tunnel on the night of 24 March 1944. A ballot was held to decide which of them could escape then and on the fateful night the lucky winners began assembling in Hut 104. Paul Royle was number 57.

But there had been a mistake in the measurements and the escape tunnel was almost three metres short of the woods beyond the perimeter wire. The escapees had to clamber out of the tunnel right where the guards patrolled. This and other delays meant that only 76 men got through the tunnel by the time it was discovered shortly before 5 a.m.

Royle was one of the men who got away. He eluded the guards and with the man next in line, Edgar Humphreys, headed through the frozen countryside for Switzerland. But they didn't get far: they were captured after a day or so by the German home guard and handed over to the Gestapo. After brutal interrogation Royle was returned to solitary confinement in the camp but Humphreys was among the 50 escapees executed on the direct orders of Adolf Hitler. Royle never knew why he was spared the fate of his companion. Only three of the escapees made it back to Britain.

The ashes of the executed men were returned to the camp, where the British prisoners built a stone memorial to their dead comrades. It remains today, tended by the local community. In the Nuremberg war crimes trials in 1947, eighteen of those who had executed the escapees were prosecuted. Thirteen were themselves executed and the rest imprisoned for many years.

Paul Royle was liberated in 1945 and later worked in the mining industry in his native Western Australia. He was not a fan of the famous movie of the great escape, particularly not of the heroic but historically inaccurate motorcycle-riding star Steve McQueen. He never observed the annual commemoration of the escape but he did give an interview on the seventieth anniversary in which he said, matter of factly: 'While we all hoped for the future we were lucky to get the future. We eventually defeated the Germans and that was that.'

Paul Royle died in August 2015 at the age of 101.

A JENOLAN JOURNEY

In 1954, a group of young men risked their lives swimming through an underground river in the Jenolan Caves. They were searching for a new cavern that might link with the stream that appeared in the Imperial Cave.

Attempts to swim the river had been made before but this was to be a full-scale assault using around one thousand pounds' worth of what was then the latest diving and communication technology, including an underwater telephone.

Garbed in all-black frogman suits, the four men who braved this dangerous journey were Russell Kippax, Owen Llewellyn, Keith White and the Frenchman Michael Calluaud. As vice-president of the Underwater Explorer's Club, Calluaud was the most experienced member of the team. He was the first in Australia to use self-contained compressed air breathing equipment under water.

The support team spent the night building a wooden platform in the cave for the divers to use as a base and preparing for all eventualities.

> The explorers' main worries were light, air (or more correctly, lack of them), cold and fatigue. All these were taken care of. Each man was completely encased from neck to ankle in a water-tight rubber suit, and wore woollen underwear. A mask and goggles covered almost all of the face. Sealed beam cat head-lights with batteries to last about an hour solved the light problem. And just for emergency each man carried a waterproof torch.

Each diver carried a knife, and a lead belt to help them submerge, and was connected to an AFLOLAUN (apparatus for laying out line and underwater navigation). This device paid out the telephone line and could also transmit a distress signal back to the platform where two reserve divers were on standby, should they be needed. Just after 11.15 a.m. the first two frogmen put on flippers and helmets and slipped into the cold clear water. They were followed at intervals by the other two. To the watching standby divers left behind, the yellow glow of the underwater lanterns slowly faded, leaving only the black darkness and silence. The seconds ticked by.

Five minutes later one of the standby divers shouted, 'A light! One of them is coming back!' The Frenchman broke the surface, crying, 'I lost him! I lost him!' The thick mud churned up by the divers had made visibility almost nil. Fortunately everyone was still in contact via the AFLOLAUN and the remaining divers underwater confirmed they had found a passage leading to a siphon that they would try to swim through.

After another seven anxious minutes of silence, the telephone crackled and Kippax reported excitedly, 'I'm through!' He described a cave over 90 metres in length and 6 metres wide.

Keith White also passed through the siphon and into this cave. He reported:

> I got a terrific feeling when I stood up in this great cave and turned my light around. I thought to myself 'No man has ever been here before.'
>
> We were standing in water about a foot deep. It trickled over the floor of the cave. All around there were fallen rocks and there was a sign of a recent fall at one end of the cave. We were very careful not to touch anything for fear of dislodging other rocks. Without our lights the cave was dark—the blackest darkness I've ever been in. The roof of the cave sloped up to 70 feet high. There were beautiful lights. Stalactites stretched down from the roof. There was a continual drip, drip, drip of water from the roof.

The new cavern was expected to contribute to the further development of Jenolan for recreational spelunking.

In those days, cave diving was a very new sport, especially in Australia. One of the greatest of the French pioneers of the activity was quoted as saying: 'Of all the gambles, this is the most perilous and foolhardy, for one's life hangs upon a thread in these narrow tubes of rocks filled or almost filled with water.'

The Indigenous peoples of the area know the caves as Binomea, or 'dark places', while Jenolan means 'high mountain'. The present name was given to the caves in 1884. Before that they were known as the Fish River caves. Europeans first officially located the underground complex in 1838, although legend has it that the caves were in use by escaped convicts some time before this. Over the years many caverns and cavities have been discovered, explored and opened up to tourism. Today Jenolan Caves is a premier tourism and recreation site. Well over 200,000 people every year make the journey into the mountains to take in the magnificent natural display.

MANHUNT

Just why police tracker Billy Benn pumped fourteen bullets into Harry Neale on 5 August 1967 has never been clear. Most say it was related to the misappropriation of sacred Aboriginal stones, often known as *tjuringa*. Neale died before a full account of the incident could be taken from him but he lasted long enough to identify his killer.

Two constables from the Northern Territory police pursued Billy but the wily tracker ambushed them in a gully, wounding both badly. Fortunately they survived, but the hunt was redoubled, for an armed and very dangerous man who knew his way through the Outback better than any white man. The police understood this and formed a pursuit party that included a number of Aboriginal trackers, including a young man known as Teddy Egan.

The police in this hastily assembled group were poorly equipped and mostly without a lot of bush experience. They had no compass or maps. One of the officers recalled that the only way they were likely to find Billy was when he shot at them.

As they struggled through the rough country, seeking signs of Billy's passing or that of his relatives who had followed him out into the bush, and waiting to be shot, the journey became a contest of mind and skill between Billy and Teddy Egan. The Aboriginal outlaws wrapped their feet in strips of blanket to hide their tracks and kept just ahead of their pursuers. But Teddy soon realised they had a dog and tracked the animal's prints instead.

As the days wore on, the police and their trackers were plagued by mishaps and accidents. One horse broke a leg and had to be destroyed. They were short of food and clothing in the cold conditions. A police aircraft flew over them from time to time but was of little help in locating the fugitives.

Water was a problem for both the hunters and the hunted. The police found Billy's old campfires with the remains of paddymelons around them, indicating he and his family had cooked them for the water they contained. The fugitives were continually digging for water in the arid land.

It was six days of rough riding before they caught up with Billy and his mob. That evening the pursuit party camped in a deep gorge. Teddy was restive, saying Billy was nearby. Just as it was getting dark, the police tracker heard a noise and went out to investigate. What happened next differs in the telling. In Constable Terry O'Brien's account, recalled many years later, they lost sight of Teddy behind a large rock, then a rifle shot echoed around the range. The police feared the outlaw had shot Teddy. Luckily not. Teddy had bravely walked straight up to one of Billy's mob, who was carrying a rifle, and ripped it away from him, then fired a shot into the air to signal all-clear.

The police were relieved. Fearing for their lives but also for a race-relations disaster if the situation got further out of hand, the officers gladly took custody of the fugitives. Billy and his people were also pretty relieved, worn out from lack of food and water. 'They were poor as crows,' Constable Laurie Kennedy remembered.

They camped overnight, with Billy held in custody, and next morning the group set out for Harts Range, a day's ride away. Billy led the way, guiding them to the waterholes for the horses. The police party appreciated how lucky they had been. As Laurie

Kennedy said, 'If it wasn't for the trackers, I believe we could have still been out there.'

Billy was flown to Alice Springs and eventually stood trial for murder. He was acquitted on grounds of insanity but served fifteen years in gaol followed by two years in an Adelaide mental institution. Teddy's bravery and skill were largely forgotten as the years went by, although at least one policeman did not forget Teddy's courage: former Alice Springs station chief Graham MacMahon campaigned tirelessly for proper acknowledgment. Six Northern Territory police commissioners came and went. Each was petitioned. All refused to recognise Teddy's service.

Through those same years Billy Benn served his time. While inside he took up painting as a form of therapy and a way of reconnecting with his faraway country. His landscapes eventually made him a successful and well known central Australian artist. When he died in 2012 he had even been the subject of a book on his life and art.

In 2015, a new Northern Territory Police Commissioner finally agreed that the heroic tracker Teddy Egan deserved an award. He was given the Northern Territory Police Valour Medal in October 2015, at the remote Yuendemu community. But the award was given to his family: Teddy Egan had died in 2011. It had taken nearly half a century for the potentially deadly journey that he and Billy Benn had taken together to deliver rightful recognition for one and redemption for the other.

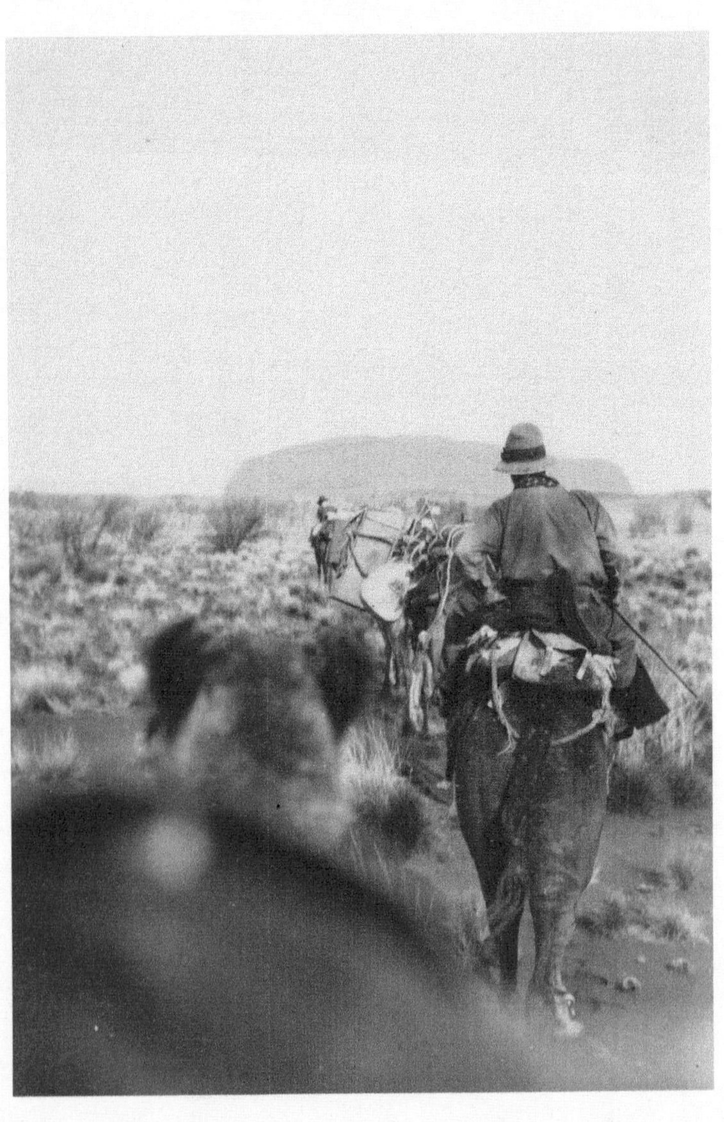

4

MYSTERIOUS JOURNEYS

The Court cannot say what particular form was taken by the catastrophe.

Board of Trade Inquiry into the loss of the SS *Waratah*, 1909

LEICHHARDT'S RIFLE

The German-born explorer Ludwig Leichhardt was perhaps the greatest and most single-minded inland explorer of Australia. His last expedition produced one of our most persistent colonial mysteries.

Leichhardt landed at Sydney in 1842, following years of scientific and medical study in his native Germany (then Prussia) and in England. He wished to explore the inland, and in 1844 led a privately funded expedition overland from Sydney to Port Essington on the Cobourg Peninsula in the Northern Territory. The successful journey, of almost 5000 kilometres, made Leichhardt a hero. He was feted in his homeland, in Britain and in Australia and showered with geographical and scientific awards.

After a partially successful attempt to cross the country from east to west in 1846–47, he assembled another expedition with the same aim in 1848. With six others, including two Aboriginal men, he left the Darling Downs in April with the intention of travelling far enough north to skirt the central desert, hoping to find a river that would then take his party to the west coast. Going across the Top End would also provide a reasonably reliable water supply for the large herd of livestock that was an essential element of the expedition.

On April 4 he wrote from Mount Abundance, describing his progress and the country he had crossed. All had gone well. The weather had been kind, the ground mostly good and there had been no accidents. The leader also expressed himself pleased with his party: 'I cannot speak in too high terms of my present party, who seem to me well qualified for the long and tedious journey which is before us.'

No more was ever heard from Leichhardt or his companions. We have been looking for him ever since and, like the journey of Burke and Wills, Leichhardt's story has moved from history into myth.

The explorers expected to be away for two or three years so initially there was little concern for their fate. The first person to express concern seems to have been another German scientist and explorer, Ferdinand (later Sir) Von Mueller. As early as 1849, he was writing to officials suggesting it was time to look for Leichhardt. But search parties did not head out until 1852, then again in 1858 and 1865–66. Explorers pursuing other conquests were also tasked to look for Leichhardt. These investigations found an old campsite and a few trees marked with an L. But that was about all until more than fifty years after Leichhardt set out on his last expedition.

Some time around 1900 an Aboriginal man known only as Jackie came across a firearm in the branches of a boab tree marked with an L on the border of Western Australian and the Northern Territory, near Sturt Creek. The firearm was burned but there was a brass plate mounted on the stock or butt of the weapon. Engraved on the plate were the words LUDWIG LEICHHARDT 1848. Jackie gave the find to his employer, Charles Harding, who threw away the wooden remains but kept the plate. He apparently treasured it and would often show the artefact to the curious. He later gifted the plate to a friend. It was loaned to various institutions and individuals but in 2006 came to rest in the National Museum of Australia, where it remains today.

The plate's authenticity has been confirmed but it is almost the only hard evidence of Leichhardt's fate. The exact location of the original find has always been murky and often contested, leading to many theories about the total disappearance of the party. As well as speculation that they died of thirst, hunger or both, it has been suggested they drowned in a flash flood or were murdered by Aborigines, among other wilder thoughts. Did they abandon their plan of sticking to the relatively well-watered north and make a fatal trek into the desert? What about the many trees that have been found over the years all bearing marks that might—or might not—have been made by Leichhardt or his men? In the absence of almost any other verifiable evidence other than the enigmatic brass plate from Leichhardt's own gun, myth takes over.

Almost as soon as Leichhardt's disappearance became an acknowledged fact there were stories about a white man living with the Aborigines somewhere in the centre of what is now the Northern Territory. In 1889, a stockman reported that an aged European man with yellow hair was living with Aborigines at the head of the Macarthur River. He spoke in what the stockman thought was German but he appeared very weak and the people in whose care he was seen were unwilling to allow him to leave. About twenty years earlier, a 'wild white man' was reported seen with a group of Aborigines along the Roper River. It was speculated that this might have been a member of Leichhardt's party, a German named Classen.

Another claim was made by a man named Hume: he maintained that he met Classen about 1870 in similar circumstances and even obtained his and Leichhardt's journals. Hume said Classen told him the expedition had mutinied at the head of the Victoria River. Leichhardt died and the rest of the party were murdered at Eyre Creek on their way home. Classen survived but as a prisoner of the Aborigines. Unfortunately, Hume was unable to produce the documents and his criminal past meant that many were not inclined to accept his account. There was also a story that an Aboriginal named Jimmie, known to have been part of Leichhardt's expedition, had also survived.

It is said there is an iron or steel chest from the expedition in the possession of Aborigines living far to the north of the Warburton Ranges or along the Plenty River. Skeletons and gold coins have been found with alleged links to the lost expedition. A lively oral tradition continues among bush people about Leichhardt's fate, and there's a mini history industry dedicated to feeding the ongoing speculation about how seven men, 70-odd cattle and horses, wagons, and masses of equipment could disappear with almost no trace. Patrick White's famous novel *Voss* plumbed the psychological and cultural enigma that Leichhardt and his men had become.

There is even an odd link between the Leichhardt myth and that other great legend of the Outback, that of Lasseter's reef. In the story of Lasseter's original discovery of his fabulous lode, told in this chapter, the perishing young prospector was saved by an Afghan cameleer and a surveyor named Harding. Lasetter and Harding together returned to the find a few years later but a poorly set watch rendered their recorded bearings wildly inaccurate. The reef was 'lost' again. It seems that the Harding who rescued Lasseter was the slightly shady Joe Harding, brother to Charles Harding, who was so proud of the brass plate from Leichhardt's gun in his possession. Coincidence, of course, but one that, along with the many other imponderables of Leichhardt's fate, only serves to intensify its enduring mystery.

NAMING THE DESERT

This is the story of a journey within a journey; an epic trek that left one man dead and the other barely living.

Earnest Giles is one of many relatively unsung explorers of the inland. Born in 1835 in Bristol, England, he came to Australia in 1850 and gathered what was then called 'colonial experience' on goldfields, in the public service and with some exploring expeditions. He later led expeditions across South Australia and the Northern Territory, seeking a route to the coast of Western Australia. He left a precise but compelling account of his travels in *Australia Twice Traversed: The romance of exploration*. On one of these journeys he was accompanied by an enthusiastic but inexperienced young man named Alfred Gibson. When Gibson asked to 'go out' with him, Giles replied:

> I said, 'Well, can you shoe? Can you ride? Can you starve? Can you go without water? And how would you like to be speared by the blacks outside?' He said he could do everything I had mentioned, and he wasn't afraid of the blacks. He was not a man I would have picked out of a mob, but men were scarce, and as he seemed so anxious to come, and as I wanted somebody, I agreed to take him.

This man would be remembered as the namesake of one of Australia's harshest environments, and in the account Giles gave of their harrowing journey.

With Gibson, William Tietkens and guide Jimmy Andrews, Giles set out for the west coast in August 1873. They struggled through mountain ranges, discovered Mount Olga (now Kata Tjute), and passed through the Tomkinson Range to Lake Amadeus. From their camp at Fort Mueller they explored the surrounding country. But after nine months they were still nowhere near the west coast. Giles decided on a last desperate reconnaissance, travelling light.

On 20 April 1874, Giles and Gibson loaded up a couple of packhorses with water and a week's supply of smoked horse meat. Mounted on a cob and a bay, they rode west from their camp at the distinctive rock formation east of Lake Christopher that Giles called The Circus (also Circus Water), leaving the other two men, with the rest of the supplies, to await their hopefully triumphal return. Giles and Gibson chatted as they rode:

> I remarked to Gibson that the day was the anniversary of Burke and Wills's return to their depot at Cooper's Creek, and then

> recited to him, as he did not appear to know anything whatever about it, the hardships they endured, their desperate struggles for existence, and death there . . . He seemed in a very jocular vein this morning, which was not often the case, for he was usually rather sulky, sometimes for days together, and he said, 'How is it, that in all these exploring expeditions a lot of people go and die?'
>
> I said, 'I don't know, Gibson, how it is, but there are many dangers in exploring, besides accidents and attacks from the natives, that may at any time cause the death of some of the people engaged in it; but I believe want of judgment, or knowledge, or courage in individuals, often brought about their deaths. Death, however, is a thing that must occur to every one sooner or later.'
>
> To this he replied, 'Well, I shouldn't like to die in this part of the country, anyhow.' In this sentiment I quite agreed with him, and the subject dropped.

Giles later discovered that Gibson had not packed enough smoked horse meat and there was hardly enough to last one man for a week, let alone two. Despite this they made reasonably good time through the landscape of casuarinas and bloodwood trees. Ants troubled Giles at night though Gibson seemed immune to their attentions.

But soon their mounts were ailing in the 'heated breeze' and the packhorses were turned loose to trek back to the last water, if they could. Giles and Gibson pressed on through what looked like 'fine, open, dry, grassy downs' with the odd patch of mulga or mallee scrub.

Around 160 kilometres from their starting point, Gibson and his mount could go no further. Giles was bitterly disappointed:

> The hills to the west were twenty-five to thirty miles away, and it was with extreme regret I was compelled to relinquish a farther attempt to reach them. Oh, how ardently I longed for a camel! How ardently I gazed upon this scene! At this moment I would even my jewel eternal, have sold for power to span the gulf that lay between!

A few kilometres along the return route, Gibson's horse died. They kept going, Gibson riding Giles's horse and the leader on foot. They drank the last of their water.

It was time to make some hard choices. Giles sent Gibson on with the horse and his treasured compass, even though he knew the young man was unable to operate it: 'I sent one final shout after him to stick to the tracks, to which he replied, "All right," and the mare carried him out of sight almost immediately.'

Giles struggled after them on foot, hoping to reach the next water hole. He made it and found that Gibson had been there and left him water in a keg. He drank it and then ate two dirty sticks of the smoked horseflesh also left for him. The only receptacle that would hold liquid was the keg Gibson had left behind, filled with water. His revolver, blanket and knife, together with his fourteen remaining matches, weighed around 22 kilograms.

Loaded like a packhorse, the explorer staggered on through the scrub, mostly by moonlight and often in a daze. He lost track of time as he tried to resist drinking his precious 'elixir of death' as long as possible. Frequently losing consciousness, Giles managed about five miles a day. Eventually he stumbled across Gibson's tracks again. The man had followed the trail of the two packhorses but they were going in the wrong direction. Giles tottered after them for a mile or so but, finding no signs, turned back to what he knew was the correct course.

Around what he thought was 27 April, after seven days in the bush, Giles was near death.

> I felt quite light-headed. After sitting down, on every occasion when I tried to get up again, my head would swim round, and I would fall down oblivious for some time. Being in a chronic state of burning thirst, my general plight was dreadful in the extreme. A bare and level sandy waste would have been Paradise to walk over compared to this. My arms, legs, thighs, both before and behind, were so punctured with spines, it was agony only to exist; the slightest movement and in went more spines, where they broke off in the clothes and flesh, causing the whole of the body that was

> punctured to gather into minute pustules, which were continually growing and bursting. My clothes, especially inside my trousers, were a perfect mass of prickly points.

He hoped for a relief party. And where was Gibson?

Giles managed to reach The Circus two days later, just as the last of his water ran out.

> Oh, how I drank! how I reeled! how hungry I was! how thankful I was that I had so far at least escaped from the jaws of that howling wilderness, for I was once more upon the range, though still twenty miles from home.

After satisfying his deep thirst, Giles looked for food.

> Just as I got clear of the bank of the creek, I heard a faint squeak, and looking about I saw, and immediately caught, a small dying wallaby, whose marsupial mother had evidently thrown it from her pouch. It only weighed about two ounces, and was scarcely furnished yet with fur. The instant I saw it, like an eagle I pounced upon it and ate it, living, raw, dying—fur, skin, bones, skull, and all. The delicious taste of that creature I shall never forget. I only wished I had its mother and father to serve in the same way.

Giles staggered back the last twenty miles or so to the remaining two men of his expedition, who were now camped at Fort Mueller beneath the ominously named Mount Destruction. None of the horses had returned. When the fortunate explorer had recovered, he and the rest of the party went looking for Gibson. Five days out, and with the water gone yet again, they gave up. Gibson had ridden into the desert on Giles's fine mount. The horse must have refused to give up, carrying its rider further and further into the emptiness. Giles named this terrible region Gibson's Desert 'after this first white victim to its horrors'.

Earnest Giles would later be noted for twice crossing the western half of the continent. He received acclaim, honours and land grants, although his alleged gambling and drinking habits robbed him of an official appointment in South Australia. He died in 1897 and is considered one of the finest bushman of the inland exploration era.

LASSETER'S FIRST FIND

The tale of Lasseter's lost reef of gold is one of Australia's best-known and oft-told yarns. Lasseter's own story ended in tragedy, with him dying alone in the desert, leaving behind a notebook and map as contradictory and subsequently controversial as his life had been. Much less known is the story of the journey Lasseter originally made—or said he did—during which he first located his fabulous reef.

Born in rural Victoria in 1880, Lewis Hubert Lasseter claimed to have served a few years in the English Royal Navy before travelling to the United States where he was married in 1903. He was soon back in Australia, leasing a farm at Tabulum (NSW) around 1908 and spending the next few years developing inventions and designs, including a design submitted for the Sydney Harbour Bridge. He enlisted twice during World War I but was discharged on both occasions. He married again, probably bigamously, in 1924 and worked in Sydney and Canberra as a carpenter, continuing to devise such things as a method for pre-cast concrete.

A short, peppery man of strong opinions and high self-esteem, Lasseter was seen by many as a crank. By 1929, he was publically claiming to be the original designer of the Harbour Bridge and sought back payment for what he said was six months' work on the plans. His assertion was not accepted. Perhaps motivated by this, and by the onset of the Depression, Lasseter began contacting people in government and trade unions about a lode of gold he had found in the desert many years before. He wanted funding for an expedition to relocate the reef to the enrichment of all involved. And he told them all the story of its discovery to back up his claim.

Lasseter gave several versions of this find. In one, he claimed to have discovered the reef in 1897 near the Warburton Ranges.

In another, he said it was in 1911, and somewhere near Lake Amadeus. Even those keen to believe Lasseter had difficulty believing the earlier date of discovery plausible as he would only have been seventeen at the time. It was not impossible that he had found the mysterious riches at that age, of course, just highly unlikely. He had already claimed to be in the Royal Navy in his youth, which operated quite a long way away from the central Australian desert. One thing that Lasseter was fairly consistent about, though, was the richness of the find: 3 ounces or more to the ton.

Lasseter usually said he had been on his way to Western Australia after seeking his fortune mining for rubies in the East MacDonnell Ranges. The rush failed when the precious stones turned out to be mere garnets but as he was already in South Australia he decided to keep riding across some of the world's harshest country. Not surprisingly his horse soon perished west of the MacDonnell Ranges but not before he had seen the 16-kilometre reef—sometimes it was even larger in the telling. It was 'four to twelve feet wide, and at places . . . four feet above the surface'. At the point of death he was miraculously rescued by an Afghan camel driver and nursed back to health by a surveyor named Harding.

Three years later, with Harding and accompanied by camels, Lasseter said he returned to the area of his original find, relocated the reef and recorded its exact coordinates. (They later discovered their watches were wrong. The bearings would have placed the reef in the Indian Ocean, according to one sceptical commentator). They took samples and seem to have had them assessed at a number of assay offices although, oddly, did not peg a claim. Harding sought funds to exploit the reef without success and died shortly afterwards. Lasseter went to America and no more was heard of the reef until he began seeking backers in 1929. The next journey he made in search of the supposed treasure was his last.

But it was only the beginning of ongoing attempts to solve the mystery of Lasseter's reef and to locate it again. Many have tried and failed, suggesting that Lasseter was a fantasist. Certainly there are many signs of folklore in the tale. The false ruby strike took place in 1887, when Lasseter would have been six or seven years old. The 'surveyor' was the stock rustler Joe Harding. Lasseter changed his name to Lewis Harold Bell Lasseter, rather suspiciously echoing the name of the author of a popular American book about a lost reef of gold. This book, *The Mine With the Iron Door*, was published in 1923 and was one of a number of popular fictions on the same theme tracking back into the nineteenth century. Like the most famous such fiction of all, Rider Haggard's *King Solomon's Mines*, these works draw on the ancient El Dorado legends of fabulous wealth hidden in impenetrable locations and usually guarded by fierce tribes.

There is even an intriguing Australian precedent for Lasseter's alleged reef. It was said that a South Australian prospector named Earle stumbled across a vast 'cave of gold' somewhere in the Tomkinson Ranges during 1895. A vast mythology quickly evolved around this story. An investigation in 1900 was thought to be in possession of Earle's map of his find. The expedition was attacked by Aboriginal people. One man was killed and another wounded. The survivors returned to Oodnadatta with no news of the fabled cave of copper and gold. Like Lasseter's reef, it is still lost.

In the end, Lasseter paid the ultimate price for his fantasies. After quarrelling with a member of his 1930–31 expedition, he went into the desert alone. When the celebrated bushman Bob Buck finally found Lasseter's remains in March 1931 there was not much left. The man who had prophesised fabulous wealth from his lost reef probably survived for up to four months with occasional help from Aborigines. He died a lonely and lingering death, leaving only his notebook buried beneath the ashes of his fire, a few letters and a legend that will not go away.

THE WARATAH MYSTERY

On 1 July 1909, the luxury steamer SS *Waratah* left Melbourne for South Africa. With over 700 passengers aboard she was well loaded. One passenger, an engineer named Claude Sawyer, feared the ship was carrying too much. At Durban he left the *Waratah*, cabling his wife that he thought the ship was 'top-heavy'. Sawyer forfeited his 8 guinea fare to Cape Town and later testified:

> I first noticed something peculiar at Melbourne, and that was when we left the port; she had a big list to port. I formed the opinion that the list was considerable when I walked in my cabin. It was very uncomfortable to walk towards the port. I suppose the floor of the cabin was inclined slightly to port. Then going through the disturbed water just before you get out to the Heads, she wobbled about a good deal and then took a list to starboard and remained there for a very long time. She went right over so that the water was right underneath me. I was standing on the promenade deck.
>
> She remained so long there that I did not like it.
>
> Then, by degrees, she went over the other way, and remained with a list to port so that it was very uncomfortable walking in my cabin, because my cabin was on the port side.

When the SS *Waratah* left Durban for Cape Town on 26 July she was carrying just over 200 passengers and crew. *Waratah* briefly signalled a passing ship that night but worsening weather conditions made lengthy communication impossible. Ships did not carry radio at that time. There was another possible sighting later in the night but the *Waratah* has never been seen since. Her disappearance has led to her being called Australia's *Titanic* and her disappearance is considered one of the most baffling mysteries of world shipping.

Searches for the missing ship began straightaway. Royal Navy ships assumed that she would be found drifting at sea, but found nothing. The shipowners financed a search vessel and in 1910 the relatives of the passengers commissioned another fruitless investigation.

An official Board of Trade inquiry into the incident interviewed many experts and other interested parties. There was disagreement on the seaworthiness of the ship, her design and the cargo stowage. The lucky passenger who left her at Durban said that his decision had been influenced by bad dreams. Details of the dreams were not given in the report but it was later stated that Sawyer had seen an oddly dressed man carrying a blood-drenched sword in his right hand.

The inquiry concluded that 'the ship was lost in the gale of the 28th of July, 1909, which was of exceptional violence for those waters and was the first great storm she had encountered'. Given the meagre evidence available, the court continued:

> In the total absence of direct evidence, and with only conflicting evidence of an indirect character, the Court cannot say what particular form was taken by the catastrophe, but the fact that no wreckage has been found in spite of the most careful and exhaustive search which was carried out, indicates that it must have been sudden. The Court, on the whole, inclines to the opinion that she capsized, but what particular chain of circumstances brought about this result must remain undetermined.

The air of mystery surrounding the SS *Waratah*'s fate deepened over time. Reports of clothed bodies being sighted cropped up, though none of these was ever substantiated, or even apparently investigated. A deckchair from the missing ship washed up along the coast. In 1915, an Irish soldier on the Western Front claimed to be the sole survivor of the disaster. During the 1930s, lumps of timber and cork thought to belong to the SS *Waratah* were found near East London, South Africa.

Supposed sightings of the wreck were made in 1925 and 1977. Searches were again carried out in the 1990s and since. Some of these have claimed success, though to date there is no verification. One wreck hunter spent over twenty years in a vain search, giving up only in 2004.

What happened and where do the *Waratah* and her dead lie? Did she suffer some mysterious catastrophe that left her abandoned and drifting into the Antarctic? Did she explode? A couple of bright flashes were seen in the blackness of the night she disappeared, possibly caused by combustion of coal dust from the large supply of coal she carried. Other theories involve the ship being sucked beneath the waves in a whirlpool. Most think the unusually slow roll of the *Waratah*, as described by Sawyer, made her vulnerable to a freak wave hitting at the wrong moment. If so, the ship would simply have capsized and gone to the bottom with little chance of anyone escaping.

The even more catastrophic loss of the *Titanic* three years later has dampened the memory of the *Waratah*'s fate, even though many similar structural and technical issues might have been involved in the loss of both vessels. We know what happened to the *Titanic* but the mystery of SS *Waratah* remains unsolved.

THE DIAMOND FLIGHT

It was March 1942. Japanese forces were three days away from taking Bandung on the island of Java. The predominantly Dutch European population was being evacuated to mainland Australia as quickly as possible. Early in the afternoon of 3 March, a Netherlands East Indies KLM Dakota passenger plane prepared to take off with eleven anxious passengers. As the Dakota was about to taxi to the runway the airfield manager handed the pilot, Ivan Smirnoff, a sealed brown paper package, telling him to look after it. A bank would take delivery of the parcel on arrival in Australia, the airfield manager said. Ivan's mind was on more pressing matters, so he dropped the parcel into the first-aid chest and took off straightaway for the safety of Broome. It was around 1.15 p.m.

As the plane climbed into the sky, the Japanese were attacking Australian coastal communities far to the south. Smirnoff and his passengers, including a mother and her eighteen-month-old baby, made their nine-hour flight mostly without radio contact. They only began to realise that Broome had been devastated by a Japanese aerial attack just before sunrise when they received a terse message: 'Airstrip is OK for the time being.' Around 80 kilometres out of Broome they saw the thick pall of black smoke left behind by nine Mitsubishi Zero fighters.

Unfortunately, three of the Japanese fighters returning from the raid spotted the Dakota and raked it with bullets. The baby was hit in the arm and her mother shot twice in the chest. Another two passengers were wounded and Smirnoff was struck in the arms and hip. He desperately threw the plane into a steep spiralling descent, pursued closely by the fighters. As the port engine burst into flame he had to act quickly. Smirnoff turned the aircraft towards the beach, managing to bring it down more or less level and then to swing its front section into the sea, extinguishing the engine fire. One of the passengers, himself a pilot, would later recall the Russian national 'put up the greatest show of flying anybody in the world will ever see'.

But although Smirnoff had piloted his plane, crew and passengers safely onto the sands of Carnot Bay, they were still in trouble. The Japanese strafed the beach, wounding another passenger, before they turned back towards their base in Timor. The passengers cautiously crawled out from beneath the Dakota where they had taken refuge. The radio was undamaged and they were able to send an SOS. Smirnoff asked a KLM official among the passengers to retrieve the stricken plane's documents, including the sealed brown paper package, but the package was lost in the surf. With more immediate concerns, the passengers and crew made a temporary shelter under parachute cloth and hoped for a rapid rescue.

Later that morning a plane appeared. The bedraggled group on the isolated beach waved until they realised it was Japanese. The pilot dropped two bombs. Both missed. The plane disappeared but later another dropped two more bombs that fortunately failed to detonate. Despite these lucky escapes, the situation of the survivors was desperate. They needed fresh water but there was none to be found. By the next morning three of the wounded passengers were dead.

Smirnoff despatched two small groups to Broome, unaware that an Aboriginal man had seen the crash and reported it to the Beagle Bay Mission, about 40 kilometres away. A rescue party from the mission met the two groups sent from the Dakota.

On 6 March, a Royal Air Force plane appeared above the survivors on the beach, dropping supplies and a message that the relief party would reach them the same night. But the party did not arrive until 3 a.m., too late to save the baby. The shattered survivors and their rescuers trekked slowly back to the mission and two days later were trucked to bombed-out Broome and relative safety.

It was only some time later in Melbourne that Captain Smirnoff became aware of the contents of the brown paper package he had been handed, when he was visited by a police detective and an official of the Commonwealth Bank. They had come to collect the mysterious parcel. Smirnoff told them what had happened and that the parcel was missing. What was in it?

The answer Smirnoff received was the start of an enduring mystery. The parcel had contained a cigar box filled with thousands of high quality diamonds rescued from Amsterdam before the invading German forces arrived. The gems had been on their way via the then Dutch East Indies to safekeeping in the vaults of the Australian Commonwealth Bank. They were valued at the time at half a million guilders, approximately twenty million dollars in today's money. Where were they?

From this point, the ongoing story of this bloody journey becomes murky. After the survivors of the tragedy were rescued from the crash site, a local beachcomber and lugger master named Jack Palmer and the crew of a powerboat travelling with him came across the wreckage. They salvaged its remaining contents and Palmer found the package, either in the plane or in the surf, and quickly discovered its alluring contents. He divided the gems up, hiding most of them beneath the sand in an aluminium container and distributing the rest among his companions, telling them to keep quiet about the find.

Palmer was on his way to enlist in the army. He reached Perth and went to the district military commandant where he told the story of the crash and his discovery of the diamonds. To prove his point, he produced two salt cellars full of small stones to the astonished officer.

By now, though, diamonds were starting to turn up in

unexpected places. One was found in the fireplace of a Broome home and another in a matchbox in a train carriage. Aboriginal people were seen with them and Chinese traders offered them for sale. Others would be found after the war, including one nestling in the fork of a tree.

An army investigation led to Palmer and two of his comrades being put on trial in 1943. Smirnoff was called as a witness but provided no new information. All three accused were acquitted as they had—seemingly—handed in the diamonds to the authorities. Palmer then served in the army. After the war he tackled a number of business ventures and appeared to be living well for the few years that were left to him.

Jack Palmer died of stomach cancer in 1950. A priest attending his deathbed is said to have asked him what he had done with the rest of the diamonds. Palmer insisted that he handed them in. Then he smiled.

There are a number of other stories stemming from the medical staff who tended the dying man. They vary in detail but all end the same way. They all state that Palmer kept a mysterious bag under his bed which he hinted might contain riches—maybe cash, maybe diamonds. The day after he died, the bag had disappeared.

Smirnoff returned to Holland after the war and continued his career as a KLM pilot. He seems never to have gone home to the USSR and died on the island of Majorca in 1956 after an adventurous life that even attracted the brief attention of Hollywood in 1944.

Stories still circulate about the 'Smirnoff diamonds'. As recently as 2012 a claim was made by relatives of the man who drove Smirnoff and his surviving passengers from Beagle Bay to Broome that the pilot knew the package he was carrying contained the diamonds. Whether he knew or not, only a fraction of the hoard was ever recovered. It is thought that the bulk of the cache, perhaps twenty million dollars worth, is still missing. Are they still buried in the sand along with the remains of the ill-fated Dakota? Were they found by others? Or did Jack Palmer simply take them and spend up big for the rest of his life?

TAMAN SHUD

On the morning of 30 November 1948, a respectably dressed man in his mid forties arrived at Adelaide station. He bought a ticket for the 10.50 to Henley Beach, then walked for fifteen minutes to King William Street where he showered and shaved at the City Baths. He returned to the station and left a brown suitcase at the cloakroom. Then he bought a ticket on a bus that had already left the stop opposite the railway station. He may have caught the bus at a later stop but in any event later in the morning he was in Glenelg, near the St Leonard's Hotel and not too far from the home of a woman who would come to be known as Jestyn.

The well-dressed man probably remained in the area all day. At some point he ate a pastie. Several people saw him in the evening between 7 and 8 p.m. At 6.30 the next morning the man was found dead on Glenelg's Somerton Beach. His last journey had ended but the mystery of his life and his death remains unsolved.

The Somerton Man, as he became known, was Caucasian with well-kept hands, broad shoulders, a narrow waist and feet and legs that, to some, suggested a dancer or perhaps a long-distance runner. He was in top physical condition but had no wallet and the labels of his clothing had been removed.

Who was he?

The autopsy revealed an unpleasant list of damages to the internal organs. The only conclusion the pathologist could reach was that the man had been poisoned but could not say what with, or how. The pastie was ruled out as causing his death.

Despite an intensive local and national police investigation, and help from Scotland Yard, the Somerton Man's identity remained a mystery. In hope that a solution to the puzzle would be found eventually, the body was embalmed on 10 December. People continued to claim that they knew his identity but subsequent investigations ruled these out for one reason or another.

On 14 January the next year, railway staff discover what was subsequently realised to be Somerton Man's brown suitcase in the cloakroom. It took this long because no left-luggage receipt was found on the body, another mystery itself. Inside the case were personal items that could only have been bought in America. These reinforced the American connection already suggested by some of the clothing on the body.

The other contents of the brown case were even more perplexing. They included a sharpened pair of scissors, a cut-down table knife, a paintbrush used for stencilling maritime cargo and a variety of miscellaneous everyday objects, such as a shaving kit and a spoon. There was other clothing from which the labels had also been removed, except for three items which bore the name T Keane or Kean. Police never found anyone of that name with any connection to the body.

Another pathologist examined the Somerton Man's remains in June. He concluded that the victim was probably poisoned and the body may have been taken to the beach from another unknown location. At the inquest a poisons expert testified that certain drugs could kill but leave no trace in the body. He would not speak the names of the drugs because they were so deadly and, at that time, freely available from a chemist. The coroner could still not determine the exact cause of death but thought it was likely murder rather than suicide.

Around this time the Somerton Man had a name change. Further investigation of the victim's clothing revealed a rolled-up scrap of paper hidden in a deep pocket. On the paper were the words TAMAM SHUD. This turned out to be a phrase from the ending of the *Rubaiyat of Omar Khayyam* and the scrap of paper on which it was printed was apparently torn from a rare edition of a translation of the famous Persian poem. The phrase is usually translated as meaning 'the end' or 'finished', relating to the poem's theme of living life to the full and dying without regrets.

In July, an unidentified man came forward with a copy of the same obscure edition of the *Rubaiyat* translation lacking the section containing the fateful words. He had allegedly found the book on the rear floor of his unlocked car, which had been parked in Glenelg around the time of the mysterious death. He did not make the connection until the mysterious roll of paper was mentioned in the press. Not only has this man's name never been revealed, neither has the reason for its suppression. The Somerton Man now began to be called Taman Shud (though the correct form is Tamam; Taman is a newspaper misprint that stuck).

In the back of the book brought forward were two telephone numbers and some indented pencil lines believed to be a code of some sort, though cryptographers were unable to decipher whatever message it might have contained. One telephone number was a bank, the other belonged to a 27-year-old woman living in Glenelg. When police tracked her down they showed her a plaster cast of Taman Shud's distended face. According to the attending officer, she was shocked near to fainting but denied knowing the man.

Despite a complex and murky series of revelations and investigations which continued until 2007 when this woman died, her real name had always been suppressed, though it was known to researchers on the case. She was known only as Jestyn, a rendering of the signature 'Jestyn' written in another copy of the *Rubaiyat* which she gave to an admirer in 1945 while training as a nurse in Sydney. That alias was abandoned when her real name was finally made public on a *60 Minutes* television show in 2013. Her married name was Jessica 'Jo' Thomson, previously Jessie Harkness. After 1947, she was known as Jo Thomson. Researchers have discovered that she had a son with some physical features very similar to those of Taman Shud. Recent DNA testing suggests that this now-deceased son had some American heritage.

Efforts to locate other copies of the unusual edition of the *Rubaiyat* have turned up more intriguing mysteries. It seems that there was no officially published edition of the book in which the final words had been omitted. Investigators were unable to establish where the editions found on the dead man or in the car at Glenelg came from. Nor could the edition of the copy given to Thomson's admirer in Sydney be traced. A New Zealand publisher did have an edition of the particular translation but it was in a different format to that found in the parked car.

Even more strangely, in June 1945 another dead man was found at Mosman (New South Wales) with a copy of the *Rubaiyat* near his body. This book was marked as the seventh edition produced by a well-known London publisher. Yet it seems there were only ever five editions of the book produced by that company.

With complex and unexplained dead ends like these, the disappearance of evidence over the years and ongoing public fascination, it is not surprising that the Taman Shud case has remained open since 1948. What is possibly the world's most intriguing cold case has been re-investigated many times by police, journalists and researchers of all kinds and is still an active issue.

Solutions to the riddle abound. They include a Cold War link to the American Project Venona espionage program and the foundation of ASIO, as well as a possible connection to the then top-secret Woomera rocket facility less than 500 kilometres north-west of Adelaide. Or maybe he was just a common crook. Whoever Taman Shud was in life, most now seem to accept that the man on Somerton Beach died from an undetectable dose of the poison digitalis. It may be possible to identify the body through genetic testing if the corpse can be exhumed.

Whichever theory appeals, or not, the last journey of Taman Shud is probably Australia's most mysterious. It will probably remain so.

ROAMING GNOMES

Fantastic journeys undertaken by garden gnomes have joined the canon of modern legends. As the stories go, garden gnomes have been going missing for decades, if not longer. It seems that these prized ornaments often disappear in the middle of the night. Some time later, maybe days, weeks or months, their disconsolate owners receive a letter or email from a distant holiday location informing them that their gnome or gnomes are having a great time. Usually there is a photograph of the gnome reclining by the pool or beside the sea. Then, sometimes years later, the vanished gnomes may mysteriously reappear in the gardens from which they disappeared.

The disappearing gnome story might have originated in the practice of stealing gnomes from gardens and placing them in unexpected locations, such as a freeway verge. This was reported, in a post to the Museum of Hoaxes blog, to be happening in Sydney in 1978. This prank seems to have evolved into stealing gnomes then demanding a ransom for their return. Some time around the middle of the 1980s, reports of gnomes simply disappearing on holidays began to circulate.

Gnome roaming has now moved onto the internet, where there are innumerable reports of their antics to be found. The roaming gnomes have made it into the movies, such as the French film *Amelie*. And it's not just the gnomes who have taken to travel. All manner of garden ornaments take off, including flamingos, rabbits and frogs.

Is it all an elaborate international prank, another urban legend or something much more sinister?

In case your gnome has taken an unscheduled trip to Bali or elsewhere and has not returned, help may be at hand. The enterprising residents of the Dardanup area in the Ferguson Valley of south-western Australia have created Gnomesville, 'the magical home to over three-thousand gnomes who have migrated here from all over Australia and around the world'. A whole roundabout is full of miscellaneous gnomes who, for whatever reasons, have not returned to their homes.

So, if you're wondering what happened to your gnome, take a trip of your own to Dardanup and see what you can find. Even if your gnome is not on the roundabout there is a shop, so you could always give another lump of coloured concrete a good home.

TIGGA'S TRAVELS

The tale of a globetrotting ginger cat entertained the world's media and social media for some months in 2015. Tigga was his name, although he was rechristened Ozzie near the end of his adventurous life.

Tigga's rise to global stardom began in mid 2015 when he was found in a garden in County Armagh, Ireland. A cat protection volunteer took him to the vet for a check-up. To everyone's surprise, Tigga's microchip revealed that he was from Australia.

But not by direct flight, it seems. The microchip also indicated that Tigga had been residing in London during 2004. He had turned up as a stray at a veterinary clinic there, though how he travelled from the English capital to Australia and then to Ireland was a total mystery.

Even more curiously, according to the electronic data on Tigga's microchip he was born in 1989, making him an incredible 25 years old. Cats are mostly long gone by then, so this one was probably the oldest living feline ever.

How did Tigga get from London to Australia and then to County Armagh? And how could he be so old?

The puzzle persisted while Irish cat protectors looked after Tigga and began a search for more information. Carers waited anxiously for news of the tomcat's background. Eventually social media provided the answer to the riddle.

Tigga belonged to a well-travelled couple who frequently moved between Ireland and Australia. They left their pet with friends in Armagh but he ran away and lived rough on the streets and in the gardens of the locals until he was picked up in June.

It also turned out that he was not as old as he seemed. A misprint in the original records meant that he was born in 1999, not 1989.

Sadly, this tale has an unhappy ending. Despite gaining an extra ten years of youth, Tigga became ill while in care. An untreatable liver condition took him away before his owners could be reunited with their roving pet. He died without fear or pain 'and surrounded by love', members of the Armagh cat protection group wrote on Facebook.

Tigga's ashes made the long journey back to Australia, ending his unusual life of travel, adventure and global stardom with one last trip.

5

COMING AND GOING

> Australian history is almost always picturesque; indeed, it is so curious and strange, that it is itself the chiefest novelty the country has to offer . . .
>
> Mark Twain on his visit to Australia, 1895

PLATYPUS DREAMING

Lovesick, homesick and seasick, a young Charles Darwin sailed into Sydney Harbour aboard HMS *Beagle* in January 1836. He was nearing the end of a four-year scientific quest that had taken him and his companions around the world collecting specimens and observing perplexing natural phenomena. But now Darwin was ready for home, even though it lay at the other end of the world. He looked forward to Sydney as a little bit of England that might help assuage his longing for home and bring a respite from the *mal de mar* that had afflicted him across the Pacific ocean. But there was nothing he could do about his love life. He had just found out that the girl who had been waiting for him could wait no longer and had married another.

At least he had the consolation of studying the young British colony and following up the puzzling things he had read about its plants, animals and landscape. Unfortunately his first impressions were not good. Drought was devastating the country and emancipated convicts were becoming wealthy and too democratically inclined for Darwin's upper-class attitudes. But his gloomy outlook would soon change as he took a trip across the Blue Mountains to Bathurst. This journey was to have momentous consequences for the world; then, now and, it's to be expected, long into the future.

At first Darwin was disappointed with the drab carpet of eucalypts that hid the shape and structure of the mountains: 'The bark of some of the Eucalypti falls annually, or hangs dead in long shreds which swing about with the wind, and give to the woods a desolate and untidy appearance.' He was expecting the dramatic scenery of the Alps. But when he saw the cascading water at Wentworth Falls and 'the most stupendous cliffs' of the Jamison Valley he sensed he was looking at something of great significance, though the fully realised thought remained just out of reach: he surmised the plunging valleys must have been carved by water flows. It would be some time before the geological process of erosion was understood.

Riding on down Victoria Pass to Wallerawang Station, then more or less at the frontier of settlement, Darwin observed and collected as he went. His amazement increased with every new discovery. The crucial moment came one evening as the young naturalist walked along a stream near the sheep station. He saw several platypuses; duck-billed, egg-laying mammals, or monotremes, with a poisonous back claw—biological impossibilities that appeared to defy the natural order.

Pondering these peculiarities for hours, Darwin began thinking in a way that would end up many years later in the world's most revolutionary and controversial idea: the origin of species and the theory of human evolution. He tentatively wondered how there could be such differences between various species of animals and how an anomaly such as the platypus fitted into the traditional Christian account of Creation. The implications of his thinking were heretical to Christian theology and he quickly dismissed his musings: 'the one hand has worked over the whole world', he wrote in his notebook.

Darwin would not present the radical implications of his platypus musings to the general public for another two decades. In the published account of his mountain journey all those years earlier, Darwin simply calls it 'a most extraordinary animal' and moves quickly on. But his Australian sojourn, which also included visits to Tasmania and Western Australia, was the start of a long interest in the country's natural history. One of his assistants on the *Beagle* cruise, Covington Symes, later migrated to New South Wales and continued to provide Darwin with specimens over the years as he developed his revolutionary idea. Others also continued to provide him with information about the antipodean landscape and its often perplexing features, including Sir Thomas Mitchell, surveyor-general of New South Wales.

Ultimately this all fed into the great theory Darwin was developing. Finally published in 1859, *On the Origin of Species by Means of Natural Selection* ignited enormous controversy and debate among scientists, theologians and the educated middle classes. Was the world and its wonders the six-day creation of an all-powerful being, as the Bible taught? Or was nature the result of a biological process of evolution and selection over millions of years? Charles Darwin's summer encounter with *Ornithorhynchus paradoxes* near Wallerawang caused those questions to be asked and answered.

The great man died in 1882. His legacy remains one of history's greatest ideas, first germinated in the Australian bush.

MARCH TO NEW GOLD MOUNTAIN

It's a long walk from Adelaide to central Victoria. But the distance and difficult terrain did not deter thousands of Chinese who made the trek during the 1850s and 1860s. Like many others at that time, the Chinese came to strike it rich on the 'new gold mountain', as they called the Victorian goldfields.

Why did they not simply sail to Melbourne and make the relatively short journey from there to the goldfields?

The European view of the Chinese at that time was deeply racist. They were thought of as 'celestials', opium addicts and unhygienic. And they were arriving in large numbers, stoking fears of competition for the yellow metal. This potent combination of prejudice and avarice resulted in the Victorian government restricting Chinese entry by levying a heavy tax on each Chinese person entering the colony by sea. The neighbouring colony of South Australia had no such levy and so hopeful Chinese diggers took ship to Adelaide. Then they walked.

Most of the Chinese who came seeking their fortunes came from troubled southern China. They were almost all young men, who had hastily married before they left the village. Often the younger sons were sent abroad in the hope they could send back money to support their families. Most had no desire to settle permanently in Australia. They hoped to find enough gold to return home wealthy, a form of economic migration known as sojourning.

The Chinese soon became the largest groups of travellers on the trail of dreams from Adelaide to the Victorian goldfields. The various routes were set out by the police and helpfully published in the Adelaide newspapers. In the early days, the main trail led from Adelaide to Wellington, then south past various vital watering holes along the coast, east towards the Victorian border, moving from one squatters' station and source of water to the next, to Horsham, along the Wimmera River to Mount Cole, then east to the River Loddon, ending at Mount Alexander. The distance was estimated at 461 miles, around 800 kilometres.

Larger and richer finds of gold were soon made at Ballarat, Bendigo and other places in Victoria and beyond, attracting ever-larger throngs of diggers to brave the hike. There were a few variations to this route, mostly a little longer, some of them rough and dangerous. Later, ships carrying Chinese to South Australia landed at Robe, around 300 kilometres closer to the Victorian fields.

Whichever way they went, the travellers carved Chinese characters in trees to let those who followed after know where to find water. The travellers were a prominent sight—and sound—in the landscape, as another traveller observed in 1854, 'between six and seven hundred coming overland from Adelaide':

> They had four wagons carrying their sick, lame and provisions. They were all walking single file, each one with a pole and two baskets. They stretched for over two miles in procession. I was half an hour passing them . . . everyone behind seemed to be yabbering to his mate in front in a sing-song tone.

As the country was completely unknown to them, the sojourners often depended on local guides to get them to the goldfields. Some of these men were unscrupulous, taking their hopeful group some way along the trail and then abandoning them after taking their money. Many were unprepared for the rigours of walking through difficult country. An unknown number died, their graves, or just their bones, marking the dangerous way.

When they did arrive on the goldfields they were greeted with discrimination and sometimes aggression. They camped together for self-protection and comfort, forming the first Chinatowns now such an unremarkable feature of Australian life and cuisine. There was serious anti-Chinese rioting in the late 1850s, notably at Buckland River in 1857. When overlanding Chinese discovered a new field at Ararat there was more trouble, eventually leading to the Chinese being dispossessed of their rightful claims by some legal chicanery trading on the general Chinese ignorance of the English language.

By 1861 over 3 per cent of the Australian population had come from China. These large numbers, together with the fierce competition for wealth and the prejudice of other diggers, made life more than difficult for the Chinese. They were accused of unhealthy practices, opium dealing, gambling and fraternising with European women. Worst of all, despite being relegated to supposedly worked-out areas of the goldfields, they managed to make money by industriousness and hard work. The only answer was a Royal Commission.

When the commission reported on its investigations into 'the conditions and prospects of the goldfields of Victoria' in 1863, it found that most of allegations were inaccurate and that the Chinese were cleaner in their habits than the Europeans. This only made matters worse for the Chinese and prejudice and violence against them continued until the easily won gold faltered and opportunities for small-scale fossicking gave way to industrialised mining techniques.

The sojourners gradually returned home as they had planned, most better off than when they had arrived. But some stayed. They joined more than three thousand Chinese who had been resident in Australia even before the gold rushes. When the gold rush was all over the population of Australia had trebled, 'Marvellous Melbourne' had been established and the economy placed on a prosperous footing from which it has only occasionally faltered ever since.

SPIDER WOMAN

She was beautiful, talented and naughty. Men loved Lola Montez, the Irish-born entertainer, and she loved some of them in return. Back in 1837, at the age of nineteen and under her proper name of Maria Dolores Eliza Rosanna Gilbert, she had been promised as a bride to an elderly judge. Instead, the spirited Lola eloped with a dashing young army lieutenant. Their marriage survived only a few years and Lola went to Spain where she learned to dance. After an unhappy debut at Her Majesty's Theatre in London in June 1843, Lola embarked on a European career of what were then considered provocative performances.

Lola became the mistress of a number of prominent men, including the composer Franz Liszt, the writer Alexandre Dumas and a newspaper proprietor named Alexandre Dujarier. After Dujarier's death in a duel in 1845, she posed as a Spanish aristocrat and went to Munich where the elderly King Ludwig I of Bavaria fell under her spell. She became an influential figure in the politics of the time, also taking lovers behind Ludwig's back. As well as showering her with riches and a house, Ludwig made Lola a countess. This move was deeply unpopular with the Bavarian aristocracy and middle classes. Serious rioting led to Lola's expulsion and the king's abdication. Lola was on the road once more.

She turned up in London the following year where she apparently married a guards officer but was then arrested for bigamy. Out on bail, Lola and her new paramour went to Spain. When he died in 1850, Lola resurrected her colourful career in Europe and America, becoming notorious for carrying a whip and a pistol, and invariably appearing at the centre of scandals and leaving a trail of court cases in various jurisdictions.

The best place for an entertainer like Lola to make real money was a gold rush. It was in gold-crazy San Francisco that she first performed the routine for which she will be forever associated: the daring 'spider dance' that involved her searching for an imaginary insect through the folds of her dress.

> The full perfection of her frame was revealed as she swung gracefully to the centre of the stage, and paused for a moment. She made it appear evident that she was entangled in the filaments of a spider's web. In a dance step, she portrayed that she was more and more confused as the fibres wrapped themselves about her ankles. The music slowed as she discovered a spider in her petticoat, which she attempted to shake loose; then she discovered other spiders, and examining her skirts, she shook them to reveal even more spiders. The fight against the spiders became more and more hectic, as she danced with abandon and fire, and at the conclusion she had succeeded in shaking them out upon the floor, where she stamped them to death . . . the audience was held spellbound, and somewhat horror struck, but when the dance ended, the applause was thunderous; and as Lola Montes [sic] addressed her audience after numerous curtain calls, bouquets were showered at her feet.

She also found time to get married and divorced again, later taking up with an actor named Noel Fallin (later Folland) who was also her manager. Together they arrived in Sydney in August 1855.

Lola Montez's tour of Australia was the stuff of legend. She opened in Sydney with a performance titled 'Lola Montez in Bavaria'. It was a short season. A couple of weeks later she and Folland boarded a ship for Melbourne, with the law close behind for unpaid debts. According to folklore, when the officer confronted her in her cabin she stripped naked and dared him to lay hands on her. He didn't and the ship sailed.

Melbourne audiences did not care much for Lola's Bavarian routine so she began to perform the Spider Dance again. They loved it but the press was outraged and demanded her arrest. She fled and performed to packed houses in Adelaide until the end of 1855. Then it was back to Sydney in January and on to Ballarat in February.

On the goldfields the diggers tossed gold nuggets onto the stage as Lola swayed through her famous dance but the editor of the local paper, Henry Seekamp, ran articles railing against her immorality. Seekamp subsequently encountered Lola in the bar of her hotel where she attacked him with a riding whip. He fought back with another whip and then they took to tearing out each others' hair. Lola sued Seekamp for libel over his articles and he counter-sued. But public sympathy was with the feisty Lola. As well as titillating audiences, Lola impressed by heckling her critics, and with stunts like being lowered down a mineshaft with one foot in a rope sling and a glass of champagne in her hand.

Lola briefly met her match when the wife of one of her promoters beat her so badly that she had to take a month's break. But she was soon back again with her outrageous dance and even more outrageous lifestyle. After more touring and more trouble, Lola and Folland sailed for San Francisco. Somewhere near Fiji, Folland was mysteriously lost overboard.

Unfazed by this inconvenience, Lola attempted to revive her American career. But her moment had passed and her novelty had palled. By 1857, she was delivering moral lectures and apparently repenting of her wicked ways, though the title of a book published under her name in 1858 suggests otherwise: *The Arts of Beauty or Secrets of a Lady's Toilet: With Hints to Gentlemen on the Art of Fascinating*. As well as 50 tips on how to intrigue men, this handy manual included chapters on 'How to Obtain a Handsome Form', 'A Beautiful Foot and Ankle' and, vitally, 'How to Prevent the Hair Falling Off'.

Perhaps Lola had some personal experience with this problem. By now the consequences of her wild life were catching up with her. She began to display the symptoms of advanced syphilis and died on 17 January 1861. *The New York Times* published a generous obituary:

> There are few leaders of the newspaper literature of the day who are not familiar with the name of that eccentric, brilliant, impulsive woman known as LOLA MONTEZ. As a danseuse, an actress, a politician, a courtezan, a lecturer, a devotee, she has occupied a large space of the public attention for many years, both in this country and in Europe. Her career, so strangely erratic, so wonderfully checquered, [sic] came to its end on Thursday last. After a lengthened period of suffering, during which the knowledge of her approaching end quickened her to renewed preparations to meet it . . .

The cigarette-smoking entertainer and woman of fortune was buried in Brooklyn under the name Mrs Eliza Gilbert. Surprisingly, her passing was barely noticed in the Australian press of the day. But Lola and her spider dance are still remembered in legend, in popular culture, and even on the internet, where she has her own Facebook page.

BLACK LORDS OF SUMMER

On Boxing Day in 1866, the Melbourne Cricket Club predictably thrashed a green team of Aboriginal cricketers. But around eight thousand people turned up to watch the match, which marked the beginning of a sporting journey considered to be one of the hundred defining events in modern Australian history.

Cricket was a favourite game in Victoria, played wherever and whenever conditions allowed. Many stations employed Aboriginal stockmen who began to take an interest in the game too. When William Hayman, owner of Lake Wallace Station, observed this he gathered together a team from the local Jardwadjali, Gunditjmara and Wotjobaluk people. Tom Wills coached the group, and also played with them. It was Hayman who arranged for the Boxing Day match. But this match, watched by so many, then led to a series of matches in Sydney arranged by an entrepreneur known as Captain Gurnett, who also wanted the team to tour England.

When Gurnett disappeared with the proceeds of the Sydney tour they were coached by a former all-England player named Charles Lawrence, who was able to obtain financial backing for the England tour. In February 1868, the thirteen-strong team left for England on the clipper *Parramatta*.

The Aboriginal cricket team arrived in May, and while they lost their first match to Surrey, 20,000 people came to see them play and they impressed their hosts:

> Mullagh is a remarkably good bowler; and though some few blunders occurred to mar the general merit of the fielding it is but fair to say that Twopenny is a first-rate long-stop; that King Cole is an energetic and indefatigable point; and that Dick-a-Dick is one of the best of long-legmen, his running and his throwing being alike admirable. With the ground, and also—which is no slight matter—with the atmosphere quite new to them, the Australians allowed themselves, by their fielding, worthy opponents to the best English cricketers.

Over the next six months, the team played a strenuous series of 46 matches, of which they lost fourteen, won fourteen and drew the remaining nineteen contests. Their performance surprised the English. Despite this more than creditable record, *The Times* newspaper described the tour as 'a travestie upon cricket at Lords'.

Regardless, the Aboriginal team was popular with the public and complemented their cricketing prowess by demonstrating traditional 'games' of their own, including boomerang throwing. One team member Jungunjinuke (also called Dick-a-Dick) impressed everyone with his ability to wield a spear and club:

> After a game played at the Oval, Dick-a-Dick showed his skill in cleverly evading cricket balls thrown at him, and so amused

> the spectators that they broke through the ring at the finish, and carried him shoulder high to the dressing-tent.

The team was away for eight months and returned to Sydney in February 1869. One member, Bripumyarrumin (also known as King Cole), died in England and was buried in London.

Upon returning to Australia, most of the team members went back to their old lives and work. Legislation enacted in Victoria to prevent Aboriginal people moving around without official permission meant that it was difficult to continue playing. A few team members did play on though. Yellanach, otherwise know as Johnny Cuzens, played for Melbourne before returning to the bush and reportedly dying in 1870. Murrumgunarrimin, or Twopenny, played for New South Wales against Victoria in the same year. Unaarrimin, also known as Johnny Mullagh, played on for at least another decade. There is a Johnny Mullagh memorial trophy and a cricket centre named after him in Harrow, Victoria.

In 2015, a number of artefacts from the tour were discovered in the Royal Albert Memorial Museum in Exeter. As well as a boomerang and two spears, there were spear throwers, clubs and firesticks. How the objects came to be in the museum remains a mystery.

STEAMSHIP TO MELBOURNE

Before the era of air travel, migrants travelled to Australia by sea. Some came in steerage, the cheapest fare; some came in the moderate comfort of second class. A lucky few came first class. Whatever their circumstances, the long voyage from home was a rite of passage during which they changed from citizens of a familiar home country to newcomers in a strange land.

In September 1874, at Gravesend docks in London, young Ally Heathcote and her family were bound—travelling first class—for new lives aboard the 2215-tonne steamship *Northumberland*.

> We went below to see our future home for the following two months, the first look at our berths was not so favourable as

> we would have liked but we must put up with inconvenience on board a vessel like the one we had chosen for the means of transport to our adopted country.

Friends and relations from their home town had gathered to send them off. 'I am sure no one left their country with more prayers than did my parents, brother and sister and I. We are leaving one home to make another in the opposite extreme of Her Majesty's dominions.' As the crowd waved from the docks, the bell was rung, the anchor weighed, a gun was fired and the *Northumberland* 'glided elegantly out of the harbour' and down the Thames.

The *Northumberland* carried migrants as well as returning Australians. Among those accompanying the Heathcotes in first class were a judge, a squatter, a member of the Legislative Assembly, a businessman and a duo of returning theatrical performers. A Rabbi was also among the company; he would make himself popular by giving music lessons and 'illustrative lectures'. In the cargo was a 'little army of songsters', 1500 canaries selected for the quality of their plumage and song. These were a rare and precious cargo, particularly in this era long before TV and radio was readily and cheaply available, where a songbird would be a valuable and melodious possession.

Ally was entertained to see porpoises during their unusually smooth passage through the Bay of Biscay. But like most passengers on these two-month voyages, she began to find it hard to fill in her spare time. Ally and her people were god-fearing folk and spent much time singing hymns and worshipping. But as they steamed south, the temperature increased along with the monotony. Even the crew found things unusually slow: 'The second mate said he wished somebody would enliven them up for the sailors say they have never had such a dull lot of passengers on board before.' In contrast, Ally thought the crew were 'a jolly lot . . . every evening on the deck they have music amongst themselves'. She imagined that 'when they cross the line they often play some tricks on the passengers. I wish they would, it would just be the thing and make us laugh.'

The first incident to break the boredom was a fight. After almost three weeks of close living even minor irritations might produce a violent reaction, as Ally excitedly recorded in her diary:

> We had scarcely got thoroughly awake this morning before we had a pugilistic encounter between two of the male passengers in our cabin, they sit at the next table to us and are constantly quarrelling over their food. There are eight of them in one mess, all gentlemen with one exception, it appears to me they have been born grumbling. They take their turns, two together for a week to cook for all the lot, and today being the last day for two of them, they thought they would end in a forcible manner. They flew at each other like prize fighters but two other men quickly separated them, but they looked as though they would murder each other, they got a little calmed but I can assure you it caused great excitement on board.

The weather grew even hotter as they entered the tropics and they were tormented by 'a brown kind of insect, a terror to tidy English matrons and maidens'. By the end of October the oppressive heat had eased: they were well out of the tropics and headed for colder and stormier climes. But they soon might have missed the bugs and heat as a massive storm rocked the ship. Ally's diary told the tale:

> We have offered up our prayers this morning to thank God for the safe deliverance we have had from (what had every appearance, and what we expected to be) a watery grave, since I left off writing last night we have had the greatest storm this ship ever encountered, about 10 o'clock last night, after most of the passengers had retired, Willie among the number (Papa, Mamma, Bert and I) were sat at one of the tables. The wind was screeching and howling through the rigging, there were three men steering at the wheel, all lashed to, the wind was something dreadful, we imagined and felt thankful that you were safe in your homes, away from all danger, and we were expecting every minute the ship would go down.

Just as they were wondering how much longer the storm would last they heard a crash up on deck and the sea began pouring in on them: 'We gave ourselves up for lost and the people rushed out of their cabins looking terrified. Ma sat quite calm, I looked at her and could see her lips moving, she was pale as death and so was Papa . . .'

Fortunately it was only some deck housing that had been swept away, allowing the waves to penetrate below. The second-class cabins were drenched and had to be bailed out. More seriously the waves almost extinguished the boilers. As Ally put it:

> the water poured down in the engine house and almost put out the fires, indeed, steam has no use, only to keep the ship straight, the sea had struck her a little sideway, had it struck her broadside nothing but a miracle could have saved her, the force of the sea the time the crash happened was so strong it turned the engine backwards.

Despite fears the ship had caught alight, they plowed on and around 11 p.m. the captain came to reassure them that the worst was over and they gave thanks.

The remainder of the voyage was calm, albeit punctuated by the unmasking of a sneak thief among the first-class passengers; 'the black sheep of the *Northumberland*', as Ally described the named and shamed miscreant.

Ally herself suffered an accidental fall when she missed her grip on a handrail. She gave her head 'an awful thump which made [her] see stars in consequence.' But she then had the pleasure of being spoiled by family and other passengers and recovered in plenty of time to anticipate the thrill of first seeing their destination.

Approaching Cape Otway the captain gave the order to shorten sail and prepare the anchor. The sailors and the male passengers 'did not require telling twice and I can assure you the passengers put a hand too, as they knew that looked well for soon casting anchor'. Ally wrote, 'all we have to do is wait as patiently as we can, and in due time, we will rid the ship and crew of our company, but it is time to close and turn in and try to sleep'.

When she woke the next morning her journey was over. The *Northumberland* passed through Port Phillip Heads on 14 November after 52 days at sea. Ally and her family were no longer in that peculiar limbo of ocean passages. Now they were landed immigrants with new lives to begin.

THE MOST BEAUTIFUL LIES

Samuel Langhorne Clemens was born in Missouri in 1835, but would eventually—after looking out for himself from the age of twelve—become the great American writer and humourist known as Mark Twain. His pen name derived from his days as a riverboat pilot where the cry 'mark twain' was the pilot's call to indicate a depth of two fathoms beneath a boat. By the early 1890s, Twain had made and lost a couple of fortunes and was repairing his finances with a world speaking tour, which included Australia in 1895. When the great American man visited he left a flurry of witty remarks and quips in his wake. Many of them are as revealing and funny now as they were back then.

On arriving in Sydney, Twain was interviewed by a local journalist and declared:

> my greatest efforts are directed towards doing the world with as little hard work as possible. I frankly admit that in regard to most things I am phenomenally lazy. I have travelled from the Rocky Mountains to Jerusalem in order to escape hard work, and I have come to Australia with the same idea.

He praised the harbour as 'superbly beautiful':

> We entered and cast anchor, and in the morning went oh-ing and ah-ing in admiration up through the crooks and turns of the spacious and beautiful harbor—a harbor which is the darling of Sydney and the wonder of the world. It is not surprising that the people are proud of it, nor that they put their enthusiasm into eloquent words. A returning citizen asked me what I thought of it,

> and I testified with a cordiality which I judged would be up to the market rate. I said it was beautiful—superbly beautiful. Then by a natural impulse I gave God the praise. The citizen did not seem altogether satisfied. He said:
>
> 'It is beautiful, of course it's beautiful—the Harbor; but that isn't all of it, it's only half of it; Sydney's the other half, and it takes both of them together to ring the supremacy-bell. God made the Harbor, and that's all right; but Satan made Sydney.'
>
> Of course I made an apology; and asked him to convey it to his friend. He was right about Sydney being half of it. It would be beautiful without Sydney, but not above half as beautiful as it is now, with Sydney added.

But when travelling by train across the New South Wales–Victoria border, Twain was stunned to discover that he and all the passengers needed to change trains due to the different gauge tracks in each colony. His much-quoted comment was, 'Think of the paralysis of intellect that gave that idea birth.'

He was happier in Melbourne, especially at the Melbourne Cup.

> The Melbourne Cup is the Australasian National Day. It would be difficult to overstate its importance. It overshadows all other holidays and specialized days of whatever sort in that congeries of colonies. Overshadows them? I might almost say it blots them out. Each of them gets attention, but not everybody's; each of them evokes interest, but not everybody's; each of them rouses enthusiasm, but not everybody's; in each case a part of the attention, interest, and enthusiasm is a matter of habit and custom, and another part of it is official and perfunctory. Cup Day, and Cup Day only, commands an attention, an interest, and an enthusiasm which are universal—and spontaneous, not perfunctory. Cup Day is supreme—it has no rival. I can call to mind no specialized annual day, in any country, which can be named by that large name—Supreme. I can call to mind no specialized annual day, in any country, whose approach fires the whole land with a

> conflagration of conversation and preparation and anticipation and jubilation. No day save this one; but this one does it.

With a writer's ear for everyday speech, Twain gently sent up the Australian accent, reporting his hotel chambermaid's morning greeting: 'The tyble is set, and here is the piper [paper]; and if the lydy is ready I'll tell the wyter to bring up the breakfast.'

He was also fascinated by the expression 'My word', seemingly in vogue at the time: 'the first time I heard an Australian say it, it was positively thrilling,' he wrote and suggested that Americans import it for their own use.

In Adelaide, Twain was impressed by the many faiths and the numerous churches, temples and chapels.

> She has a population, as per the latest census, of only 320,000-odd, and yet her varieties of religion indicate the presence within her borders of samples of people from pretty nearly every part of the globe you can think of. Tabulated, these varieties of religion make a remarkable show. One would have to go far to find its match.

Twain was moved to consult a table of statistics recording the adherents to the faiths professed in Adelaide, and arrived at a total of just over 320,000, including 1719 practitioners of 'Other Religions'. There were:

> Agnostics, Atheists, Believers in Christ, Buddhists, Calvinists, Christadelphians, Christians, Christ's Chapel, Christian Israelites, Christian Socialists, Church of God, Cosmopolitans, Deists, Evangelists, Exclusive Brethren, Free Church, Free Methodists, Freethinkers, Followers of Christ, Gospel Meetings, Greek Church, Infidels, Maronites, Memnonists, Moravians, Mormons, Naturalists, Orthodox, Others (indefinite), Pagans, Pantheists, Plymouth Brethren, Rationalists, Reformers, Secularists, Seventh-day Adventists, Shaker, Shintoists, Spiritualists, Theosophists, Town (City) Mission, Welsh Church, Huguenot, Hussite, Zoroastrians, Zwinglian.

> About 64 roads to the other world. You see how healthy the religious atmosphere is. Anything can live in it. Agnostics, Atheists, Freethinkers, Infidels, Mormons, Pagans, Indefinites they are all there. And all the big sects of the world can do more than merely live in it: they can spread flourish prosper. All except the Spiritualists and the Theosophists. That is the most curious feature of this curious table. What is the matter with the specter? Why do they puff him away? He is a welcome toy everywhere else in the world.

Twain visited the goldfields of Victoria and in Ballarat thought the Eureka Stockade 'the finest thing in Australasian history. It was a revolution—small in size; but great politically; it was a strike for liberty, a struggle for a principle, a stand against injustice and oppression' and 'another instance of a victory won by a lost battle'.

And on Hobart he wrote:

> Hobart has a peculiarity—it is the neatest town that the sun shines on; and I incline to believe that it is also the cleanest. However that may be, its supremacy in neatness is not to be questioned. There cannot be another town in the world that has no shabby exteriors; no rickety gates and fences, no neglected houses crumbling to ruin, no crazy and unsightly sheds, no weed-grown front-yards of the poor, no back-yards littered with tin cans and old boots and empty bottles, no rubbish in the gutters, no clutter on the sidewalks, no outer-borders fraying out into dirty lanes and tin-patched huts. No, in Hobart all the aspects are tidy, and all a comfort to the eye; the modestest cottage looks combed and brushed, and has its vines, its flowers, its neat fence, its neat gate, its comely cat asleep on the window ledge.

He concluded with a perceptive summary of the Australian experience:

> Australian history is almost always picturesque; indeed, it is so curious and strange, that it is itself the chiefest novelty the country

> has to offer, and so it pushes the other novelties into second and third place. It does not read like history, but like the most beautiful of lies. And all of a fresh new sort, no mouldy old stale ones. It is full of surprises, and adventures, and incongruities, and contradictions, and incredibilities; but they are all true, they all happened.

Of course they did, Mark!

SONS OF EMPIRE

It was once the practice in many British families for the eldest son to inherit while sons born later (and all daughters) had to make their own way in the world. Although this custom preserved family wealth—as long as the first-born was not a wastrel—it condemned many younger sons of middle-class families, and a few penniless aristocrats (actual or assumed), to rove the roads of the empire, earning their keep as best they could. There was a well-worn trail from Britain through southern Africa, Canada, New Zealand and Australia along which these wanderers travelled by tramp steamers, train and foot, often working their passage through the world's byways. Rudyard Kipling wrote a poem on this theme. He called these men 'the lost legion' of 'gentleman rovers abroad' and wrote of their wanderings in Sarawak, up the Fly River, along the Oil Coast and on the wallaby track with 'the swag and the billy again'.

Kipling also hymned the lost legion in some of his other poems. In 'The Song of the Banjo', written in 1894, he refers to the industrial troubles in Australia at the time:

> By the bitter road the Younger Son must tread,
> Ere he win to hearth and saddle of his own,
> 'Mid the riot of the shearers at the shed,
> In the silence of the herder's hut alone . . .

London was the pivot around which the adventurers revolved through the empire, including Australia. In another poem, an unnamed writer describes those who roamed the roads of empire before World War I in search of adventure, riches, love or fulfilment of some kind. The war called many back to fight for the empire from which they had previously wandered, their experiences and assumed character now being turned to a common good; a righteous fight ending in a likely death.

> The younger son he's earned his bread in ways both hard and easy,
> From Parramatta to the Pole, from Yukon to Zambesi;
> For young blood is roving blood, and a far road's best,
> And when you're tired of roving there'll be time enough to rest!
> And it's 'Hello' and 'How d'ye do?' 'Who'd have thought of meeting you?
> Thought you were in Turkestan, or China or Peru!'
> It's a long trail in peace-time where the roving Britons stray,
> But in war-time, in war-time, it's just across the way!
>
> He's left the bronchos to be bust by who in thunder chooses;
> He's left the pots to wash themselves in Canada's cabooses;
> He's left the mine and logging camp, the peavey, pick and plough,
> For young blood is fighting blood, and England needs him now.
> And it's 'Hello' and 'How d'ye do?' 'How's the world been using you?
> What's the news of Calgary, Quebec and Cariboo?'
> It's a long trail in peace-time where the roving Britons stray,
> But in war-time, in war-time, it's just across the way!
>
> He's travelled far by many a trail; he's rambled here and yonder,
> No road too rough for him to tread, no land too wide to wander,
> For young blood is roving blood, and the spring of life is best,
> And when all the fighting's done, lad, there'll be time enough to rest.
> And it's good-bye, tried and true, here's a long farewell to you
> (Rolling stone from Mexico, Shanghai, or Timbuctoo!)
> Young blood is roving blood, but the last sleep is best,
> When the fighting all is done, lad, and it's time to rest!

A large body of romance and fantasy was built up around the figure of the younger son. He featured in boys' own adventures and ripping yarns set in many different countries. The reality though, as always, was rather different. Some did stop rolling, perhaps settling down in the Australian bush in the pearling industry or mining and a few 'made their pile', either by luck or good management, possibly with a faint air of nefariousness involved. But more often, the demands of a life lived almost perpetually on the road, moving from place to unsanitary place, working in unhealthy conditions and climates, and the consequences of drink, drugs and heedless sexual encounters meant that many more younger sons did not get too old.

The intergenerational journeying of the younger sons of the empire mostly came to an end with World War I. But the idea and the image of the rough diamond wanderer lived on in popular culture, particularly through movies and boys' annuals right in to the 1960s.

THE GREAT WHITE FLEET

In an early example of a 'captain's call', in 1907 American President Teddy Roosevelt decided to send a large fleet of his battleships on a voyage around the world. On 16 December that year sixteen ships of the United States Atlantic Fleet steamed past the presidential yacht in Hampton Roads, Virginia, to begin a cruise that would last fourteen months.

This tour of the gleaming white vessels with golden bows was to be a global statement of American naval power. They would dock at twenty ports on six continents in the first ever round-the-world trip by a fleet of steam-powered steel warships. The 14,000 sailors and marines aboard the ships would cover 70,000 kilometres by the time they returned home. In August 1908, the 'Great White Fleet', as it had come to be known, reached Australia.

Newspapers kept the public informed of the fleet's progress. In early August 1908, some 100,000 New Zealanders greeted the fleet at Auckland in a massive display of public and official interest. The Australian press was also flooded with adulatory stories. Well before the ships were due, the country was in a state of high excitement bordering on mass hysteria. As one newspaper screamed, 'Everybody is talking fleet.'

Sydney's Catholic community planned to welcome the Americans with an illuminated southern cross at the top of St Mary's Cathedral. On Thursday 20 August, when the fleet docked, the cathedral bells would ring. The remaining week of the visit would be a nonstop cavalcade of parades, choirs and concerts, as well as banquets, at which the toast would be to 'Our allies, friends and brothers: the American nation', which had been proposed by the Catholic archbishop of Sydney. Arrangements for mass and other Catholic observances were also made on a large scale.

But this was just a small part of the larger festivities planned by the city. All major public buildings and many private structures would be outlined in electric light bulbs. On the General Post Office, the official centre of the city, 'AUSTRALIA'S GREETINGS' would be writ large in lights. Roads were to be lit up, as well as statues, and even trees; 'the giant fig tree in front of the old Education building will be spangled with hundreds of coloured lights'. And so on and so on. Some feared that the power supply would not be able to cope with such extravagance and that there would be a catastrophic blackout in the middle of the celebrations.

At 11.37 a.m. on the appointed day, the gleaming armada steamed through the heads to a tumultuous welcome, as pleasure craft and official vessels rushed out to greet them.

Prime Minister Deakin was effusive:

> Australians will receive the men who man these splendid battleships with unbounded enthusiasm, not only the gallant tars, but also those gallant artisans who toil in the hidden caverns of these 16 monsters of the deep. Our welcome is enthusiastic, not because of the giant strength of the great Republic, but be cause it is a nation of kinsmen, and kinsmen we are proud of.

He went on to talk of the fleet, and America, as a mighty force for peace, progress and freedom in the world.

> In this grand mission they do not stand alone. There is another great flag waving beside the Stars and Stripes, the flag that once waved over our ancestors and still flies over us—the Union Jack of our beloved motherland—the flag that's braved a thousand years, the battle and the breeze.

It is claimed that over half a *million* Sydneysiders went to watch the fleet sail in, or over 80 per cent of the total population of the city at that time. This unlikely number would have meant that only those too young, to old or too infirm didn't participate. Nevertheless, it's undoubted that the crowds were the largest in Australian history to that time and it is thought that most people in Sydney had seen the fleet.

And the fleet had seen them. After a few days partying the sailors were beginning to wilt. One is said to have stretched out on a park bench with this sign above him:

> Yes, I am delighted with the Australian people.
> Yes, I think your park is the finest in the world.
> I am very tired and would like to go to sleep.

After the clamour of Sydney, the Americans sailed on to Melbourne where they spent another week in celebrations. *The Sydney Morning Herald*, naturally, reported that Melbourne's decorations were 'No comparison with Sydney'. But as in Sydney, the crowds that turned out to welcome the Americans were larger than those to celebrate Federation in 1901.

At the end of Fleet Week, as they called it in Melbourne, there was a 'great state luncheon' and yet another march, and then on a dull and misty morning most of the fleet sailed for Albany in Western Australia. Although Adelaide was not due for a visit from the fleet, much to the city's annoyance, there was a little satisfaction: under the heading 'The best laid schemes of mice and men . . .', Adelaide's *The Register* exulted in telling the story of a distressed supply ship in the fleet needing to put in to port at Semaphore due to foul weather. It was not much, but it was better than missing out entirely on what was possibly the greatest popular celebration in Australian history.

Although the fleet arrived at Albany on another wet and grey day, the event was described as 'a brilliant scene' in the local press. Despite the rain there were yet more marches, and the fleet spent the better part of a week taking on coal and enjoying the breathless hospitality of the small community. On 20 September, the fleet steamed past Rottnest Island *en route* for Manila, giving the residents of Fremantle a last long loving look at the 'majestic array' of American sea power. Signals and despatches were exchanged, in accordance with naval etiquette, and then they were gone.

Effusive editorials on the significance of the visit ran on in the press for weeks. According to one writer, the object lesson of the fleet's visit was clear:

> The welcome of the American Fleet to Australia was founded, as stated, upon pure racial love and affection; and all future relationship in the officers of the Atlantic or Pacific, should be one, indivisible and eternal. The Australians were not carried away with thoughts of republicanism by the presence of what has been termed the 'Great White Fleet.'

This attitude was borne of the widely held fear of invasion from the north by the 'yellow peril', and offers one reason for the enthusiasm for the visiting Americans. Many saw the American fleet as their potential saviours should the country be attacked from Asia. It was not until the armada reached Australia that it was called the Great White Fleet.

Whatever the reason, there's no doubt enthusiasm for the fleet's visit seemed boundless at the time. Composers penned florid songs, poets extolled, and patriots thundered at the relative greatness of American and British navies. Journalists considered the implications of an Australian–American alliance and politicians decreed holidays. The Americans were generally impressed with Australia, if a little exhausted by it. A considerable number of sailors did not go back to their ships.

The fleet returned to its American starting point in February 1909. Nothing quite like the size and excitement of this naval carnival has been seen in Australia since.

THE MIGRANT LORD

In the mid 1920s a British Member of Parliament and son of the Earl of Bathurst voyaged to Australia on a migrant ship. Under the assumed name George Bott, Lord Apsley travelled third class in a cramped cabin with a group of British migrant men. His wife Lady Viola Apsley travelled first class on the same ship for one section of the voyage, planning to join up with her husband again in Australia.

When this unusual journey came to the attention of the Australian press in May 1925 they naturally wanted to know why Lord Apsley had decided to travel so humbly. He told them that in the course of his work as a parliamentary secretary, he had been privy to allegations in parliament that immigrants to Australia found no work and suffered 'brutal' treatment at the hands of the locals. Though these instances were likely atypical due to extenuating circumstances, he nevertheless 'wanted to take [his] chance with other fellows and see how the ordinarily experienced "Pommy" got on when he landed and what happened to him' so he registered on board 'as an ex hunt servant with no agricultural experience'.

When George Bott landed he reported to the immigration bureau, as did all migrants. He was given a job on a Gippsland farm at 20 shillings a week and his keep.

> After 10 days on that farm I moved up into the Mallee, where I worked for a farmer who had taken up a block of virgin country three years ago at 8/6 an acre, and converted it into a farm with a nice homestead. There were 300 acres under crop (there will be 400 the next year), two dams, 50 sheep, two cows, two pigs, and poultry. The farmer had fenced all his land with sheep-proof fencing, put up a windmill and installed a telephone. Though, he

> had been offered £4 an acre he and his wife, both English, were too fond of it to sell.

George worked on this industrious farm for three weeks and 'was sorry to leave'.

The temporarily working-class lord was keen to point out that immigrants who drifted back to Melbourne 'and hang about trying to discourage others and beg money from them are mostly those who do not want work and never should have come here, and those willing but never taught to look after themselves, cannot cook, cannot mend, or even wash their own clothes, and are quite helpless'. Wherever he went in Australia 'as an unknown and nameless stranger' he had met with 'kindness and goodwill from every class of people in town and country'.

After reassuming his true identity, Lord Apsley lived at the state government house in Melbourne. After 'restocking his wardrobe', he was due to talk with migration officials and to call on the prime minister. He then continued his journey to Darwin where he had arranged to tour the far north-west in a newly designed British half-track vehicle that was billed to 'revolutionise transport both for military, and civilian use in desert country'.

The no-nonsense, roll-up-your-sleeves Lord Apsley was frequently interviewed and spoke publicly about his views, inspiring a lively debate in the Australian press about the virtues and vices of assisted migration. With his supportive wife he published a book of 'ripping yarns' about his unique journey titled *The Amateur Settlers*, which gave advice to intending migrants.

But their adventures didn't end there. He and Lady Apsley later lived under the assumed names of Mr and Mrs James with group settlers in Western Australia to gain further on-the-ground experience for their investigations. The 'groupers', as they were known, were British migrants assisted to settle the state's south-west wilderness through the state government's Group Settlement Scheme. Even this early in the program's existence, it was showing signs of strain.

Mr and Mrs James spent two weeks with their group. She

minded the house as did all the wives. He joined the men as part of the communal workforce, felling the forests and using gelignite to clear stumps from the land.

Of their experience, Viola Apsley subsequently wrote that 'the best equipment for a woman to take to Australia is grit, common sense, adaptability and a touch of the saving grace of humour. Capital or brains are not so necessary.' Lord Apsley wrote:

> I believe Australia must have a rosy future. She has much more to offer the average person than this country has at the present time. My final impression is that though no one should leave England who has a happy home in this country, to all those who have no prospects inn the Old Country and nothing of their own but healthy minds and bodies, Australia offers a happy Home and a Future of their own making.

Apsley claimed that the disastrous group settlement scheme had a 'romantic side' similar to Saxon England. This would have been a surprise to the many disillusioned groupers. Even before the migrant lord and lady arrived to find out for themselves what it was all about, significant numbers had already walked off their unviable plots of rock and jarrah. Many more would walk off after the amateur settlers went home and no new settlements were established after 1928.

6

JOURNEYS OF THE HEART

> Pray Sir be good enough to let my husband know you have had a letter from me, and beg him to take care of my dear children.
>
> Mary Talbot, transported convict, 1791

THE LADY ON THE SAND

The slight figure boarding Louis de Freycinet's *Uranie* would hardly have attracted a second glance. Ship's boys as young as ten were not uncommon in the early nineteenth century. But this 'boy' was the beautiful wife of the captain dressed as a man. The year was 1817 and 23-year-old Rose and 35-year-old Louis had just married. It was a truly romantic marriage for love. Rose was a commoner and de Freycinet an aristocrat. So hopelessly in love were the couple that they could not bear to be separated and Louis broke every rule of the French navy to have her with him on what they knew would be a very long journey.

De Freycinet needed to modify his ship to cater for a female passenger and it was not long before word of the unauthorised passenger made it ashore, causing great official consternation. But by then *Uranie* had sailed. The story delighted the French public and the de Freycinets became celebrities in their absence. The authorities decided to allow the romantic duo to proceed.

They were bound for the great south land via the Cape of Good Hope and Mauritius on a round-the-world voyage of scientific discovery.

A year after leaving France the expedition anchored in Shark Bay (Western Australia) to conduct scientific observations and map the area. But Rose's husband also had some unfinished business in this part of the great south land. In 1802, de Freycinet had been with the Baudin expedition when they discovered the beaten-out dinner plate left there by Willem de Vlamingh to mark his visit to the unknown south land in 1697. De Freycinet and other officers had wanted Baudin to remove the plate and take it back to France for posterity. But Baudin had refused. De Freycinet had sworn that he would one day return and take the plate, so that it wouldn't be 'swallowed up by the sands, or else run the risk of being taken away and destroyed by some careless sailor':

> I felt that its correct place was in one of these great scientific depositories which offer to the historian such rich and precious documents. I planned, therefore, to place it in the collections of the Académie Royale des Inscriptions et Belles-Lettres de L'Institut de France.

He duly retrieved the plate and conveyed it to the academy, where it immediately disappeared. It was not seen again until 1940 when it was found in a box of old junk in the basement of the academy.

Rose kept a journal of her travels, recounting the sights she saw and the adventures she experienced with her husband. She also wrote many letters home. Her first view of New Holland, as the west coast of Australia was known at the time, did not impress her. She saw a 'low and arid coast' with 'nothing in the sight to ease our minds, for we knew we would find no water in this miserable land'. She would later go ashore with Louis and spend a few nights under canvas but the 'stay on land was not a pleasant one . . . the country being entirely devoid of trees and vegetation'. In the cooler parts of the day she collected shells and read in her tent.

On one of these trips off the ship, Rose went ashore in a small boat but was unable to land because the water was too shallow. A couple of sailors had to carry the captain's wife to the beach in all her finery. When they reached the sand a group of ten or so Aborigines approached, making strong signals for the intruders to return to their ship. 'I was afraid, and would willingly have hidden myself,' she wrote home. But the Aborigines retreated, leaving Rose, Louis and some officers to picnic on the beach beneath a canvas shade they had brought from the ship along with the food. This they supplemented with some local oysters 'far tastier than all those I had, sitting at a table in comfort, in Paris'.

What the people of the region might have made of this strange scene is not recorded. They may have thought that the strangers picnicking on their beach—Rose in her fashionable finery and the sailors in their colourful uniforms—did not present a very serious threat. In any case, just a few days later, friendly contact with the Aborigines was established when they exchanged some of their weapons in return for tin and glass trinkets.

The French sailed north to Timor, then to the Maluku Islands, the Caroline Islands, the Mariana Islands and Hawaii, then the Sandwich Islands, before again heading south. In November 1819, they arrived in the growing colony at Port Jackson. Here the de Freycinets were welcomed enthusiastically. The governor sent a military band to play them along the river as they travelled inland to meet him at his Parramatta residence. There were endless parties and the French were provided with a house and facilities to pursue their scientific work. But on their first night in the house they were robbed of their silver service, table linen, the servants' clothing and other items. Rose wrote home: 'You know the purpose of this colony and what sort of people are to be found here in plenty; you will therefore not be astonished at this misdeed: might one not say it is roguery's classic shore.'

Rose departed on the *Uranie* on Christmas morning. Aboard were two Merino rams, adding to the black swans and emus they had already collected on their journey. Also aboard was a convict stowaway suffering the effects of too much Christmas cheer. He was handed over to the pilot but when they got out to sea another ten escapees were found. They joined the crew as the ship set a course for the Falkland Islands in search of an abandoned French settlement.

Here the *Uranie* was wrecked, though the expeditioners managed to save their notes and around half of their samples. They eventually made it back to France where Louis was court-martialled for losing his ship. He was cleared of the charge and ultimately feted for his scientific achievements. Rose and Louis were a celebrated couple until Rose died of cholera in 1832. Louis died in 1841. The de Vlamingh plate they retrieved was gifted back to Australia in 1947.

PLEADING THE BELLY

Young Mary Talbot came to London from Ireland with her stonemason husband and at least one child in about 1787. There her husband suffered a work accident that left him unable to provide for his family. With no other means of support, Mary became a thief. In February 1788, aged 22, she was caught stealing a bolt of printed cotton valued at 17 shillings. Her defence at the Old Bailey was that she had been drunk at the time and had mistakenly picked up the material. Witnesses refuted this tale and she was sentenced to seven years' transportation to New South Wales, then barely established.

Later that year she was taken from prison and placed aboard the convict transport *Lady Juliana* with her baby. In company with some other convicts Mary managed to escape. She went into hiding but was recognised, apprehended and tried again in January 1790. She claimed her escape was motivated by the lack of nutrition aboard the ship, making her unable to feed her baby. Found guilty of returning from a sentence of transportation she was sentenced to death. It was then discovered that Mary was pregnant, enabling her to 'plead the belly', a common-law practice that allowed her execution to be delayed until after the birth. As was often the case in these situations, Mary's death sentence was eventually commuted to transportation for life.

In court, Mary said that she would prefer to die rather than leave her three children: they were the reason she had escaped from the *Lady Juliana* in the first place. She was cautioned that her death sentence could still be reinstated but she continued to cry out for death. She had to be taken from the court in convulsions. While in prison she continued to bewail her fate but to no avail: she was eventually transported without her children and without the chance to farewell her husband. Among other female convicts, some with children, she embarked for Australia aboard the *Mary Ann* in February 1791. Mary described the voyage in a letter to a friend who had tried to have her transported together with her family to America. Her graphic letter was sent from the Cape Verde Islands on 29 March 1791:

> We sailed from Portsmouth the 23rd of February, with the wind much against us, and were so much in danger, that we feared we should have shared the fate of a ship which was lost within sight of us.
>
> Our good Captain very kindly dropped anchor at the Nase, but did not stop more than one night, and sailed for the Downs, where we sent our pilot on shore. On the 25th and 26th, along the Coast, we had a violent storm, which lasted 24 hours; during every moment of its continuance we expected to perish, and were washed out of our beds between decks, while the sea-sickness and the groans and shrieks of so many unhappy wretches, made the situation we were in truly distressing; for there were 138 women and five children; two of the latter born after we sailed, and one only died on our passage hither, where we remain no longer than is necessary to repair the ship and taken in water.

The *Mary Ann* arrived in Sydney just 143 days after leaving England, a speedy passage. But despite her hopes for reprieve and to be reunited with her children, the forlorn mother and wife died only seven weeks later and was buried on 28 August 1791. The fate of her husband and children is unknown.

MY HEART IS STILL UNCHANGED

'My heart is still unchanged': these were the words of John Nicol as he recounted his life story in the harsh Edinburgh winter of 1822. A self-described 'child of chance', his heart still belonged to the convict Sarah Whitlam and the child she bore him aboard a convict transport bound for Port Jackson more than thirty years before. 'What is become of her, whether she is dead or alive, I know not.'

John Nicol led an adventurous life in the 35 years before he became steward aboard a convict transport in 1789. He had sailed in whalers, fought in sea battles and visited many ports in many counties. He had also found time to learn the cooper's trade. Eventually, the wandering life his soul craved led him to join the crew of the *Lady Juliana*—the same ship young Mary Talbot had escaped the previous year—which was then bearing 200 women to penal servitude in New South Wales. It was to be a long voyage from the River Thames, but there were compensations:

> When we were fairly out to sea, every man on board took a wife from among the convicts, they nothing loath. The girl with whom I lived, for I was as bad in this point as the others, was named Sarah Whitlam. She was a native of Lincoln, a girl of a modest reserved turn, as kind and true a creature as ever lived. I courted her for a week and upwards, and would have married her on the spot had there been a clergyman on board.

According to Sarah, she had been 'banished for a mantle she had borrowed from an acquaintance. Her friend prosecuted her for stealing it, and she was transported for seven years.' This all mattered not to John. Even before he knew her story, he was entranced:

> I had fixed my fancy upon her from the moment I knocked the rivet out of her irons upon my anvil, and as firmly resolved to bring her back to England when her time was out, my lawful wife,

> as ever I did intend anything in my life. She bore me a son in our voyage out.

And a long voyage it was. South to Tenerife, an extended stay in Rio, another layover in the Cape of Good Hope. Some of the convict women proved difficult to manage. An incorrigible few were imprisoned and occasionally whipped. There was a fire, a miscarriage and antics too many to recount in the 364 days the *Lady Juliana* took to reach Port Jackson.

On their safe arrival, Nicol's impression of the south land was good, though he saw little of the place: 'It is a fine country and everything thrives well in it,' he wrote. He was employed in revictualling the ship for the return voyage though 'any moments I could spare I gave them to Sarah'.

John and Sarah's time ashore together with their son, also named John, seemed too short. 'The days flew on eagles' wings, for we dreaded the hour of separation which at length arrived.' Nicol offered to forfeit his wages to stay with his beloved, but the captain needed him and he was taken aboard 'not without the aid of the military'. Nicol would have spirited Sarah back aboard the *Lady Juliana* if he had been able. But in the end he had to sail for China without her.

He was deeply troubled by the separation: 'Everything brought her endearing manners to my recollection.' He worried about the company in which she was forced to remain: 'to leave her exposed to temptation in the very worst company the world could produce was too much to think of with composure'. But there was some comfort in the knowledge she kept his Bible in which they had written both their names. When he returned to England he planned to go back to Australia with enough money to somehow buy Sarah's freedom. Eventually he shipped out aboard a whaler, intending to return to Port Jackson.

While at sea his ship encountered a vessel bound from New South Wales with an escaped convict aboard. Incredibly, the escapee had news of Sarah. She had left the colony for Mumbai, then known as Bombay. But the convict had no news of their son.

Nicol was plunged into despair. 'My love for her revived stronger at this time than any other since I left her. I even gave her praise for leaving . . . She did so to be out of bad company, my mind would whisper.'

Recovering his spirits, Nicol decided to make for India. He joined a Portuguese ship returning to Europe. After many delays he finally returned to England, hoping to add to the money from his whaling trip and planning to find Sarah.

While eluding the press gangs, which at that time were forcing men to fight in the Royal Navy, Nicol travelled to Lincoln to visit Sarah's parents. But they knew even less of their daughter's travels than he and so the wanderer went back to sea. Four years after leaving Port Jackson he landed in Batavia, modern-day Jakarta, still trying to reach Sarah's last-known destination in India. No ship was bound in that direction.

Time heals all wounds, goes the proverb, and the years of separation were beginning to cool John Nicol's affections. 'Indeed,' he wrote, 'I must confess, I did not feel the same anguish now I had endured before.' He reasoned that she must have cared little about him if she simply left the colony without writing to him, or even to her parents. He would try to find word of her once more in Lincoln, and then would return to Scotland and settle down. But on the way he was finally caught by a press gang and spent the next seven years fighting the French.

He was eventually released from service, considerably richer but now with 'the thoughts of Sarah . . . fad[ing] into a distant pleasing dream'. His strong passion 'was now softened into a curiosity to know what had become of her'. But again, no one in Lincoln had any news of her and as he 'was now too old to undertake any love pilgrimages' Nicol returned to a city he no longer knew and in which none knew him. He wandered around the country, eventually marrying a cousin and becoming a successful tradesman.

At the outbreak of the Napoleonic wars, the navy once again needed bodies and Nicol was forced to sell up and move to the country to avoid the press gangs once more. Eventually Napoleon was defeated in 1815 and it was safe to return to Edinburgh where, yet again, much was changed. His skills were little in demand. His wife died a few years later and he was reduced to near penury. The old mariner had no family or friends and could not obtain a pension from the navy. By the time he told his tale he was living on a few potatoes and 'coffee' made from toast scrapings. He was too proud to beg. He ended his story thus: 'I have been a wanderer and a child of chance all my days, and now only look for the time when I shall enter my last ship, and be anchored with a green turf upon my breast, and I care not how soon the command may be given.'

And Sarah? The day after John Nicol sailed out of Sydney Cove she married another convict. With him and her two children she did set sail for Bombay in 1796 but what became of her after that nobody knows.

FOOTSTEPS OF THE SAINT

The ancient religious tradition of pilgrimage is as popular today as ever. Believers band together to retrace the steps of a religious figure or to visit a site of special significance. There are many pilgrimages in Australia, though the most trodden paths are probably those concerned with Australia's only officially recognised saint, Sister Mary MacKillop.

Mary MacKillop's life and work were certainly inspiring and continue to provide a spiritual and practical example to many today. There are a number of local pilgrimages based on the life of St Mary MacKillop, including visits to The Rocks in Sydney, the town of Penola in South Australia and Brisbane. There are also pilgrimages to Rotarua and Auckland in New Zealand, where she also established schools. But the major event is the annual National Pilgrimage, known as 'In the Footsteps of Mary MacKillop'. The Sisters of Saint Joseph organise and accompany the eleven-day pilgrimage, which covers significant sites in South Australia and New South Wales.

Mary MacKillop was the first child of Alexander McKillop and Flora McKillop nee MacDonald, born in Fitzroy in 1842.

(She later changed the original spelling of her surname.) Mary and her seven brothers and sisters had an unstable childhood, moving often and struggling to get by. Mary became the chief provider for the family and began work as a clerk at the age of fourteen. Four years later, in 1860, she moved to Penola in South Australia to work as a governess, where she met Father Julian Tension-Woods. They shared a strong Roman Catholic faith and a concern for educating the young at a time when schooling was difficult for poorer people in the bush to access. Woods wanted to found a new order to address these and other issues and at the age of 24, Mary became the head of St Joseph's School in Penola.

She had begun wearing a black dress, as a symbol of her commitment to her faith and a practical reflection of the poverty and simplicity which would become the basis of the order she would lead. In 1867, Mary became Mother Superior of the Sisters of St Joseph of the Holy Cross. The order had just funded a new school building, and operated by a set of rules that emphasised service and poverty. The MacKillop approach to education was revolutionary at the time: the school was open to all who wished to learn, whether they could afford to pay or not. The sisters also ministered to the poor, sick and the weak and, remarkably for the period, were responsible for having a child-abusing priest returned to Ireland from rural South Australia in 1870.

In 1869, Mary and a group of sisters moved to Brisbane to further develop the order and her radical approach to education, which was a great success. But there was trouble back in South Australia, where she returned in 1871. The order's practice of poverty, which neccessitated begging in the streets, was seen by some as inappropriate. There were also rows about doctrine. Mary's fierce independence brought her into frequent conflict with the church hierarchy. A commission of inquiry was established and the recommendations it drew clashed with most of Mary MacKillop's beliefs and practices. She was unwilling to accept them and was excommunicated—apparently invalidly—in September 1871, though this dire edict was lifted five months later. Schools were closed and the order itself came close to being shut down.

To save her order, Mary travelled to the Vatican to seek official approval. Upon reaching Rome in 1873 she met Pope Pius IX. Despite her earlier excommunication, she returned to Australia in 1874 with the necessary approval to continue, though under the original rules set by Tenison-Woods, a condition which led to an unresolved disagreement between her and the Father. Mary was also continually embroiled in battles for control of her order. But the work continued and by the early 1890s 300 sisters of St Joseph were teaching and ministering to the poor throughout Australia and New Zealand.

Mary MacKillop died in 1909, following a tumultuous life of faith and service. Her reported last words were typical of her life and approach:

> Whatever troubles may be before you, accept them cheerfully, remembering Whom you are trying to follow. Do not be afraid. Love one another, bear with one another, and let charity guide you in all your life.

She was already a legend in her own time and the Archbishop of Sydney who attended at her death is said to have extolled her saintliness. Her achievements were widely recognised and admired far beyond the Catholic church. A long campaign for official recognition—or canonisation—of her life and work resulted in her canonisation on 17 October 2010 in Rome as Saint Mary of the Cross. She is Australia's first and only saint recognised by the Catholic church. Her example continues to inspire the work of the Sisters of St Joseph and many others, regardless of their beliefs.

Stories about her include the hardened murderer moved to prayer on seeing tears stream down from Mary's eyes. She sat with the dying at their request, shared her food with the hungry and tended the sick. One of her best-known sayings was, 'Never see a need without doing something about it.'

Mary MacKillop's legend lives on in many aspects of Australian life, in the form of scholarships, and organisations for charity, health and education. Many Australians will still recall being taught and disciplined by the Brown Joeys, so-called for their distinctive brown habit. There is even a rose and a hotel named after her. The eighth of August is Saint Mary MacKillop's feast day.

AN AUSTRALIAN LADY TRAVELS

On New Year's Day in 1892, an 'Australian lady' left London's Tilbury Docks on a mail boat *Oroya* bound for 'the sunny South'. She had a female companion and they were to be joined by their two gentlemen when their ship reached Naples.

This was to be no hardship voyage. The first luncheon was chicken and champagne. This was followed at four o'clock with afternoon tea and 'a very special cake from Buszard's'. By 6 p.m. it was nearly dark and they were thinking about getting ready for dinner

> when there came a sudden shock a tremendous crash, bang, a commotion on dock, and a general stampede. 'Whatever is it? Are we going down? Has the end of the world come?' asked a timid old lady. 'Someone got the influenza, mum,' replied a flippant steward.
>
> I ran up hastily, and there saw a small schooner 'impaled' on our steamer, and falling into the sea below were several terrified-looking seamen. Others were struggling to get up, and were aided by willing hands from the *Oroya*. Eventually the five sailors were safely taken on board, but alas the poor Danish captain was drowned. He was seen to run below to his little cabin probably thinking he would try to save some of his small belongings, but the attempt was fatal to him, and we never saw him again though his cries were heard once. One of the officers wanted to go after him, but fortunately was not allowed to, for if he had what with the darkness and the confusion he would surely have been drowned.

The Danish ship had been carrying coal to France, and operating without navigation lights. The captain had been the only married man aboard and the passengers on the *Oroya* took up a subscription for the survivors and the dead captain's family.

Continuing their journey, they docked at Gibraltar and the ladies 'had a very jolly drive across into Spain', where they purchased souvenirs 'more curious than beautiful'. And so on to Naples, the passage eased by games of patience, whist, chess and 'a little music'. In Naples they were 'glad to find the boys waiting for us on the pier', where they were

> beset with the usual crowd of fascinating-looking foreigners beseeching us to buy flowers, corals, cameos, all of which we sturdily refused at first, though it always ended by giving in and getting some of everything before we got back to our ship. The vendors came down so in their prices, that we felt we had driven a good bargain this time, only to find, alas, that our tortoiseshell combs were bone, our coral necklaces wood, our cameos false, and our jewellery set in brass and tin.

At Port Said, they went ashore and rode through the town on donkeys, 'half the population scampering at our heels, and all laughing and chatting and gesticulating at once. One of the Arabs wanted to buy Miss Sydney, and offered £200 for her on the spot. We asked him if he had not got a wife, and he said, "Yes, beauty lady, but only two; I want many more."'

On the next leg, the passengers formed an amusement committee and were entertained by a magician and each other's talents as singers. A fancy dress ball was planned 'and great was the planning and numerous the secret meetings held for the purpose of a good surprise in the shape of something novel in fancy dress'.

It was 'a frightfully hot morning' when they reached the next port of Colombo, in what is now Sri Lanka but was then known as Ceylon. 'The coolies were swarming up the gangways with bags of coal, looking like so many black gnomes.' Then:

> We, and most of the others, went on shore, where we had rickshaw rides all over the place, a trip by rail to Mount Lavinia, and on our return a bath and cool drinks at the Grand Oriental Hotel, that abode of luxury and lemon squashes, long lounges, and cool

> verandahs. Such a luncheon, too, with punkkas waving and corks popping, curry that only an Indian cook can turn out, and fruit and flowers of tropical hue on all the tables.

On the way back to the boat, they were 'amused to see numbers of little natives who had evidently been converted by the good nuns, and who wore for sole costume a little scapular suspended round each dusky neck':

> On the ship some of the men throw sixpences into the sea, and the little blackfellows dived from the ship, and even from the boats above, bringing up the money in their mouths.

But once more there was tragedy:

> One of their number was drowned almost before our eyes in a catamaran, which was upset near the shore. No one seemed to care much; even his relations lifted him up carelessly and bore him home stoically, returning to finish, bartering with us before the ship departed.

After Colombo, a Great Cricket Match between the first- and second-class passengers 'was the principal topic of conversation in our little world for days'. Then the cakes ran out but disaster was averted by the ability of the ship's baker to produce as many as the passengers required.

As the equator was crossed 'the heat was trying, but nights were delightful'. They ploughed on via Albany in Western Australia. At their destination, Melbourne, they 'were ever so long getting to the pier', anxious to greet waiting friends and family. Even so, and after all their adventures and pleasures aboard, 'it was good to be at home again . . .'

This was how the privileged travelled in the great age of ocean voyaging. From the secure heights of the first class lounge, they journeyed very comfortably, looking down on the lives and deaths of those less fortunate.

LES DARCY'S GIRL

Among its vast collections, the National Museum of Australia holds a tiny gold locket that once belonged to the sweetheart of boxing legend Les Darcy. The delicate nine-carat gold locket is worn from handling. It contains a miniature portrait of Les together with a lock of his hair, thought to have been clipped from the champion's head as he lay dying in Memphis, Tennessee. The locket belonged to the woman who rushed from Sydney to the doomed boxer's bedside in 1917. Her name was Winnie O'Sullivan.

The object of Winnie's enduring affection was the remarkable young boxer from a coal mining community in the Hunter Valley in New South Wales. Born in 1895, Leslie Darcy first came to public attention as The Maitland Surprise Packet in 1912. The following year one of his early local victories provided enough money for his parents to buy their own cottage.

It was the beginning of a career in which he was rarely bested. His stunning footwork was honed by practising Irish and Scottish dancing and he enjoyed the natural advantages of a long reach and great strength. Darcy was also musical, playing both the harmonica and violin. He was also considered one of the finest gentlemen to step into a ring; his respectful treatment of friends and opponents, good humour and film star looks quickly making him a public idol.

When he was narrowly—and controversially—beaten by the American Fritz Holland at the Sydney Stadium in July 1914, 2000 of his enraged supporters tried to burn the building down. Two months later he again lost to Holland over three fouls he allegedly delivered in the last three rounds of the fight. Over the next six months Darcy lost only one out of six high profile fights. He faced Holland for a third time in March 1915 and won on points. At just twenty years of age he was a national celebrity.

That year, Darcy met and fell deeply in love with Winnie O'Sullivan. The O'Sullivans owned the popular Lord Dudley Hotel in Sydney's Paddington where the champion enjoyed socialising with Winnie's show-business set. They wanted to become engaged but Winnie was only nineteen. As Winnie would later write, 'Mother said I was too young, and I mustn't have a ring until we could announce the engagement, so Les gave me a diamond bracelet instead.' Darcy fitted into the family easily and the pub became his second home. He even helped out behind the bar after returning from a fight. Darcy's easy way, big toothy grin and warm personality made him everyone's friend. Well, almost everybody. His brilliant career soon ran into trouble.

The Gallipoli campaign plunged the country into war and grief as the casualties mounted. The government was desperate for men to enlist, especially young men. The popular press began to question why the great fighter had not volunteered to fight. After receiving white feathers in the mail, he signed up in an emotional response. As he was not yet 21, he needed his parents' permission, which his mother refused to give, after which he was further vilified in the papers, a galling contrast to his previous lionisation.

He began to receive offers to fight in the United States, which was not then at war. Keen to ensure the financial security of his family, Darcy wanted to go. But he and his management fell out with potential backers and he sought a deal with the Commonwealth government instead. The deal struck was that in return for a passport, Darcy would post a thousand-pound bond against his return after contesting the title and promise to enlist when he got back. This arrangement fell through, however, largely due to the machinations of one of Darcy's former backers, Hugh D. McIntosh, the owner of the Sydney Stadium and a man with considerable influence with the newspapers. Three days before his twenty-first birthday, and a day before the results of the bitter conscription plebiscite would be known, Darcy stowed away aboard the *Hattie Luckenback,* bound for the United States. Such was the need for secrecy that Darcy told no one he was going, not even Winnie.

When the news got out, Darcy was vilified as a coward and a 'shirker' by the popular press at home, although the reaction of the American newspapers would be exactly the opposite. When he arrived in New York in December 1916, his first act was to telegraph his mother that he had arrived safely and to ask her to telephone Winnie.

Then Darcy was feted by reporters, cheered on stages, honoured with dinners and even appeared in vaudeville shows. No other visiting boxer had ever received such a welcome and reports of his doings even drowned out war news in the American press:

> Darcy is always smiling. He is quiet and modest in his manner, and boasting seems to be entirely lacking in his make-up. His twinkling grey eyes disappear entirely when he laughs heartily. His hair is brushed straight back over his massive head in true college boy style. When he smiles he displays two rows of even white teeth . . .

All this was widely reported back home. But crucial questions remained unanswered: when and where would he fight? And who would he challenge?

While his management tried to arrange a bout, the negative depictions of Darcy from the Australian press began to filter through to the American papers. The United States was about to enter the European conflict and patriotic war mongering was on the increase. The governor of New York state banned Darcy from fighting, and other states followed suit. So he travelled to Memphis, Tennessee, a city with a strong sporting tradition. Here the mayor and local interests were happy to have Darcy fight, especially as by then he had registered to become a United States citizen. In a private match, Darcy defeated the main American heavyweight contender in two rounds, even though the Australian was suffering from a mysterious sore throat at the time.

Impressed, the Memphis sports organisation agreed to organise a title fight but suggested that Darcy enlist in the American forces. He joined the aviation section of the Reserve Signal Corps as a sergeant. Darcy was given two weeks' leave from service to prepare for the bout. But despite being described as the most perfect specimen of manhood the enlisting officer had ever seen, Darcy collapsed during training. He had blood poisoning caused by two unhealed front teeth broken in a fight in Sydney the previous year. The teeth had spiked back into the bone beneath his gums and become ulcerated. This developed into inflammation of the heart, then pneumonia. It was soon clear that the champion was losing his last fight.

Before all this, Winnie had been missing Darcy, and so she had begged her reluctant parents to let her go to him. They agreed only because she would be effectively chaperoned by some of her showbiz friends bound for America to try their luck in Hollywood. And Winnie promised to return to them.

Winnie left with her friends on 17 March and while in San Francisco managed to telephone Darcy, who told her that he was doing well and not to come to Memphis until he had proved himself in that ring. While in Los Angeles, she heard about Darcy's case of tonsillitis. But one Saturday night Winnie received a telegram saying that Darcy was sinking fast and asking her to come at once. 'I was just paralysed with worry,' she later recalled.

It took three days to reach Memphis, and Winnie was unable to see Darcy until the following day. When she did he said, 'Oh, Winnie, when they told me you were here I thought they were joking me.' He joked about dying but Winnie was distressed at his wasted appearance and the bandages swathing his arms. Darcy rallied, but two days later his sister asked Winnie not to be too long with her visit, so she briefly spoke to him and then said goodbye. But as she reached the door, Darcy's sister called her back. Winnie ran to embrace him once again, but the champion was already dead.

His body was embalmed and received a sportsman's funeral in Memphis attended by the greats of American boxing. The coffin, draped in the Australian and American flags, was shipped to San Francisco amid widespread mourning, and then back to Australia. There was 'barely breathing space' at the dead hero's requiem mass at St Joseph's in Woollahra. They say that nearly half a million mourners filed through the church to view the dead champion one last time. A massive crowd followed the casket from the church to Central railway station. Street sellers did a strong trade in memorial buttons and a man sold a ballad sheet in the streets reflecting the inaccurate belief that the Americans killed Les Darcy:

Way down in the USA
Where poor Les Darcy died
His mother's only joy
Australia's bonny boy

How they longed for that night
To see Les Darcy fight
How he hit them
How he beat them
Every Saturday night

The critics 'round the door
Said they had never saw
A lad like Les before
Fight on the Stadium floor

They said he was a skiter
But he proved himself a fighter
But we lost all hope
When he got the dope
Way down in the USA

Les was finally laid to rest in his home ground at East Maitland cemetery but Hugh D. McIntosh's press interests continued to vilify the champion, attacking what they portrayed as the graveyard canonisation of Les Darcy, 'the shirker'. But Les Darcy's legend ultimately bested the gutter press and has lived on long after the newspapers of the day have been forgotten.

Winnie married in 1921. Once asked by the writer Ruth Park whether she thought that Darcy might have ended up as a 'tubby publican' if he had lived, she replied, 'No, he would have been a farmer: I was agreeable, the man mattered, not the place.' She kept the gold locket but never spoke to her husband and children about her love for 'Australia's bonny boy'.

CAB ACROSS THE NULLARBOR

Bea Miles was one of Sydney's great eccentrics. Born in 1902, Bea, or just B, had a difficult relationship with her conservative middle-class family from an early age. At Abbotsleigh school she made political comments and wrote essays criticising World War I, which was then raging. An inheritance allowed her financial independence but conflicts with her father over what was then considered her immoral bohemian lifestyle continued. After a brief enrolment at Sydney University, Bea contracted encephalitis. The disease reportedly sharpened her independent outlook, and what some considered her anti-social behaviour, allowing her father to commit her to the insane asylum at Gladesville in 1923.

Bea remained in the asylum until 1925 when an article about her plight titled 'Mad house mystery of beautiful Sydney girl' on the front page of the *Smith's Weekly* newspaper led to her eventual release. Bea then became a notorious ratbag about town, sleeping rough, jumping into stationary cars with a demand to be given a lift and reciting Shakespeare on street corners to anyone who would pay. But her main pastime was boarding taxis and refusing to pay the fare. Three race-goers encountered Bea in the mid 1950s:

> The lady was large, very vocal; and she wore a worse-for-wear tennis shade rakishly tilted over one eye. She sat beside the worried-looking taximan piloting yours, etc., and a couple more males to try our luck at the races. She offered to bet us a couple of bob each that the taxi wouldn't pass more than 39 cars on our way from Ashfield to Canterbury. Recovering, we declined politely. Foiled, the lady went to work on the driver, issuing loud commands on the route to be taken. The driver, not so politely, said 'nertz.'

> Outside the racecourse, we three mere males alighted, but the large, vocal lady with the tipped-over eye shade refused to budge. 'Stone the crows,' moaned the taximan, giving us an anguished look as we left him stranded with—Bea Miles.

On being abused by unhappy taxi drivers, Bea was sometimes known to bend the passenger door right back on its hinges to show her dissatisfaction. She had a few friends in the taxi business, though, and they were happy to drive her on some legendary journeys. John Beynon took Bea from Sydney to Hobart, Adelaide and the long way to Melbourne through Broken Hill. But Bea's greatest trip needed two taxi drivers: Beynon and Mrs Sylvia Markham. The two drivers secured the greatest fare of their lives when Bea booked them to drive her to Perth—and back again.

The details of this epic of public transport have become muddied over the years but it seems that Beynon, Markham and Bea left Sydney early in January 1955. They made it to Perth after about seven days of very hot travelling, in the age before automobile air conditioning. Bea spent four days there, apparently behaving herself, and then they set off back to Sydney.

Bea was paying one shilling a mile for the trip. That worked out to be around 300 pounds one way across the Nullarbor. Every 100 miles, Bea handed over a five-pound note to her driver. It all added up to a lot of money at the time.

On the way back, in Eucla, Bea explained the reason for her unusual journey in a telephone call with a journalist in Perth:

> Primarily I undertook the trip to collect flowers for the Sydney herbarium but the weather has been so blazing hot—up to 108 dig(rees) [sic] at Madura—I've not seen a flower worth collecting along (the) Eyre-highway. However, we are having a lot of fun and the open-air life suits me fine.

The journalist also spoke with Sylvia Markham, who said: 'I got a bit of a shock when asked to drive across Australia and back, but I'm glad I agreed.' Sleeping outside each night, as they had on the way, the intrepid three expected to be in Adelaide about 24 January and back in Sydney a few days later. All up, the cab fare for the round trip was 600 pounds.

Bea continued her wayward life. She claimed to have been convicted of charges 195 times, 100 of them fairly. As she aged, Bea's antics became increasingly irritating. She wore out the already thin welcome she had at places like the State Library of New South Wales, where she was in the habit of spending the day reading, and was banned in the late 1950s. Now old and ill she was taken in by the Little Sisters of the Poor at Randwick in 1964. One of the many colourful quotes attributed to her comes from this period: 'I have no allergies that I know of, one complex, no delusions, two inhibitions, no neuroses, three phobias, no superstitions and no frustrations.'

Gems like this, together with Bea's utter irreverence towards authority, the police, the law and respectability in general, made her a folk hero to Sydneysiders. In 1961 her portrait was entered in the Archibald Prize by artist Alex Robertson.

Even at the end, Bea went out in outrageous style. When she died in 1973 her coffin was covered in Australian wildflowers and a jazz band played 'Waltzing Matilda', 'Tie Me Kangaroo Down, Sport' and 'Advance Australia Fair'.

Bea's larrikin life has featured in a musical, in a poem by Les Murray, and in Kate Grenville's 1985 novel *Lillian's Story* and the subsequent film of the same name. Now mostly forgotten, her legend is kept alive through the occasional media article and in the B Miles Women's Foundation.

A CRUSH OF CRABS

While first discovered in 1615, Christmas Island was rediscovered and named on Christmas Day 1643. The small uninhabited speck in the Indian Ocean was not settled until the late nineteenth century when rich phosphate deposits were mined with an imported workforce of Malay, Chinese and Sikh people. Japanese forces occupied the island in 1942. After World War II the island became first a dependency of Singapore, then part of Australia in 1958. This diverse history gives the island the unique character it has today.

Its culture is not the only unique feature of Christmas Island: it is the location of what has been described as a wonder of the natural world. Once a year at the start of the wet season, usually between October and November, the millions of red land crabs that populate the island forests make a journey to the sea. For a week or so they swarm across the island. They mass across roads, where their hard shells have been known to puncture tires, so tunnels and plastic barriers and bridges have been constructed to divert them off the streets as they crawl, clicking and crackling, towards the ocean.

This annual migration is so the crabs can mate. The males usually arrive at the beach first, where they build burrows in which to mate with the females. After this, the females stay in the burrows for a couple of weeks. Then their eggs are spawned in the last quarter of the moon at the turning of the high tide. The eggs wash out to sea, where they hatch and the larvae spend three or four weeks washing round in the ocean. Meanwhile, the females return to the forests. Their larvae wash back to shore and become young crabs that then crawl back across the island for nine days until they reach the same forests in which they live until reaching maturity after four or five years. Then they take their turn in the yearly parade.

The crawling crabs have become an international tourist attraction. While the yellow crazy ant, introduced from Africa, poses a threat to the population, at the time of writing this seems to be under control. Tourists ask if the crabs can be eaten. The answer is no, though the crabs do eat each other.

Since 2001, the island has been the location for a controversial asylum seeker reception and processing facility for those who have undertaken journeys of a very different kind.

ON THE HIPPIE TRAIL

Between the mid 1960s and 1979, the overland route between Istanbul and southern India, and sometimes beyond, was a rite of passage for the young adults of the postwar baby boom. Hundreds of thousands, possibly more, adventurous men and women took to the often rough roads that led from Turkey through what is now Iran to Afghanistan, Kathmandu and, ultimately, Goa. There were a few side trips along the way, including to Kashmir, Chitral and Manali. The appeal of these exotic locations was partly the availability and legality of marijuana and hashish.

Although most of the kids travelling the trail wore tie-died garments and beads, relatively few of them were actually hippies. The hippie movement evolved mainly in San Francisco and its adherents practised free love, pacifism, drug use, alternative life-styles and, at the extremes, the overthrow of the capitalist state. While a few committed individuals continued to follow the hippie creed, by the late 1960s the movement had mostly fallen apart and its outward appearance had become a popular culture fashion style. Most of the long-haired men and lightly clad women seeking spiritual enlightenment, with or without bodily pleasures, in the Middle East and India ended up as accountants, lawyers, doctors and other useful members of society.

The favoured modes of transport along the trail were jointly purchased cars, usually old bangers, campervans and buses. Many people now recall a legendary Magic Bus that took you from Amsterdam as far along the trail as you could afford. But the magic bus did not exist as such: it was basically a booking agency that organised coach travel from place to place along the adventuresome way.

Public transport was another option. The often erratic nature of these systems suited the carefree ethos and budgets of travellers and brought them up close and personal with local people and their customs.

While many travellers began their journey in London or Europe, Australians often took the trail in reverse. It was just a matter of flying to southern India or elsewhere on the trail and then they were off. Local communities along the trail had quickly adapted to the welcome boost to their economies from these comparatively affluent Westerners and there was a well-developed network of accommodation, travel arrangements and, of course, access to the all-important dope.

The trail was basically a global link between Australia and the northern hemisphere. Australians travelled along it to seek out adventures abroad in an earlier version of today's backpacking gap year. Or they returned home along it, winding up their year or two or more of expatriation with a last fling before settling down to work, marriage, children and all the banalities of everyday life they had managed to escape for a while.

Often recollected in later life, the journeys made by young Australians in those days can be found in accounts on social media. Many of the elements in the stories are similar: the bus rides; the companions, good and bad; exotic locations; robbery; epic binges on alcohol and marijuana; trouble at borders; tummy bugs; and, invariably, going home when the money ran out.

For all its excess, indulgence and youthful frolics, the hippie trail had its dark side. The French serial killer of Indian and Vietnamese heritage, Charles Sobhraj, specialised in 'cleaning' Western adventurers. Born in 1946, the smooth and well-mannered Sobhraj was just the right age to fraternise freely with the young men and women along the hippy trail. He progressed from robbing them to conning them, or both. He is thought to have graduated to murdering them in 1975.

Sobhraj was believed to have murdered at least twelve people when he was caught in 1976. Sentenced to long prison terms, he nevertheless managed to live well inside and through various manipulations of the justice system he was released in 1997. After returning to Nepal in 2003, he was arrested for a murder he had committed there in 1975. He received a sentence of life in prison, during which he has continued his flamboyant attempts to stage-manage the authorities and the media. In September 2014, Sobhraj was again convicted of murder in Nepal. The Serpent, as he has been dubbed, is spending the next twenty years in gaol.

Sobhraj is not known to have murdered any Australians but his intriguing repellence led the artist and journalist Richard Neville to interview him for *Oz* magazine back in 1975. Neville co-authored a full biography of Sobhraj with Julie Clarke in 1980. The book was a global bestseller and inspired a number of television documentaries. When interviewed for *GQ* magazine in 2014 Sobhraj expressed no remorse for his crimes.

The hippie trail wound down in 1979 when Iran sealed its borders and Russia invaded Afghanistan. Overland travel was now too dangerous for most, though some of the same generation who blazed the trail, now retired, continue to have intrepid overland adventures, if now following safer routes.

DOING THE DOUGHNUT

Between 1976 and 1984 TV audiences were plagued by an earworm. It was the catchy theme music to one of the country's most popular shows, 'Ask the Leyland Brothers', hosted by Mike and Mal Leyland. In each show the brothers took their four-wheel drives and a camera to places that most Australians had never seen, and probably never would. The adventurous Leylands virtually invented the figure of the television outback adventurer and naturalist, paving the way for the The Bush Tucker Man and Steve Irwin who came afterwards.

They first appeared on Australian screens in 1963, turning their filmed holidays into travel shows that would eventually fascinate millions of viewers. Among many other places, they journeyed along nearly 2500 kilometres of the Darling River system, across Australia through the Simpson Desert, and filmed rain cascading down Uluru for the first time.

Later, their partners Laraine and Margie Leyland featured in the adventures, providing a compelling family holiday feel to the shows. This and the ongoing popularity of Leyland brothers travel films, series and specials are often credited with the invention of a new tribe—the legions of retired baby boomers widely known as Grey Nomads.

Equipped with caravans or increasingly sophisticated campervans, couples over 55 often rent, or sometimes even sell, the family home and just take to the road. Some have definite travel plans, others are content to wander wherever the road leads them.

Although the motorised rambles of the grey nomads are not a single journey, the route they tend to take, either all at once or in different stages, is usually a circuit around the coastline, sometimes known as 'doing the doughnut'.

At any one moment, countless grey nomads are encircling the entire continent in a never ending journey that has some similarities to the traditions of 'beating the bounds' carried out in many parts of Britain. In these events, there is usually a procession around the parish boundaries or other significant areas through which the rights of the parishioners or villagers are asserted and displayed. These traditions are often several hundred or more years old, while the grey nomad tradition is a relatively recent Australian development. But there is definite sense of the grey nomads, in spirit at least, demonstrating that they belong to the country and that it belongs to them. There is more than a hint of pilgrimage in many of these trips.

Those who take these journeys are often motivated by a desire to see Australia and to travel to places they have heard or read about but never before been able to visit. Often these are iconic locations such as Uluru or the Nullarbor Plain. They may also be attracted by the legends of the bush and Outback, undertaking journeys that favour country towns and the appeal of 'the wide brown land'. Some now also espouse ecological principles and interests and are keen to experience the great Australian wilderness and perhaps learn something of Indigenous culture.

Others are keen to work. The fruit and vegetable picking industries rely heavily on casual labour supplied by grey nomads. Driving into the local caravan park and working for a week or two, maybe a bit longer, is considered a great way to meet local people, help out with the local economy and provide funds for continuing their travels. Many enjoy volunteering, helping farmers rebuild fences after devastating bushfires or assisting straitened rural communities in other practical ways.

The grey nomad ethos is one of adventure, camaraderie and humour. Grey nomads tend to be independent of mind and although on the road are definitely not disengaged from current affairs, often voicing strong opinions in get-togethers in caravan parks and on social media.

A group ritual is 'happy hour'. Around mid afternoon the grey nomads roll their outfits into campsites and caravan parks, park, then bring out the chairs and settle in for a getting-to-know-you session fuelled by cups of tea or something stronger.

So numerous are the geriatric gypsies, as some call themselves, that a whole industry, providing entertainment, travel equipment, guidebooks and maps, has built up around them. Buying the right 'rig' or travelling home is a popular topic. Finding work, hobbies to fill leisure time, events of interests, telling stories of their experiences—all these are part of the endless journey of the grey nomads.

7

THE TRACK

I've humped my drum from Kingdom Come to the back of the Milky Way.

Bush poem, late nineteenth century

THE ROAD WEST

Almost as soon as Blaxland, Wentworth and Lawson struggled across the Blue Mountains in 1813 the fledgling colony of Sydney needed a road to follow the route they'd forged. Fortunately just the man to build it was ready, willing and able: ex-army officer William Cox was around fifty years old when he offered his services to the governor. Lachlan Macquarie nearly fell over himself to accept:

> having recently received from you a voluntary offer of your superintending and directing the working party to be employed on this very important service, I now most readily avail myself of your very liberal and handsome offer of superintending and directing the construction of this road; and do invest you with full power and authority to carry out this important design into complete effect, Government furnishing you with the necessary means to enable you to do so.

Cox was given 30 convict labourers and tradesmen and eight soldiers to guard them. They were instructed to build a road from Emu Plains to the newly established settlement at Bathurst. The tradesmen needed for road building were a blacksmith, a shoemaker, a stonemason and carpenters.

> The road thus made must be at least 12 ft. wide, so as to permit two carts or other wheel carriages to pass each other with ease. The timber in forest ground to be cut down and cleared away 20 ft. wide, grubbing up the stumps and filling up the holes, so that a four-wheel carriage or cart may pass without difficulty or danger.
>
> Thirdly: In brush ground it is to be cut 20 ft. wide and grubbed up 12 ft. wide. Any small bridges that may be found requisite to be made must be 12 ft. wide. I conceive this to be a sufficient width for the proposed road at present; but where it can with ease and convenience be done, I should prefer the road to be made 16 ft. wide.

On 17 July 1814, Cox mustered his men and equipment, including the purpose-built caravan in which he would sleep along the way. The next day, with the weather clear and frosty, they began cutting a path down the banks of the Nepean River. There were problems with the tools and the provisions but the men worked well and Cox felt that they were setting out making good progress.

By 26 July they were at the foot of the mountains. Now the road builders had to go up. The cliffs were steep and stony, thick with tough ironbarks. One of the superintendents resigned in early August. Two Aboriginal men, Coley, or Coleby, a Darug man, and Joe of the Mulgoa people, joined the group. The weather remained cold but mostly fine and they continued to make good progress, despite increasing sickness among the men as well as accidents, especially from splinters. The sergeant in charge of the soldiers died in late August, from natural causes it seems.

On the night of 8 September the wind 'blew a perfect hurricane'. But work on the road and bridges needed to cross swollen streams continued well and mostly cheerfully. By late October they had blasted, burned, hacked and grubbed a road out of the unyielding land for almost 40 miles. It was now clear that the road was never going to be very level. The work was slowed down by rains but began again at full speed as October turned into November. For the first time they sighted Aboriginal groups. There was no contact but Cox had the smith make eight pikes for self-defence.

Now the bullocks became a problem. The fresh beasts supplied by the government stores were too wild to harness. The continually damp conditions were also oppressing the men so Cox cheered them up on 3 November with an issue of spirits. But illnesses and accidents increased in the unpleasant weather and rugged conditions.

The crew struggled on, digging, levering, hewing and blasting. By mid November the smith was having trouble keeping their tools in working order, so quickly were they blunting and breaking. There was more cold rain and more issues of grog. The ground was often worse than anticipated and the crew's bullocks went missing for ten days. But still Cox's men forged ahead, over creeks, up and down the ridges.

By 8 December, Cox was at the halfway point, near Mount York, about to build the steep descent to the valley below. Some of his men were malingering and he was forced to deliver a dressing-down. Two days later they completed yet another bridge. On 11 December, Cox sent six married men back to complete the mountain descent with orders that they be discharged when they had finished. He and the remainder pushed on, many of his men spending most of the day working in water. They were rewarded with a gill of rum every night. The rains returned but the road thrust forward. By Christmas Day there were three bridges left to build and just another five miles of road. As it was a holiday, each man received the now-customary gill of spirits as well as a new shirt.

By New Year's Day Cox was finishing a three-day reconnoitre of the area. He was greatly impressed with the country and grazing potential around the Fish River. When he returned he had a bullock slaughtered and the meat given to the men as a welcome relief from the usual salt pork. 'When the men were mustered this morning they were extremely clean, and looked cheerful and hearty,' he observed contentedly.

Two weeks later the road was finished. The end of Cox's way overlooked the Macquarie River in what is now the Bathurst Peace Park. For the time and place it was an engineering triumph, a feat of hard labour and Cox's logistical and management skills. The road was now open from the coast to the western plains, allowing the expansion of the frontier.

The governor toured the road later that year and pronounced himself pleased with the results. He commended William Cox, Esq. particularly:

> for the important service he has rendered to the colony in so short a period of time by opening a passage to the newly-discovered country, and at the same time assuring him that he shall have great pleasure in recommending his meritorious services on this occasion to the favourable consideration of his Majesty's Ministers.

When it was over there were rewards. Cox received 2000 acres of the western lands now accessible thanks to his and his men's efforts. His chief assistants were given substantial grants of land and livestock and even Cox's servant got two cows. The convicts were all pardoned, given tickets-of-leave or emancipated. The Aboriginal men got nothing.

The roadbuilder lived on until 1837, a wealthy man and pillar of the colonial community. His road was added to, changed and subsumed in later developments but can still be seen in places. The longest mostly intact stretch runs over a kilometre along the Old Bathurst Road.

But ease of access was not the only aim for this new road: Cox, his convicts, soldiers and the two Aboriginal men had built a road that finely balanced two competing needs. Like the best thoroughfares, it was designed to allow people and traffic to pass over it in either direction. On the other hand, the governor was under orders from London to control population movements, as the government was keen to regulate land settlement and the advance of the frontier. And Cox's road was almost impassable in some places, especially on the steep inclines, allowing Macquarie to simultaneously point to a great achievement for his colony as well as dampening a too-rapid population movement inland. A more than satisfactory result for a colonial governor.

ROADS TO RUIN

At the end of each shearing season, hordes of happy shearers made a classic Australian journey. Clutching their swags and a hard-earned cheque for many pounds, they set off from the stations they had called home for a few months and humped their drums back to wherever they had come from in the first place. Most of them had the best intentions of returning to wives and families with enough money to tide everyone over, more or less, until the next season. Some actually made it home. But for many the story, told in the bush song 'The Road to Gundagai', had a much less happy ending.

This particular journey began when a couple of shearers 'started out from Roto when the sheds had all cut out'. They 'humped their blues serenely and made for Sydney town with a three-spot cheque between us, as wanted knocking down'. Three hundred pounds was a great deal of money back in those days but the danger signs were already there: the song says their cheque wanted knocking down, or spending in a hurry.

The shearers cross the Murrumbidgee, trek through Narrandera and past Wagga Wagga. Eventually they make camp at Lazy Harry's 'not five miles from Gundagai'. Unfortunately, Lazy Harry's is a shanty: a rough type of pub specialising in 'lambing down' thirsty shearers with big cheques. The delights of this establishment are 'beer to knock you sideways' and 'girls to make you sigh'.

> Well we chucked our blooming swags off and we walked into the bar,
> And we called for rum-an'-raspb'ry and a shilling each cigar . . .

The barmaid who served the 'poison' gives the shearers the wink and the spree is on. The money lasts a week—then 'the cheque was all knocked down'.

So we shouldered our Matildas and we turned our back on town,
And the girls they stood a nobbler as we sadly said good-bye,
And we tramped from Lazy Harry's not five miles from Gundagai.

The song ends with the hungover and broke shearers continuing their now difficult journey back to Sydney and whatever might await them there.

Being lambed down is a frequent theme of bush songs. One of these, usually known as 'Across the western plains', has a fair claim to be the greatest hangover song of all time.

Well, I'm crook in the head and I haven't been to bed,
Since I first touched this shanty with my plunder,
I see centipedes and snakes and I've got the aches and shakes,
And I'll soon be shifting out over yonder.

This bloke has lost his horse along with his money and has no choice but to continue his dismal journey to search for work.

I'll take that Old Man Plain and I'll cross it once again,
Until me eyes the track no longer see,
And my beer and whisky brain looks for sleep but all in vain,
And I feel as if I had the Darling Pea.

So hang that blasted grog, that hocussed shanty grog,
And the beer that's loaded with tobacco,
Grafting humour I am in and I'll stick the peg right in,
And I'll settle down once more for some hard yakka.

Then the chorus repeats again, reminding us that the alcohol provided at the shanty was probably adulterated with tobacco, increasing the effect:

And it's all for the grog, the jolly, jolly grog,
The beer that's loaded with tobacco,
I spent all my tin in a shanty drinkin' gin,
Now across the western plains I must wander.

In 1925, a Tasmanian newspaper reminisced about the old days when this song was sung and the life it describes was lived by many itinerant bush workers:

In the bad old days of the Coast, as well as other places, as far as the 'old hands' were concerned, rum was the national drink, and many of the old fellows could swallow it like drinking new milk. In the early days of Latrobe a good many of those old fellows, who led a nomadic life, would come down to Sassafras for the harvest and potato digging, and as there were some good workers among them, at the end of the season they would have good cheques, coming to them. During the time they were working they would deny themselves various necessaries, so that, they could have a good 'rum-burst' at the finish.

Well, about a mile out of Latrobe, on the road to Moriarty, there used to stand an old two-roomed place which was always known to us kiddies as the 'Swipers' Hut', and this place was often tenanted by as many as a dozen of these old follows at the one time. On wet days one of their number would be deputed to bring rum out by the gallon from Latrobe to the old camp. Needless to say, the carousals there were often fast and furious. Many a time other boys and myself would hide in the scrub that surrounded the hut, and listen to the wild singing, and, I am sorry to say, cursing that went on.

Another lambed-down shearer turned up in a newspaper column in 1894:

I'm a broken-hearted shearer, I'm ashamed to show my face,
The way that I got lambed down is a sin and a disgrace;
I put a cheque together, and thought that it would do,
So I just slipped into Orange for to spend a week or two.

I thought I was no flat, so resolved to cut it fat;
I dressed myself up in my best, put a poultice round my hat;
I went to have a nobbler at a certain house in town,
Where the barmaid she was cautioned for to lamb a fellow
down.

I would get up in the morning to have a glass of stout;
She cost me many a shilling, for she was in every shout.
She would toss me up at Yankee Grab, and keep me on the booze:
But somehow or the other I was always bound to lose.

My money getting short I resolved to know my fate;
I asked this pretty barmaid if she would be my mate,
When she said, 'Young man, on my feelings don't encroach,
I'm a decent married woman, and my husband drives the coach.'

I had two-and-six in silver and half-a-bar of soap,
A box of Cockle's pills and a pot of Holloway's;
I thought to turn a farmer and grow pumpkins near the town,
But she squashed all my pumpkins when she had me lambed
down.

I had two old shirts, but they were all in rags;
A pair of moleskin trousers and a hat without a crown.
This was my ten years' gathering when clearing out of town;
But it's nothing when you're used to it to do a lambing down.

BY TRAIN TO HOBART TOWN

Early in 1876, the mayor of Geelong took a trip to Tasmania, then popularly referred to as the Tight Little Island, a reference to its English character. While there he took the train from Launceston to Hobart and back again, describing his eventful journey in a letter to his constituents. They would have been very amused at his entertaining yarn and may have quietly decided not to travel by train if they ever visited Tassie.

> The carriages and engine having to turn sharp curves are made, the first to travel on two sets of wheels called the Bogie principle, whilst the latter have the doors at each end, not fastened. They are connected together with a pin, which allows them to move to the right or left easily.

The trains aside, the track itself seems to not quite have been built with the care and attention needed:

> Without mentioning the particulars of our down journey other than to say that the rails being very light and placed on small sleepers without the necessary weight to keep them down, floated on the water when the flood came, and were in many places clear of the permanent way, in others the soil had been washed from under the sleepers.

As a result of these long washed-out sections of track much of the mayor's 'train trip' actually took place by coach—which he drove himself:

> After waiting some time four horses were brought knocked up, having just come a journey of 27 miles. We started with a very heavy load, and it was not long before the pace was reduced to a walk. The coachman asked me if I could drive, I answered in the affirmative, at once arranged the reins in the most scientific manner possible, and there I sat in my glory whilst the coachman got down and ran or walked alongside the horses, which, by means of a tickle now and again with the whip, he succeeded in making go at the rate of fully four miles an hour.

The picture the mayor offers of the sight they must have made on the road sounds like the beginning of a joke: a mayor, a priest and a coachman caught the train one day.

> Anyone meeting us must have thought we were a comical turn-out—myself driving, a priest on the box next me holding

> an umbrella over my head, the coachman running by the side cracking his whip, and some of the passengers also stretching their legs alongside of him.

Despite these hiccups the merry band arrived safely at Hobart Town, although likely a little damp. On the return trip, finally on the train again, this travelling mayor ran into the vexed issue that would come up time and time again in early Australia: the different train track gauges in each state. Perhaps betraying his parochial preference for his own state's rail gauge, he found Tassie's narrow gauge to be highly inferior:

> The line, I may mention, is on the narrow gauge, 3ft. 6in. wide. The carriages have no springs similar to those used on the Victorian lines, but rest on spiral wire springs, and these, when travelling fast, nearly shake the inside from you. During the latter part of the journey I was glad to stand, as when we were travelling at the rate of forty miles an hour to make up for lost time the motion was almost unbearable.

And when the rattling wasn't the problem, it was the want of it—they were late to start out and later and later thereafter:

> The hour at which it was announced the train would start was 8.30 sharp, but at that hour everything apparently had to be got ready. The water was carried in three four-hundred gallon tanks lashed on a truck, coals on a truck behind. However we got off at last at about 9 o'clock, and progressed steadily for about an hour and a half when the train came to a full stop. We all jumped out to see what was up, and found the draft of the boiler was so strong that the small pieces of coal had been drawn through the tubes so as to choke the three or four bottom rows; the back pan had to be opened and cleaned out, then steam was again raised, and away we went.
>
> After some time we stopped at a station to drop some freight, which occupied some time, as it consisted of two bags of sugar.

But the Victorian mayor showed a good sense of humour, despite the delays, and was not above rolling up his sleeves and pitching in to help get the train going:

> Away we went again, and were suddenly brought to a dead stop. On looking out I saw some of the passengers collecting wood to assist in livening the fire, so I ran back, and shouted 'All hands forward to collect wood,' and amid general laughter we all lent a hand.

In fact the accumulation of problems seems to have lent the trip an air of levity and adventure and unreality:

> Suddenly another stop was made at Jerusalem. Having got to this remarkable locality we all jumped out to amuse our selves while the freight for the thriving place was deposited on the sand. Some of the passengers played at duck stone; others threw up one stone and tried to hit it with another; a priest amused himself playing with his dog. I saw the goods unloaded; they consisted of two or three bags of sugar, some packages of canvas and a case, the whole being saturated with boiled oil. It appeared they had placed a kerosene tin of boiled oil on the top of the goods, and had succeeded in piercing the tin by carelessly placing some scythes against it.
>
> After a great deal of time had been lost in discussing this accident, and who was to remove a box covered with boiled oil from the van, the hands generally objecting to touch it, we made another start.

Good fun aside, water would insist on plaguing this trip in one way or another. During the first leg, there was too much of it washing away the track, and on the return trip, it was the getting of it that posed the problem:

> in about an hour [we] pulled up over a creek, at which we were to take in water by bucketing it up. After some discussion about

> a rope, during which some of the passengers suggested that we should tie our pocket handkerchiefs together, they set to work. The chief engineer, with the rope, dropped a bucket into the stream, hauled it up, handed it to the man who took the tickets, and who transferred it to the second engineer, and the latter emptied it into the 400-gallon tank. Meanwhile, a garden being near, a number of passengers, accompanied by the third engineer, rushed and helped themselves to fruit. After some time the ticket collector, finding the bucketing rather hard work, sang out for the third engineer to assist, the latter thereupon was seen rushing up with both hands filled with fruit, and took the place of the first engineer, being cautioned not to break the bucket, as that was the only one they had.
>
> The watering was completed in about half an hour; we made another start, and an hour afterwards pulled up at the large tank, at which I supposed a sufficient supply of water would be taken in in about ten minutes. Not so, however; when they tried the hose, which was new, they found it impossible to get either end on, so had to use a V-shaped piece of wood to support it near the aperture in the tank, and the poor fellow who held this got well soused with water.

The mayor and his well-shaken travelling companions arrived back at Launceston at 8.30 p.m. 'All's well that ends well,' he wrote, 'and I thoroughly enjoyed my trip to Hobart Town.'

TRUDGING THROUGH PURGATORY

Henry Lawson's trek from Bourke to Hungerford marked him for life. The literary critic and editor A.G. Stephens, not a man given to overstatement, described it as the 'journey of a damned soul trudging through purgatory'. Lawson set out on the journey at the suggestion of J.F. Archibald, his editor at the *Bulletin*, who provided a train ticket to Bourke and a five-pound note in the hope that Lawson would write some stories to further fuel his verse debate with 'Banjo' Paterson about the good and bad aspects of bush life. With his mate Jim Gordon, Lawson struck out in the midsummer heat of 1892 on a 450-kilometre walk.

Lawson never wrote a complete account of his experience but came back to it in one way or another in much of his subsequent writing. He did write a story called 'Hungerford' that gives some idea of the parched emptiness of the outback, 'a blasted, barren wilderness':

> One of the hungriest cleared roads in New South Wales runs to within a couple of miles of Hungerford, and stops there; then you strike through the scrub to the town. There is no distant prospect of Hungerford—you don't see the town till you are quite close to it, and then two or three white-washed galvanized-iron roofs start out of the mulga.
>
> They say that a past Ministry commenced to clear the road from Bourke, under the impression that Hungerford was an important place, and went on, with the blindness peculiar to governments, till they got to within two miles of the town. Then they ran short of rum and rations, and sent a man on to get them, and make inquiries. The member never came back, and two more were sent to find him—or Hungerford. Three days later the two returned in an exhausted condition, and submitted a motion of want-of-confidence, which was lost. Then the whole House went on and was lost also. Strange to relate, that Government was never missed.
>
> However, we found Hungerford and camped there for a day. The town is right on the Queensland border, and an interprovincial rabbit-proof fence—with rabbits on both sides of it—runs across the main street. This fence is a standing joke with Australian rabbits—about the only joke they have out there, except the memory of Pasteur and poison and inoculation. It is amusing to go a little way out of town, about sunset, and watch them crack Noah's Ark rabbit jokes about that fence, and burrow under and play leap-frog over it till they get tired. One old buck rabbit sat up and nearly laughed his ears off at a joke of his own about that fence. He laughed so much that he couldn't get away when

I reached for him. I could hardly eat him for laughing. I never saw a rabbit laugh before; but I've seen a possum do it.

Hungerford consists of two houses and a humpy in New South Wales, and five houses in Queensland. Characteristically enough, both the pubs are in Queensland. We got a glass of sour yeast at one and paid sixpence for it—we had asked for English ale.

The post office is in New South Wales, and the police barracks in Bananaland. The police cannot do anything if there's a row going on across the street in New South Wales, except to send to Brisbane and have an extradition warrant applied for; and they don't do much if there's a row in Queensland. Most of the rows are across the border, where the pubs are.

At least, I believe that's how it is, though the man who told me might have been a liar. Another man said he was a liar, but then he might have been a liar himself—a third person said he was one. I heard that there was a fight over it, but the man who told me about the fight might not have been telling the truth.

One part of the town swears at Brisbane when things go wrong, and the other part curses Sydney.

The country looks as though a great ash-heap had been spread out there, and mulga scrub and firewood planted—and neglected. The country looks just as bad for a hundred miles round Hungerford, and beyond that it gets worse—a blasted, barren wilderness that doesn't even howl. If it howled it would be a relief.

I believe that Bourke and Wills found Hungerford, and it's a pity they did; but, if I ever stand by the graves of the men who first travelled through this country, when there were neither roads nor stations, nor tanks, nor bores, nor pubs, I'll—I'll take my hat off. There were brave men in the land in those days.

It is said that the explorers gave the district its name chiefly because of the hunger they found there, which has remained there ever since. I don't know where the 'ford' comes in—there's nothing to ford, except in flood-time. Hungerthirst would have been better. The town is supposed to be situated on the banks of a river called the Paroo, but we saw no water there, except what passed for it in a tank. The goats and sheep and dogs and the rest of the population drink there. It is dangerous to take too much of that water in a raw state.

Except in flood-time you couldn't find the bed of the river without the aid of a spirit-level and a long straight-edge. There is a Custom-house against the fence on the northern side. A pound of tea often costs six shillings on that side, and you can get a common lead pencil for fourpence at the rival store across the street in the mother province. Also, a small loaf of sour bread sells for a shilling at the humpy aforementioned. Only about sixty per cent of the sugar will melt.

We saw one of the storekeepers give a dead-beat swagman five shillings' worth of rations to take him on into Queensland. The storekeepers often do this, and put it down on the loss side of their books. I hope the recording angel listens, and puts it down on the right side of his book.

We camped on the Queensland side of the fence, and after tea had a yarn with an old man who was minding a mixed flock of goats and sheep; and we asked him whether he thought Queensland was better than New South Wales, or the other way about.

He scratched the back of his head, and thought a while, and hesitated like a stranger who is going to do you a favour at some personal inconvenience.

At last, with the bored air of a man who has gone through the same performance too often before, he stepped deliberately up to the fence and spat over it into New South Wales. After which he got leisurely through and spat back on Queensland.

'That's what I think of the blanky colonies!' he said.

He gave us time to become sufficiently impressed; then he said: 'And if I was at the Victorian and South Australian border I'd do the same thing.'

He let that soak into our minds, and added: 'And the same with West Australia—and—and Tasmania.' Then he went away.

The last would have been a long spit—and he forgot Maoriland.

We heard afterwards that his name was Clancy and he had that day been offered a job droving at 'twenty-five shillings a week and find your own horse'. Also find your own horse feed and tobacco and soap and other luxuries, at station prices. Moreover, if you lost your own horse you would have to find another, and if that died or went astray you would have to find a third—or forfeit your pay and return on foot. The boss drover agreed to provide flour and mutton—when such things were procurable.

Consequently, Clancy's unfavourable opinion of the colonies.

My mate and I sat down on our swags against the fence to talk things over. One of us was very deaf. Presently a black tracker went past and looked at us, and returned to the pub. Then a trooper in Queensland uniform came along and asked us what the trouble was about, and where we came from and were going, and where we camped. We said we were discussing private business, and he explained that he thought it was a row, and came over to see. Then he left us, and later on we saw him sitting with the rest of the population on a bench under the hotel veranda. Next morning we rolled up our swags and left Hungerford to the north-west.

THE STARS FOR A LANTERN

'Whalers' or swagmen were a common sight on bush tracks and stations well into the twentieth century. They arrived at sunset anticipating the handout of provisions and accommodation that was in those days expected—and usually given—under the code of bush hospitality. Their wanderings usually followed a well-worn track between stations and along rivers such as the Darling. Usually characters with a dry sense of humour, and sometimes well-educated and widely read, many finished their wandering in lonely graves along the tracks they travelled.

In the 1930s, an unknown writer reminisced about the 'hardened old sundowners' he met many years before at Weintenigi Station, a couple of hundred kilometres out of Broken Hill.

All through the shearing they had been camped at the 'Bagman's Hut', at one time a regular feature of Darling River stations, but which is now practically a thing of the past. On the day of the cut-out all these old bagmen marched up to the cook's head-quarters to get their final hand-outs. With the typical free-handedness of his class, who are generous, more so when they do not have to foot the bill, the cook loaded them well up. The next morning they started off up the river to the next shed.

One old chap particularly drew my eye. He must have been all of 65 years of age, and yet the load he was lumping would have caused a pack mule to roll its eyes. His swag was a neat roll complete with canvas sheet. From its straps dangled billycan and frying pan, and out of the top the inevitable fishing-line showed. This latter is a regular tool of the river whalers, for there are plenty of Murray cod to be had in the waters of the Darling and its tributary rivers.

On each shoulder, swinging by the necks were two sugar bags. They were well and truly full. The old chap stopped at the store, and asked me 'how were the chances for a bit o' terbaccer'. I gave him a plug—I was allowed so many pounds per annum for that purpose—and remarked upon his swag.

The sundowner replied:

'I've carried more than that from some stations. That lousy cook only gave me 25 pounds of flour and a bit of tea, sugar and butter.' Further inquiries showed two tins of jam, one of honey, two of baking powder, half a leg of mutton, and innumerable odds and ends of his own. Together with his 'knot', the whole must have weighed a full 80 pounds.

When asked how far he planned to trek that day, the whaler replied:

I've been on the river now for seventeen years, and I never do more than my six miles a day. I go up as far as Bourke, and then work my way back down the other bank. I ought to get to Wentworth again in time for a bit of fruit picking.

> I was still curious, and asked him if he didn't get tired of that kind of life. His answer, more expressive than polite, conveyed the impression that there wasn't any better life going. Plenty of grub, nothing to do, and all your life to do it in!

The swaggie humped his heavy load onto his back, thanked his benefactor for the tobacco and 'set out up the river bank to do his six miles per day for the rest of his life. Who knows what stories may lie behind some of those figures as they tramp their beats up and down the great river, with the sky for a roof and the stars for a lantern.'

HARDSHIPS OF THE TRACK

In the depths of the Great Depression an older generation of swagmen met with a new generation doing what they had begun thirty or more years before. Times were tough, but in many places they always had been and the old hands were not necessarily sympathetic to the new battlers hopping 'rattlers' and smoking cigarettes instead of the pipes favoured in an earlier era. One unnamed bloke had such a poor impression of the youth of 1933 that he was moved to share his thoughts:

> He drifted along to my place the other afternoon with a sugar-bag over his shoulder, and said carrying the swag was a cow of a game.
>
> 'Look here, mate,' he went on, as he tackled the supper the wife gave him, 'I struck the border, and it was a terrible experience, I managed to get tucker, but my feet ached something awful.'

The old timer said nothing to the whingeing young man, but he wrote plenty in his letter to the newspaper, recalling his time carrying a swag—or a 'curse', as he called it—from Broken Hill.

> Rolled in the 'curse' was a 6 x 8 tent, fly, two blankets, a couple of pairs of trousers, and the same number of flannels. I left Broken

> Hill with 3/6 in my pocket, and headed for Menindee, which was 76 miles [120 kilometres] away. I tramped 36 miles [57 kilometres] with only a spell of 15 minutes, and struck a wretched shanty at 9 p.m. Here I had a drink of a miserable decoction called beer, slept in a hard bed, and breakfasted on goats' chops and damper, washed down with a black stewed substance. Those back-blockers lived hard in those days.

The country he passed through was 'one vast desert' with not enough wood to boil a billy and no water to put in it anyway. It was hot, dry and desolate with only one shanty that was not deserted and looked 'like a battered pelican in a wilderness'. In all that distance he passed no other travellers.

> Nine miles [15 kilometres] further on I struck a station, where I entered the hut and found the men at dinner. There was no friendly greeting, only a crushed and heartbroken, grunt and the remark, 'Help yourself'. There was stewed mutton, damper, brownie, and tea in a bucket, into which I dipped my pannikin. The men had a sour, worn, depressed look, and the meal finished in perfect silence.

After another 6 miles (10 kilometres) he encountered a plague of caterpillars coming down from the Darling. Later he passed through country where 'they must have had the hearts of lions and insides of emus' to survive.

> Seventeen miles (28 kilometres) further on I came to Menindee. I was glad to see it. I could tell you a lot more about the rest of that journey to the Queensland border, but what's the use? Now do you wonder why I smile when I hear some of these modern train jumping 'tourists', with their cigarette and sugar-bag swags, talking about the hardships of the track?

And that's how tough it was in the bad old days!

BACK OF THE MILKY WAY

The author of this anonymous poem manages to give the harsh realities of the track an unusual appeal. Like all good yarns this one finishes with a flourish that brings it back down to earth. The places visited stretch across much of the continent and the incidents mentioned are a mixture of historical, commonplace and sometimes obscure. The overall effect is a poetic nutshell of the great unending track of the Australian imaginary.

A few translations: the 'Myall track' probably means to travel through rough country; 'the great Byno' is probably a reference to Bynoe Harbour in the Northern Territory; the 'cup' mentioned in verse 5 is not the Melbourne Cup as no horse or jockey named 'Bowman' is recorded winning that race; Bathurst is known as 'the city of the plains'; the shearer's strike took place in the 1890s (see 'Razing the *Rodney*' on page 200) and 'flying stakes' is a form of open horse race. To 'hump your drum' is to carry a swag.

I humped my drum from Kingdom Come
To the back of the Milky Way,
I boiled my quart on the Cape of York,
And I starved last Christmas Day.

I cast a line on the Condamine
And one on the Nebine Creek,
I've driven through bog, so help me bob,
Up Mungindi's main street.

I crossed the Murray and drank in Cloncurry
Where they charged a bob a nip.
I worked in the Gulf where the cattle they duff,
And the squatters let them rip.

I worked from morn in the fields of corn
Till the sun was out of sight,
I've cause to know the Great Byno,
And the Great Australian Bight.

I danced with Kit when the lamps were lit,
And Doll as the dance broke up;
I flung my hat on the Myall track
When Bowman won the Cup.

I courted Flo in Jericho,
And Jane at old Blackall,
I said farewell to the Sydney belle
At the doors of the Eulo hall.

I laughed aloud in the merry crowd
In the city of the plains;
I sweated too on Ondooroo
While bogged in the big bore-drains.

I pushed my bike from the shearers' strike
Not wanting a funeral shroud;
I made the weights for the Flying Stakes
And I dodged the lynching crowd.

I've seen and heard upon my word,
Some strange things on my way,
But spare my days, I was knocked sideways
When I landed here today.

KIANDRA TO KOSCIUSZKO

Even as late as the 1930s parts of the country were little travelled, particularly the snowfields between Victoria and New South Wales. In the summer of 1934, a party of six led by Colin Gilder of the Millions Club, an association of businessmen fostering a population of one million for Sydney through British immigration, set out to walk from Kiandra to Kosciuszko. The keen skiers took three days to cover about 100 kilometres, mostly at an altitude of over 1800 metres. The group wanted to correct the recorded locations of the huts vital to the survival of walkers and skiers.

The going was not too rough. They encountered fog at the top of Happy Jack Valley and slept their first night in an improvised gunyah.

They spent their second night at Mawson's Hut, named for the famous Antarctic explorer, where it was 72 degrees Fahrenheit in the shade. But within fifteen minutes it dropped to 57 degrees Fahrenheit on the back of a southerly. 'You could almost see the mercury dropping in the thermometer,' Gill said.

At Mawson's Hut they met Dave Williamson who had 3500 sheep 'summering' in the high country. Dave had been bringing flocks up from the low country each summer for 30 years.

When the fog cleared they were able to see a valley of snow-covered downs and everlasting daisies. Colin Gilder described it as the most extensive view he had ever seen.

> There was water everywhere, and on the tops of some of the dividing ranges it was almost possible, by stretching both arms out to touch with the one hand the waters that, flowing ultimately to the west. Joined the great Murray River system, and with the other those which flowed into the Pacific Ocean.
>
> They had a magnificent view from Gungartan. They could see as far north as the mountains around Yarrangobilly Caves, they could see the hills that surround Canberra, they could see Table Top Mountain at Kiandra; in another direction they could look over Dalgety; they saw the whole of the New South Wales main range; and they were able to look into Victoria as far as Mount Feathertop.

The intriguingly named Millions Club was especially active in the 1930s and included politicians as well as businessmen among its membership. At its 60th anniversary in 1962 the Millions Club changed its name to the Sydney Club. It is now part of the Union, University & Schools Club. Gilder and his companions pursued their skiing passion through the Millions Club but later formed the Sydney Ski Club in 1937.

A FORGOTTEN WAY

Older than the pyramids or the Silk Road, the Bundian Way is a path through what is mostly still wilderness, complete with spiders, snakes and native flora and fauna. It travels through Aboriginal country rich in traditional camping sites, artefacts and spiritual significance. It has also become part of the pioneer heritage of settlement and an early example of Aboriginal people helping newcomers move safely through the bush between the coast and the high country.

People have travelled this track for thousands of years. Running for over 360 kilometres from Targangal (Mount Kosciuszko) to Bilgalera (Fisheries Beach in Twofold Bay), the Bundian Way allowed people of the Yuin, Ngarigo, Bidhawal and Monaro communities to move efficiently between their traditional grounds into the high country and down to the coast. In summer the track led them to the swarming Bogong moths, good eating when barbecued. In winter, people could access and enjoy the seafood riches of Twofold Bay, including whale meat. These travels also allowed for trading and for social and ceremonial gatherings.

Snaking by the towns of Thredbo and Delegate, the track was later used by settlers in the region to move stock. But over time the memory of the track faded and it was only due to the efforts and knowledge of the local Yuin–Monaro people, a naturalist bushwalker and a bit of luck that it was found again.

As John Blay tells it, he spent many years walking in the area, coming to appreciate its environmental diversity and uniqueness. He had heard of a mysterious path from the mountains to the sea and began searching for it in 2001. But after a couple of frustrating years he was no closer to finding the elusive way.

Then he had a bit of luck: he came across a Bombala dingo trapper named Harold Farrell. Farrell was in his eighties and knew the track from his younger years when he had followed it himself. Even better, he was able to point John to where it lay. The next day, Blay found the track exactly where Farrell had told him it would run.

Since then, and together with the Eden Local Aboriginal Council and elder Uncle Ossie Cruse, Blay has walked and surveyed the route of the Bundian Way. Their research has confirmed the course and extent of the elusive track and they aim to have it all open for walking as funds and resources become available. In 2016 the first stage in opening the track to walkers was initiated with a 12-kilometre stretch along Twofold Bay.

Many of those who have walked all or part of the track have found their journey to be inspirational, even healing. Uncle Ossie and John Blay hope that the cultural and historical significance of the ancient pathway will one day be fully available to anyone who wishes to connect with the spirit of the land.

ALL TYPES AND SIZES OF POWER AND HAND
MOWERS. SCIENTIFICALLY. GROUND

8

WORKING WAYS

> She has undertaken all kinds of work, from waiting in cafes to milking on [a] dairy farm . . .
>
> Of Shirley Howard, riding from Sydney to Darwin, 1939

HURDY-GURDY GIRLS

The story goes that the hurdy-gurdy girls originated in the German state of Hessen, then an independent country, in the early nineteenth century. Hessian farmers made brooms during the winter to sell the next summer. This cottage industry grew very quickly, especially when the farmers discovered that sex sells: pretty young ladies dancing to the loud and piercing sound of a hurdy-gurdy attracted customers for their brooms like nothing else. The idea quickly spread and before long hurdy-gurdy girls, also known as hessian broom girls, were becoming a nuisance on the city streets of Europe, America and Australia.

It wasn't just the lovely ladies attracting attention: the 'hurdies' were extraordinarily discordant instruments. The hurdy-gurdy is a medieval instrument played by turning a rosined wheel that rubs along a number of strings, including drones, in imitation of a fiddle bow. There is a basic keyboard along the outer edge. The instrument is very loud and penetrating, ideal for street music and attracting attention to whatever wares might be on sale.

From at least the 1850s, descriptions of hurdy-gurdy girls began to appear in the Australian press. By the time they reached Australia, hurdy-gurdy girls were often playing the less audibly confronting and easier to manage concertina or, according to some accounts, were dancing to street organs. They were in Melbourne in 1857 and Cowra in 1861. In 1860, they were in Bathurst: 'Those ubiquitous German girls with cracked voices and broken-winded instruments parade the streets from daylight till dark, and become a pest to anyone who has once been soft enough to reward their excruciating melodies.'

It was much the same story wherever there was a gold rush. The early years of Forbes were busy and bustling. Miners, shepherds and the occasional bushranger came and went, day and night. The town was filled with theatres, and concert and dancing halls. Shoeblacks, buskers and the hurdy-gurdy girls all did a roaring trade along the thronging streets. They also entertained in the dance halls and saloons.

By now though, the originally innocent hurdy-gurdy-girl business had long since fallen prey to the sex trade. Unscrupulous agents would convince their parents to allow the girls to travel with them in return for a share of their earnings. But these earnings were from prostitution, not advertising. Increasingly, the hurdy-gurdy girls were deemed to be of low moral character, though men visiting dance halls considered it a great honour to win a dance with one of these musical damsels. Fatal brawls between men keen to dance with a hurdy-gurdy girl were not unknown.

As the wilder gold rushes ended, Australian society aspired to a more settled and respectable character. The colourful but elusive hurdy-gurdy girls faded away with the saloons and dance halls that had provided them with a living of sorts.

COBB & CO TO MELBOURNE

English comic opera singer Emily Soldene was not deterred by much, it seems. In 1877, she was part of a visiting troupe performing in Sydney and Melbourne. They had a successful season at Sydney's Theatre Royal, though the condition of the theatre and the takings compared unfavourably with their recent tour of the United States. Soldene was a hit with the crowds and the season finished with a benefit concert in her name. The governor and his lady were present along with the local elite. She was presented with a jewel casket in the form of an emu egg decorated with Australian silver.

Then it was time to leave for Melbourne. The company was worried about the reception they would receive in the southern city, for people said, 'What went in Sydney was a dead frost in Melbourne.' Most of the company made the trip by steamer but Soldene and three of her fellow performers decided to see something of the country and took the adventurous overland route on the Cobb & Co Royal Mail coach:

> Such a journey, on a 'Cobbs' coach, drawn by six young horses, who galloped up mountains and flew down them, driven by coachmen more or less under the influence of the weather. One told us he had been out on a 'burst to a wedding, not slept for three nights,' but should be all right when he had a 'nobbler'. We looked forward with much pleasurable anticipation to the 'nobbler', but were horrified when we saw it—'half a tumbler of whiskey'. Our driver tossed it off. He had not overstated its merits. It pulled him together splendidly, not that it made any difference in his driving, which was dare-devil and perfect, as was that of all the other boys.
>
> Fancy a track of soft sand, cut into deep ruts, piled high up in banks, winding in and out of trees, sharp corners, unexpected fallen trunks, monster upturned roots, every kind of obstacle, six horses always galloping, the coach banging, creaking, swaying from side to side!! Then suddenly down we go, down over a mountain as steep as the side of a house, down into and through a rushing and roaring, tumbling, bumping, yellow river!! Splash, dash. Then with a 'Houp!' 'Hi!' and a big lurch, out again and up the opposite side galloping always galloping, breathless; the driver

> shouting, cracking his whip, and the horses shaking the water from their side, tossing their heads, and jingling their harness; then out on to the level, soft and springy, covered with mossy turf and beautiful trees like an English park; away over more sand, and leaving the mossy turf, and plunging through sharp, cutting, stiff, rusty looking, tall grass, growing in huge tufts, far apart.
>
> At last we come to a hut, full gallop, and the driver, without any preparation, pulls the horses up on their haunches . . . It was all lovely except for the jolting, and my hands were blistered with holding on. I liked to sit on the box, though it made one sick, not with fright exactly, but with excitement and the anticipation of some possible calamity.

No calamity befell them other than an unfavourable impression of Gundagai, then a gold mining town, which, 'like every other mining town I have ever seen, was distinguished by a marvellous display of rubbish of all sorts, old boots, tin cans of every description, meat cans, old stays, old bonnets, old bats, old stockings, heaps of more cans, strewn for miles. It takes all the romance out of the scene.'

The intrepid entertainers survived the journey and need not have worried about their reception in Marvellous Melbourne. They opened at the Opera House and, as Soldene put it, 'falsified our expectations by making a big success'.

Emily Soldene was a talented performer, able to sing in both serious and popular styles. She was successful enough to establish and manage her own company with considerable acumen. Her policy was to employ attractive ballet dancers for the chorus: 'The result, a minimum of voice, perhaps, but certainly a maximum of good looks and grace . . . They felt the music, were full of life, and, like a blooded horse, were anxious for a start.'

Left a widow two years after her Australian tour and with four children to support, Soldene continued touring and performing. She returned to Australia in 1892 but the tour was a failure and she was forced to take up an offer to work as a journalist. For seventeen years she wrote a weekly column of London gossip for

Australian newspapers. She also wrote a novel and a scandalous memoir naming names and delighting her readers. She died in 1912.

ACROSS THE BORDER

In the spring of 1881, a young man identified only as 'a young Bendigoian' left Victoria's Mount Hope for Mount Browne in the arid 'corner country' of New South Wales. An experienced bushman, he travelled with another man, named only as Charley M, in a light wagon drawn by a pair of horses. Their journey was primarily to search for plant and insect specimens but also to survey for gold reefs, as the Albert goldfields, to which they were headed, were in the grip of gold fever.

Preparations for the journey were careful: 'In packing up for a long journey into the bush, it is a good plan to get everything ready you intend to take and put them on the ground before you commence to pack up, then go carefully through them and turn out everything you can possibly do without, and it is wonderful what you can do without when you have not got it.'

The naturalists crossed the border between the colonies at Moama, where they had to satisfy the excise man that they were not carrying any items that would attract an intercolonial duty fee. They hid their half a gallon of best whiskey in a bag of oats and their tea—then a taxable item—in a bag of chaff.

> The examination of our trap by the New South Wales excise man seemed a disappointment to him especially as he noticed we had both got a pair of brand new boots on, and none but old pairs on board. He took a second look into my Naturalist's box, but as everything was marked with a death's head and cross bones and branded 'poison' he merely remarked that he supposed I was going to collect bugs and beetles as well as nuggets. He brightened up a little when we told him we intended to buy our stores at Deniliquin as the New South Wales goods were generally better than the Victorian ones, and wished us good luck and a good journey.

Safely past the excise man, and now into New South Wales, the only thing they now had to fear was the supernatural.

> From Moama to Deniliquin and thence to Hay is the ground, nearly as well trodden as Pall Mall and not much more feed on the road for horses or cattle. We camped one night at the 'Boundary Gums', near Hay. This is the place where the famous 'trotting cob', without a head, takes his midnight rounds to wake up the sleeping stockman if there are any strange horses in the station paddocks.

The travellers were assured that many had seen the apparition with their own eyes, but they did not. Their horses were still grazing happily in the squatter's paddock despite the threat of the headless cob. As they went, they found 'the price of stores rose very fast at each approaching township, and out of all proportion to the rates of carriage between the two places. Deniliquin was dearer than Echuca, and Hay much dearer than Deniliquin.' The price of tea more than doubled between Hay and Wilcannia. Despite the prices, they pushed on, living partly off the land and collecting specimens.

> From Hay to Booligal is one immense plain without a stick of firewood for over fifty miles, and salt-bush makes very inferior fuel; however, we did very well as we determined to take back tracks and go by way of Hilstone, both for the sake of feed and for the purpose of seeing the country. As there had been a heavy fall of rain round Cowl Cowl and Wulbar, the grass was very good but the roads heavy.

At Ballangerumble there was double disaster. The Bendigoian naturalist went out for a stroll:

> It was rather late when I got back to camp and pretty dark by the time I had pinned out my specimens, and before I had finished Charley announced the fact that 'tea was ready', and brought me

> a pannican full to go on with and after asking me if I should like a bit of cold turkey for my supper, he said, 'I say, I don't think this tea tastes quite right, it's very weak'. I said, 'perhaps it wants some more sugar, Charley'. He therefore put some more in and after giving it a good stir, quietly said, 'try your tea and tell us if there is anything the matter with it'. I therefore took a good drink as it was nice and cool, and did not perceive anything amiss until I got it down, but the flavour at once induced me to go and look into the billey, upon examining which I found a good handfull of my 'longicorn beetles' floating about in the hot tea mere bloated corpses of their former selves.

The naturalist had placed his dried beetles in a tin that looked very much like the tea box. Surviving beetle tea, they encountered various travellers along the way. On the main Wilcannia 70-mile track they 'passed several parties bound for the diggings and a mixed assortment they were . . . One day we passed a party consisting of two spring carts, four pack horses, two goats, a white cockatoo, two men and a boy; also two women both with babies, and the family carriage in the form of a perambulator tied to one of the spring carts and the whole party seemed as happy as sandboys.'

They moved on to the goldfields capital of Milperinka, now a ghost town, but then the main settlement of the region, if one with some postal problems:

> From here to Cobham lake the country consists of sand flats and scrubby country; the lake is a beautiful sheet of water about a mile and a half long, with a beautiful sandy beach. Fifteen miles further brings us to One Tree, a waterhole two miles from Milperinka Creek by running up which we arrived at Milperinka town-ship, the capital of the Albert goldfields of New South Wales. This capital consists of eight buildings and two shanties, and is about the meanest township ever called by that name even in New South Wales. It is the seat of Government and a post town, but the post-master not being in possession of a stamp to deface the postage

> stamps or to stamp the name of the township, etc., is obliged to write all these particulars on all letters that pass through his hands and to make a deliberate cross over her Gracious Majesty's two-penny countenance at the corner of each letter.

Once again the travellers were shocked by the prices on the diggings which, they claimed, were maintained by a ring of Wilcannia storekeepers. Despite the prices, the diggings were thronged with people arriving hopefully or leaving in disappointment.

> The gold field consists of three main rushes. First the 'Four Mile', eight miles from here; 'Mount Browne' four miles further on; and the 'Granite', 30 miles further still and close to the Queensland border. There have been some good patches of gold obtained at all these places, but for yields we are obliged to trust to what other people tell us, and I am sorry to say that liars even exist at Mount Browne.

The anonymous Bendigoian finished his traveller's tale with a description of the relatively liberal regulations governing the diggings and noted that everyone was 'dryblowing', or obtaining gold by shaking a wooden cradle of earth and allowing the wind to blow the soil away to reveal any fleck of gold it might contain. We do not discover whether he tried his hand at fossicking but his account gives a first-hand view of the colourful and often improvised nature of colonial life and travel.

WAY OF THE CHARLATAN

In 1898 and 1899 a popular English travel magazine published a serialised account of one man's journey through the south seas and into northern Australia. Louis de Rougemont's story was a colourful one, involving shipwrecks, cannibalism and a host of daring adventures. According to de Rougemont he had lived among the Aborigines for 30 years, marrying into the 'tribe' and eventually becoming a chief. He saved two white women from a fate worse than death, and escaped attacks by the savage local fauna, hostile natives and Europeans. He even described flocks of flying wombats.

Despite absurdities like this, de Rougemont could also write plausibly about aspects of Aboriginal practice, as he does here about the message stick tradition:

> I ought to mention that before leaving my black people I had provided myself with what I may term a native passport—a kind of Masonic mystic stick, inscribed with certain cabalistic characters. Every chief carried one of these sticks stuck through his nose; I, however, invariably carried the passport in my long, luxuriant hair, which I wore 'bun' fashion, held in a net of opossum hair. This passport stick proved invaluable as a means of putting me on good terms with the different tribes we encountered. The chiefs of the blacks never ventured out of their own country without one of these mysterious sticks, and I am sure I should not have been able to travel far without mine. Whenever I encountered a strange tribe along the line of march I always asked to be taken before the chief, and when in his presence I presented my little stick. He would at once manifest the greatest friendliness, and would offer us food and drink. Then, before I took my departure he also would inscribe his sign upon it, handing it back to me, and probably sending me on to another tribe with an escort. It often happened, however, that I was personally introduced to another tribe whose 'frontier' joined that of my late hosts, and in such cases my passport was unnecessary.

Improbable though most of these yarns were, they made an immediate impression on the reading public and were widely reprinted. Eminent scientific authorities were quoted in support of de Rougemont and he was even invited to lecture to the British Association for the Advancement of Science in Bristol before professional anthropologists and geographers. But it was his story of riding on the back of a turtle that led to his exposure as a hoaxer.

Sceptical journalists at London's *Daily Chronicle* invited de Rougemont in for a chat. They made sure to include a barrister in the group who plied him with awkward questions to which he was unable to provide satisfactory answers. Eventually, the Australian journalist M.H. Donohoe wrote a detailed exposé of de Rougemont's fantasy.

The true story was that Louis de Rougemont was in fact a Swiss–Austrian named Henri Louis Grien (or Grin, sometimes Green). While originally from a farming background, as a young man Grien had worked as a courier for a well-known actress of the era and then travelled to Australia in 1875 as a butler to the Western Australian governor. He then drifted round the country working in the pearling trade, and as a cook, a waiter and a photographer, before finally becoming involved with mining syndicates. He married in 1882, leaving seven children with his wife when he deserted her sixteen years later. He floated across to New Zealand, where he set up as a spiritualist and eventually worked for his passage to London, arriving in March 1898.

While Grien had certainly travelled to and through Australia, the bulk of what he passed off as his own experiences were those of Harry Stockdale, an artist and explorer with extensive bush experience. Stockdale had headed an expedition to the north-west in 1884–85 and kept a detailed journal of the expedition (see chapter 2). Grien seems to have known Stockdale and by some unexplained means also came into possession of the journal, which he used as a basis for his confection. Stockdale's mention of 'flying possums', presumably Eurogliders, became de Rougemont's flying wombats.

De Rougemont also made clever use of other known facts that gave his work an air of credibility. When the explorer Ernest Giles attempted to cross the continent from east to west in 1873–74 he reluctantly included an enthusiastic young man named Gibson in his party. Gibson disappeared in the course of the expedition (see 'Naming the Desert'). De Rougemont claimed to have stumbled across him out in the desert, raving and lost. The story went that Gibson lived with de Rougemont and his Aboriginal wife for two years, recovering his mind only shortly before he died.

After the hoax was exposed, Henry Lawson wrote a characteristically tongue-in-cheek appreciation of de Rougemont:

Now, that it is all over and forgotten, I cannot, for the life of me, see where was the sense or need in the howl that was raised against de Rougemont whose descriptions or pen pictures of savage life and scene in remote and unknown territory of remote and hitherto unknown Australia are the most romantic, interesting and perhaps the most reliable of any writing, in connection with Australia, published by an English magazine up to date. What, in this connection, had Australia to get mad about?

I must admit that I felt just as wild as any of de Rougemont's critics at the first go off; but that was mainly because he got there with his scenery and savages before I did with mine. He crowed low and roosted high until the glorious opportunity came; then he seized it. And he made a bigger splash in three months than any other Australian writer has begun to make in a hundred years. Seeing that, as Australian booksellers and publishers know well, English and Scottish editors and publishers are constantly writing and enquiring after Australian copy, and Australian writers, what excuse would we have for bucking if the most conceited and least literary globe-trotter on the seven seas were to write us upside down and back to front from one end of Australia to the other—from the Gulf to the Bight, from Sydney to Perth, and publish it in the biggest magazine in the world?

If we won't send 'em facts—and the fiction too—if we are too easy going and careless, or tired, or haven't got sufficient confidence in ourselves to do that—what are they to do? You don't suppose a British journalist is going to hump swag, dig, shear, go droving, knock down his cheques in the city, fence, grub, cut scrub and dig tanks and get lambed down at bush shanties, and 'run in' at bush towns, and have the Out-Backs horrors and perish of thirst on the great awful blazing plains for the best part of a life time, in order to get at the local colour of the Australian Bush? Or tramp the cities with the unemployed and doss in the Domain—to be knocked up and moved on by a policeman every hour or

> so—so as to obtain concrete facts concerning Australian city life and the pessimism necessary to the life of Australian literature?

The hoaxer continued to spruik his fantasies after his exposure, enterprisingly appearing in the South African music hall in 1899 as 'The greatest liar on earth'. But the same trick failed miserably when he toured Australia in 1901: he was booed from the stage. He remarried in 1915 under his pen name, although by then he had long fallen from public view.

Henri Louis Grien, alias Louis de Rougemont, died in poverty in 1921 under yet another name—Louis Redman. As the *Daily Chronicle* observed in its recollections on the occasion of the hoaxer's death, if Grien had simply written his story as a work of fiction 'it might have been selling to this day, and the author might have ended his days in greater comfort, if not luxury'.

RAZING THE RODNEY

At the end of 1894, the western districts of New South Wales and Victoria were ablaze with one of the most extensive and bitter industrial conflicts in Australian history. The row had erupted over a contract from pastoralists—hit by the falling price of wool—that unionised shearers could not accept. By the time of the 1894 shearing season, the talking was over and the fighting had begun. All sides used violence in support of their positions. But the arson attack on the paddle steamer *Rodney* in August 1894 marked the height of the conflict; an extreme act by union shearers and considered Australia's only act of inland piracy.

The *Rodney* left Echuca with 50 non-union workers hired by the pastoralists to replace the striking shearers. The scabs—as the strikers called these men—were under heavy police guard and were jeered by unionists on the bank. At Swan Hill, Mildura and Wentworth the boat and its growing cargo of scabs was stoned and abused. The *Rodney* was ultimately headed for Tolarno Station on the Darling River, which was blockaded by 400 striking shearers. Police were on their way from the north to break up the strikers while the *Rodney* steamed towards the station from the south.

Little did the police know the paddle steamer would never get this far. Long before the *Rodney* reached the station, the union shearers planned to stop the steamer by snagging her with wire or cable stretched across the river beneath the waterline. They would then board the boat and burn it. The pastoralists got word of this plan, however, and warned the steamer's captain. He decided to tie up for the night of 25 August in a billabong about 50 kilometres north of Pooncarie. The next morning he would make a fast run to the blockaded station to evade any ambush.

But the unionists were not to be outmanoeuvred by the change of plans: at around 4 a.m. and in the dark, the *Rodney* was boarded by a group who had disguised themselves with mud streaked down half their faces. Even so, the man on watch saw them approach and called out a warning. The captain tried to get his craft started but the ship never left the bank, as 'At the same moment his fireman, who was untying the rope which held the steamer to a tree on the river bank, was accosted by armed men, who said they would blow the fireman's brains out if he touched the rope.' The crew's resistance was effectively over:

> In a few minutes about 30 of the mob boarded the steamer. Not long afterwards the number was increased to 150. They worked systematically in gangs. One gang sought the free laborers, and bundled them and their swags ashore; another seized the captain after a short struggle. He was not much hurt. Another looted the steamer of everything useful and portable, while another procured kerosene, which was emptied over the boat from stem to stern, saturating well the chaff in the hold. Lights were then applied, and the steamer soon became ablaze.

Meanwhile the scabs had been forced at gunpoint to a nearby island, where they were marooned. The flaming hulk drifted downstream, threatening to set the bush alight as it veered from side to side. The arsonists gave three cheers as one of them played 'After the Ball (is Over)' on a concertina.

The same day at Wilcannia, further along the Darling River, another savage chapter in the strike was playing out on Nettalie station. Around one hundred union men turned up at the Grassmere woolshed, where the shearing was about to begin with scabs wielding the tools. A tense standoff developed, as armed police were guarding the woolshed and refused to hand the scabs over to the unionists. Afraid of further negative press, the strike leaders rushed to Grassmere, hoping to contain the violence. But as the strikers entered the shed, the police and a scab opened fire, wounding two unionists. One would later die as a result of his wounds.

When word of these events reached the press, the eastern colonies reacted with fear and threats. The New South Wales government issued a proclamation stating 'all subjects of her Majesty are called upon to render assistance in protecting persons from outrage or molestation and in maintaining law and order.'

Large rewards were offered for identifying and capturing the union leaders involved. Pastoralists and others in the industry who had not already done so began to arm themselves. There were calls to hang the arsonists of the *Rodney*. Eight unionists were eventually tried for the crime but they were provided with alibis by their mates and were all acquitted.

Arson, confrontations and gunfights continued throughout Victoria, New South Wales and Queensland well into 1895. This foment led to the birth of the modern Labor movement. Another result of these strikes was the unofficial national anthem, 'Waltzing Matilda', based on the story of a union shearer in conflict with the pastoralists of central-west Queensland.

The burned and sodden bones of the *Rodney* can still be seen, lying low in the Darling River near Polia Station, about 40 kilometres north of Pooncarie.

THE MAGIC LANTERN MAN

In the days before film, entertainers travelled through bush and city with magic lantern shows. The magic lantern, lit first by a lamp, and later with electricity, projected black and white or coloured images from glass slides onto a large screen or a wall. The pictures were accompanied by a presenter narrating the show and sometimes singing songs as well. Joe Watson was one of these magic lantern men who travelled the tracks to entertain audiences far and wide.

Born in Boorowa in New South Wales in 1881, Watson's first jobs were as a bullock boy and rouseabout. But at the age of sixteen he joined Paddy Doolan and Ted Hurley's magic lantern show. Doolan and Hurley drove a double-storied wagonette containing the magic lantern through the bush towns of the east coast. Young Joe was excited by the open road and the adventures he fancied he would have in his new life. And, to boot, he was now in 'show business'.

> Well, we would arrive in a town or sometimes a large station property, and line up a program, usually for the Sunday night. Paddy would make a big show of the arrival, lots of noise and banners. We'd charge the public 2/6 each for a night of magic lantern slides and mechanical films (with barrel organ accompaniment). I remember visiting the station of Mr A.D. Middleton and 'showing' to 30 or 40 shearers and rouseabouts.

Watson's job was to work the lantern and, later on, the early film projectors they also carried. Hurley organised the gate and house while the blind Doolan nevertheless managed to bellow a voiceover to whatever was on the screen: travelogues, dramas, murders, boxing matches and even horseraces. Doolan had been a juvenile convict, transported in the 1840s and blinded by accident and through incompetent treatment.

Watson described a typical show:

> We had pictures of animals in the London Zoo, Countries of Europe, the Royal Family, and slides of the popular scandals of the day—the Dick Marr Case, Paddy Crick Case, the Dean Case, the Tichborne Claimant, The Butler case of Sydney and a series on the Goldfields, and, of course, a series on the Ned Kelly Gang.

> The murders and bloodthirsty subjects were always the most popular, even with the womenfolk.

Doolan was also an accomplished singer and concertina player, and serenaded the audience, adding a musical dimension to the night's entertainment. To supplement the income from the show, Watson and his companions also sold the words and music of Doolan's songs and, on occasion, sold holy pictures door to door during the day.

Just as Watson hoped, the travellers did have plenty of adventures on the road. One of them involved the largest damper in the world:

> It must have been at least twelve feet in diameter and was cooked on a large bullock wheel. We were travelling along this road after a couple of successful lantern showings. On the horizon I could see a cloud of dust and a group of men riding on horses. They were armed with poles and were obviously intent on bashing our heads in. They thought we were the escort for the strike breakers as there was a savage strike on at the time and the shearers were all camped down by this river, and waiting for the scabs to come through—they were coming up from Victoria—the home of scabs.
>
> Luckily one of the horsemen recognised Doolan. We joined with their camp and saw this massive damper being made to feed the four hundred men at the camp. We had it with cocky's joy and it tasted good because it stuck to your ribs.

On another occasion he met Jim Kelly, the surviving older brother of Ned Kelly, and even went to his home for tea. The story of the Kelly Gang was also one of the trio's most popular offerings, thrilling audiences wherever they went. Doolan would accompany the show with a rousing sixteen verses of 'The Ballad of the Kelly Gang', a tongue-in-cheek account of the Kelly Gang's depredations. As Watson sang it in the early 1970s, then aged 92, the ballad begins:

> Oh! Paddy dear and did you hear, the news that's going round,
> On the head of bold Ned Kelly, they have placed two thousand
> pound,

> For Byrne, Steve Hart and Dan, two thousand more they'd give,
> But if the price were doubled, sure, the Kelly boys would live . . .

The ballad ends with a comment on the inability of the Victoria Police to track the bushrangers down:

> But now where they've gone is a mystery,
> The Bobbies cannot tell [spoken with laughter]
> And, until I hear from them,
> I'll bid you all farewell!

Watson picked up many songs, stories, poems, toasts and ditties on his travels and was an accomplished performer himself. Later in life he ran a pub in his home town and also became mayor. His amazing life, travels and repertoire of traditional lore were fortunately recorded by folklorist Warren Fahey and now form part of Australia's extensive folk heritage.

TRAVELLING TEACHERS

The job description for a nineteenth-century travelling teacher in Queensland was intimidating: 'he must be able to splice a broken pole, mend a wheel, doctor a sick horse, and, if threatened by fire or flood, be able to extricate himself and his boy and save His Majesty's property'. These tough-as-nails educators were also expected to treat sandy blight and other eye problems as they rode from isolated outback station to small bush hamlet, teaching the Three Rs to shy bush children.

In the latter half of the century the rural population of Queensland was great but widely scattered. One anxious parent wrote to the Department of Public Instruction:

> I am writing to ask your department for some assistance to educate my family . . . I have four boys respectively 7, 6, 3 and 1 years of age. I live 8 miles from the nearest provisional school at Mt Brisbane and there is no probability of a school ever being nearer . . .

There were increasingly loud calls for the government to provide education for outback children and end what one reforming minister of parliament called 'compulsory ignorance'. In 1901, a trial Itinerant Teaching Service was established, sending teachers on the first of many unusual but valuable journeys around the state's rural regions, a service that ran until 1930. Each travelling teacher was supplied with:

> a specially designed buggy, four to six horses, and complete camping out equipment. He has also the services of a boy from fourteen to eighteen years of age to attend to the horses, help to pitch the tent, light the fire, lower sliprails, open gates, and do numerous little things which a handy youth can do. The teacher is expected to make his own arrangements for camping and food, and thus relieve parents of this responsibility; he receives a special allowance from the department for this purpose.

As well as being a very competent handyman, these men also needed to be good bushmen, as well as:

> tactful so as to gain the goodwill of the parents and of owners whose lands he must cross. He should also be of kindly disposition so as to win the confidence of shy bush children; should be of trustworthy character, for his work can seldom be inspected, as his duties take him to homes which are far away from the beaten tracks and which can often be reached only through lonely country patrolled by police in search of cattle duffers, or of new chums who are lost . . .

Irish-born Thomas Johnson was the first of these intrepid teachers to travel the byways of the Balonne electorate on the Queensland–New South Wales border. The 38-year-old Johnson was a kindly man but a stickler for getting things right—an ideal teacher. With his young assistant he travelled almost 2500 kilometres in 1901, visiting over one hundred homes.

By the end of the year Johnson had also visited families in

the Cunnamulla area, including sixteen families previously not known to live there. He moved south to the border in April, then east to the Balonne River. Between May to August he visited a further 43 families as he followed the river north, including a side trip to Mungindie in the east. Then it was west towards the Warrego River to educate the children of another fourteen families, finishing up in the Thirsty Downs area.

In their buggy, the teacher and his assistant carried reading primers, books of tables and arithmetic, as well as texts on geography and grammar, which they distributed to the far-flung students. The families all also received a large atlas, providing a window onto the world beyond southern Queensland. Children were also provided with pencils, chalk, slates, pens, ink and exercise books to work in.

Johnson provided basic instruction and guidance in using the books and usually left a local person in charge of furthering the education process. Sometimes it was a parent or a sibling, but it could be anyone capable and willing to take on the responsibility of teaching the children.

The fathers of the children who were visited worked in a range of bush occupations, as boundary riders, fencers, carpenters, 'prickly pear contractors', dingo trappers, shearer's cooks and railway gangers. Others were overseers, bailiffs and station managers. They were united by their common need for an education for their children.

By 1911, there were around eighteen travelling teachers following various routes. One of them, a 'fully certificated' Mr Patullo, covered:

> an area of from 25,000 to 30,000 square miles and extends from Woolgar, by way of Nundah and Winton, to Longreach and Barcaldine in the south, thence north to Aramac and Muttaburra, and on to Hughenden. The district is in the artesian area; the country is flat, open downs covered with Mitchell grass. Mr Patullo is provided with a buckboard trap and six horses, which are worked in relays—two at a time.

In the first six months of 1911 Mr Patullo had already travelled over 3500 kilometres. It was noted that these teachers would need to be extremely hardy to endure such a lot of travelling. As well as their other necessary accomplishments, it was essential that they 'have a disposition which renders the work congenial to himself else he would be a travelling misery and a complete failure whatever his scholastic attainments'.

By that time, ten years into the program, the teachers were expected to visit each of their families four times a year. They usually stayed for a few days at a time, correcting work set previously and planning the next stage of the children's education. Mr Patullo found that the children he taught had many handicaps and disadvantages due to their isolation but

> their powers of observation were remarkably keen. The children in many cases have a hard life and are often set at a very tender age to do the work of an adult. Yet, with all these things to contend with, they are bright and intelligent and make excellent use of the opportunities for education which the travelling school provides.

The journeys of the travelling teachers came to an end around 1930 when an alternative, a school for primary education by correspondence, was established. Long before then, Thomas Johnson left his outdoor school to marry Amy O'Brien and take up a position in a state school. He retired as a head teacher in 1932 and died at the Brisbane suburb of Annerley in 1937.

THE ROAD URCHIN

In the middle of the Great Depression 30-year-old carpenter Harold Wright emigrated from England. Like many others at the time he went on the road in search of work. And like most, he found that there was not much work around.

So in 1935, he crafted a wooden wagon into a mobile home cum workshop and office and travelled around Victoria sharpening tools, kitchen knives, mower blades and anything else that had become blunt. He called this unique carriage the Road Urchin and spent the next 34 years on the move, living and raising a family within its cramped confines.

At first the wagon was drawn by a horse. It soon became a familiar sight to those living in the Riverina, and well beyond into Queensland and western Victoria. Later it was drawn by tractors or at one time fitted onto a truck chassis: the saw doctor continually redesigned the vehicle.

In Brisbane around 1940, Wright married Dorothy Jean McDougal, known as Jean. She lived with him on the wagon, reportedly taking charge of the fees paid for his services. They had a daughter, Evelyn, who also lived with them on the road.

Wright made a point of decorating the wagon with bright colours and trinkets to advertise his services: 'I painted it up brightly and wrote signs and decorated it to make it attractive to the public. I called myself "The Sharpening King", thinking this would attract more business and make life a bit easier.'

Among the wagon's many features were displays of family photographs, newspaper clippings and some of Wright's own creations. One of these was in the form of a notice attached to the outside of the wagon. It read:

> Fair Go, Mates!
> TO CAMERA MEN AND WOMEN
>
> Observe! I have put endless thought, time and energy, which has made photography of this unusual outfit possible. When taking photos of this unit, it would be much fairer to me if you would also purchase one of my Souvenior [sic] Brochures of Home and Workshop, with Story and Pictures.
>
> Thanks from The Battler
> ONLY 15 cents

During the day the wagon looked 'like a bower bird's nest on wheels'. At night, with coloured lights ablaze, the wagon looked like a circus tent.

The family travelled with pet dogs and cats as well as chickens. In the heat of the day they would often park beneath a shady tree. The unusual sight attracted the local farmers who would come over for a look. Once they found out what the strange contraption was all about they would usually go back to their farms and return with all the tools that needed sharpening. Sometimes there were so many edges to be restored that Wright and his family stayed overnight and the farmers would take them home for a meal and a shower.

In this way the saw doctor travelled the country from town to town for many years until his death in 1969. Harold kept a map of their journeys which was lost and Jean sold the wagon to a scrap dealer where it would have probably rotted away, but for a stroke of fate: in 1977, Peter Herry, who had often seen the wagon as a child, fortunately stumbled across it in Wangaratta. He purchased it, saving a unique slice of Australia's vast nomad history. The National Museum of Australia purchased the saw doctor's wagon from Herry in turn in 2002, installing it in the foyer of the museum where it intrigues everyone who visits, young and old.

JUMPING THE RATTLERS

The era always known as the Great Depression devastated the lives of everyday Australians in the early 1930s. Many were forced onto the roads and railways to search for work. Catching illicit rides on goods trains became an art practiced by many unfortunates, known variously as 'bagmen' or sometimes by the American term 'hobos'. In 1932, the skipper of the yacht *Symbol* gave temporary shelter to one of these men.

> He was a young Australian, about 22 years of age, formerly a bank clerk in Brisbane. When the banks retrenched he was thrown out of work, and, unable to obtain another position, when his meagre savings were gone he was forced to 'roll up' a few clothes in a blanket and go on the track in search of work, and decided to

make for North Queensland, where he hoped to obtain work on the sugar plantations.

When travelling in the more densely populated Southern Queensland he was often given lifts on his way by passing motorists. However, after a while, when he reached country where there were no roads he was compelled to travel in goods trucks, and became one of a great band of young unemployed men who roam over Queensland by taking rides in freight trains—'rattler jumpers' being their nicknames.

Of course, the police were out to check this illegal riding on trains, and I was told of many amusing experiences in this respect. On one occasion, he and three others were returning from Western Queensland, where he had journeyed in search of work in the mines, to Townsville, and at each township on the plains they went into a police station for their weekly rations. They had obtained rations there the previous week, and the sergeant, a good sort, recognised the party.

'Did you fellows come in by train?' he asked them. When they replied in the affirmative, he said: 'How the blazes did you get past those policemen of mine? I've had three of them meeting every train each way in order to catch some of you rattler jumpers.'

When they explained that they had come in on the mail train and dropped off about a mile from the station, he almost exploded. 'I've a good mind to run you in, for I've got a good fortnight's work here, and could make use of your fellows. But I'll get you yet, for I'll have every train watched, and you will have to walk out 20 miles to the nearest siding if you want to get away.'

Of course, this was all said good-naturedly, and one of the hobos said: 'Well, I bet you my ration ticket, Sarge, that your, "boob Johns" won't catch us.' The sergeant replied: 'I'll bet I have you fellows working in my garden before the week's out.'

They parted on good terms, the hobos returning to their open-air camp by the railway.

Later on the sergeant told his policemen that they had been called 'boob Johns' and instructed them, to catch the four men.

Not only were the hobos watching the police, but they also

went down to every train that came in and watched the three policemen systematically searching the trains, at the same time making encouraging remarks. In the evenings a policeman would come down and have a yarn with them over the camp fire and an old black-tracker was often prowling about watching them.

At last the four decided to shift camp, as the provisions were running low. They thought out a plan of campaign. They made a big fire and then wrapped some large stones up in old empty bags and left them lying around the fire. Then they walked two miles along the line in the opposite direction they actually intended to go, and caught the train that was travelling slowly up grades to the first siding.

Here they waited for the down train containing about a dozen trucks of silver lead ingots. These steel trucks have false bottoms, which can be lifted up in order for coal to be loaded, and having located a truck in which the ingots were not stacked over the trap-door, they got inside with their swags, let the hatch drop on themselves, and then worked their way to either end of the truck, where it would be almost impossible for them to be found.

About half an hour later the train was in the station. Sure enough, they heard the policemen clambering up the sides and searching the trucks, and heard a constable say: 'No sign of them in here.' An hour later the train was passing over the plains and the four hobos had got through.

When they reached the next town ship they sent an unstamped postcard to the Sergeant, saying: 'Dear Sarge, I think the boys are too smart for your Johns. Please send ration tickets you lost to us in Townsville.'

According to the writer of this account, he found someone who gave the mischievous bagman a job in a shipping office, hopefully bringing his illegal rail journeying to an end.

But 'jumping the rattler' was not entirely new in the 1930s. Even in the 1920s it was common to see large numbers of men dropping off goods trains before they pulled into the station. One of these bagmen boasted that he had travelled all around Australia without paying a fare. His most recent trip, early in 1925, had begun at Sydney from where he had an uninterrupted train ride to Bundaberg. Three days later he left comfortably seated in a Ford motorcar being conveyed by rail to Rockhampton. Another train brought him to Sarina on the coast of Queensland, where he 'came a terrible gutzer' hopping off, a heavy fall that was a frequent and painful experience for jumpers. He boarded another goods train that night bound for Mackay, intending to travel on to Townsville 'as soon as a train suited'.

In August 1930, a fifteen-year-old boy appeared at the Newcastle Quarter Sessions as a victim of indecent assault by a railway guard. He was asked by a solicitor:

> 'What have you been doing since you left school? Running all around the country hopping trains?'
>
> 'Yes.'
>
> 'You call it "jumping the rattler" don't you?'
>
> 'You can call it that', the boy indifferently replied.

When asked where he lived, he replied simply, 'Nowhere. On the track.'

The guard, who claimed to have only given the hungry boy and his mate a meal, was found not guilty.

SYDNEY TO DARWIN ON A NINE-BOB PONY

Work was still hard to find in Depression-era Australia when, in February 1937, 25-year-old self-described 'jobless authoress' Shirley Howard announced her intention of riding horseback the 12,800 or more kilometres from Sydney to Darwin. Howard planned to gather material for a book as she worked her way around the country over the next two years, starting from Sydney's General Post Office.

This 'unusual woman', as the papers called her, purchased a pony at the Flemington saleyards for just 9 shillings in 1932 ($40 or so today). Howard named her Mary Lou and rode her from

Sydney to Cairns the same year, and from Sydney to Adelaide via Melbourne a few years later. But these rides were just limbering up exercises for her planned epic crossing to Darwin and, perhaps, down through Western Australia and back to Sydney.

Howard began her epic journey on 22 February 1937, heading north from Sydney. But after only a few days, Mary Lou came down with cattle sickness in Port Macquarie. Howard walked and hitchhiked to Grafton, arriving on 4 May. She had to return to Sydney and find work as a waitress until the following July.

After this false start she was back in Grafton in August 1938 to contest a dispute over a horse she claimed to have purchased. After a court hearing in which the other party said he would rather shoot the horse than have Howard ride it, the police magistrate found in Howard's favour. The magistrate decided that Howard had more right to the animal—known as Kermen—than the stockman who had detained it. She rode on to Lismore where she stayed for three weeks or so selling soap to local housewives to cover the expenses for her ride. She then continued her quest for Darwin, making next for Brisbane.

Journalists were amazed that a woman might attempt such a feat. Asked if she ever felt lonely on her rides, she replied, 'Why should I? I feel just as lonely in town when I am by myself.' Questioned about the dangers she told reporters, 'If an accident is to happen, it will just happen, that's all.'

The press was particularly shocked by Howard's preferred camping spots: in cemeteries. Was she not afraid of 'bagmen'? Howard replied that there was no chance of swaggies dropping their swags in a graveyard.

But Howard did not 'cast off her femininity when on these trips', as a newspaper reassured readers. She sent her luggage ahead by train, and so during her stay in Grafton she appeared in a brown coat and a black dress 'with a natty brown sailor's cap'.

While in Brisbane, Howard accepted a wager that she could ride the 362 kilometres to Grafton in 48 hours. She covered the first 200 kilometres in 36 hours and with this record-breaking speed was on track to win the 50-pounds bet (about $4000 in today's value). But her horse Kerman injured a fetlock between Murwillumbah and Tweed Heads.

On 6 April 1939, Howard and the recovered Mary Lou left the Brisbane General Post Office at 10 a.m. bound for Darwin. Shirley Howard kept to a travel itinerary of 50 miles a day and by mid April had reached Maryborough, after stopping at towns on the way to earn money. Between Brisbane and Maryborough, she had survived accidents and an attack by a 6-foot tree snake. Described as 'independent and a battler', Howard was still selling soap and taking any available work.

> Miss Howard has had a variety of experiences and met all manner of people. She has undertaken all kinds of work, from waiting in cafes to milking on [a] dairy farm, mending a tank for three feeds ('I cleaned and soldered it and hoped to earn a few bob'), woodcutting ('I chopped a load of wood for a baker, and he gave me a loaf of bread'), shoeing horses for a blacksmith, and so on.
>
> Shirley had also 'taken short cuts and been lost, helped pull cars out of bogs, and been given £1 for a month's work on a dairy farm after sacking herself by cleaning up the cow bails—'for shame's sake'.

At this stage of the trip, the faithful Mary Lou was now accompanied by the thoroughbred Kermen as a pack horse, on this epic trip to Darwin and beyond.

But we don't know with any certainty what happened between that point and sixteen months later, when, on 26 August 1940, Howard rode into Sydney. She claimed to have reached Darwin after leaving Brisbane and then made her way back to Sydney through Western Australia.

The brief accounts don't say which of Howard's horses she was riding when she returned to Sydney—possibly Kermen—but we do know the horse was rigged with a battery-operated automobile headlight and a tail-light. Perhaps people, and therefore the papers, were more preoccupied with the war than by a woman riding a horse. Even so, there are no press mentions of Howard's movements after her arrival in Maryborough the previous year. Considering the fascination of the newspapers with Howard's ride up until that point, it seems unlikely that her arrival in towns and cities in the Northern Territory, Western Australia and South Australia would not have produced at least some copy.

Sharp-eyed readers of this one brief mention of her return to Sydney might have noted that Howard was not reported to have actually ridden all this way, only that 'she went to Darwin and thence to Western Australia and back to Sydney'. They might also have been surprised to read that in three years her stated age had mysteriously risen by seven years to 32.

Did Shirley Howard make that very, very long ride, even if only in various stages? Probably not, at least not all of it. What began as a youthful adventure and genuine search for employment in the Depression might have turned into a publicity-seeking enterprise by 1940. When she entered Sydney on her well-lit mount Howard was still insisting she would write a book about her adventures. It never appeared. But let's admire her sense of adventure, her courage and her determination to travel in her own way and in her own time.

FOREIGN FABLES

For most of us, important journeys take the form of holidays. But pleasurable and relaxing as these are meant to be, things can go wrong. Back in the 1960s, folklorists around the world began picking up an odd story. The details of the time and place varied wherever the tale was told but the basic plot was much the same.

The story went that a family was travelling by car across a deserted part of the country on a long-anticipated holiday trip. Dad was driving, Mum was in the front passenger seat and the kids were in the back with their grandmother. Somewhere in the middle of nowhere, Granny suddenly died.

The car screeched to a halt and the horrified family spilled out onto the road, aghast at the body of their granny growing cold in the back seat.

What should they do?

They couldn't leave the body by the side of the road, and neither the parents or the children were keen to sit next to a corpse for the considerable distance to the next town. There was nothing else for it but to hoist granny up onto the roof rack and get to a police station or hospital as quickly as possible. With the body strapped above them, the family tore along the road to town.

When they finally arrived it was very late at night and most of the small town was closed up. But they managed to find the local police station. Parking the car at the entrance, the family all rushed into the building, leaving the stiffening corpse of Granny where they had strapped it on top of the car. Distressed, the family approached the astonished desk sergeant to report Granny's unexpected demise.

After taking down the details on the official form, the sergeant asked the family to accompany him back to the car to identify the body and have it properly removed. They pushed open the doors of the police station. Their car had disappeared. Along with Granny.

The father gasped, the mother fainted and the kids screamed. The sergeant was unimpressed, suspecting a prank. But the family recovered sufficiently to convince him that the body of their grandmother had indeed been on the roof rack of their now unaccountably vanished vehicle. The car and body were never found.

One of the things that the different versions of the tale had in common was the location of Granny's death. It was usually said to have happened in a remote area, often on or near a border between countries, states or regions. And, of course, it was all true, wherever the tale was told. In Australia, the favoured location was somewhere on the Nullarbor Plain or just the Outback. And it wasn't always Granny who died; sometimes it was an aunt or another female relative.

What could this creepy travel story mean? The incidents described never took place. The tale is a contemporary legend or urban myth. And like many other unsettling yarns it seems to hint at the dangers inherent in journeys, especially as those who tell these tales always insist that they are true, usually because they heard it from 'a friend of a friend' or perhaps read it in the newspapers or on social media.

Another often-told legend of journeys to exotic places concerns the favourite Australian holiday location of Bali. In this one a holidaymaker (usually female) is enjoying the sun on a Bali beach when she feels a small sting on her cheek. She starts upright and slaps at her face, revealing a small black spider has bitten her. As there are no apparent ill effects and the stinging goes away she forgets about the incident and enjoys the remaining week or so of her holiday. When she returns home she notices that a small blister has formed on her face where the spider bit her. The blister gets bigger and bigger and eventually she rubs it too hard and it bursts. A host of baby spiders crawl out.

In some versions this happens on the way home or in a doctor's surgery. Sometimes the baby spiders number in their thousands. Sometimes the woman was holidaying in Penang, Vietnam, or somewhere else. Like other urban legends, this one has been around for a long time and relates to many other such tales of bodily invasions, toxic contaminations and generally dreadful things that could happen to you during a journey of almost any kind.

Urban legends tell us you could be kidnapped at Disneyland, attacked by Greek vampires or bitten by snakes infesting any number of amusement parks and venues. Even in Australia you need to watch out for yowies, bunyips and blood-sucking yaramas.

Much ink has flowed in analysing these and the many other similar stories that have been circulating for decades. Are they a warning to be careful when away from home? Especially in remote or different places? Seems reasonable. What about the consistent features, like the death of the female relative? Maybe it has to do with the very reasonable universal fear of death. Or perhaps it is a reflection on the youthful orientation of modern society with the consequent discomfort with ageing. Whatever we might try to make of these allegedly true and unsettling tales, there are certainly a good number of them on the theme of travel, holidays and other journeys. Best to stay at home.

COME ON BOYS
JOIN US

9

LEAVING

> Play on your golden trumpets, boys, and sound your cheerful notes.
> The Cyprus Brig's on the ocean, boys, by justice does she float.
>
> Van Diemen's Land convict ballad, 1830

BY JUSTICE DOES SHE FLOAT

In August 1829 the overcrowded brig *Cyprus*, carrying 33 Van Diemen's Land convicts in iron chains to the dreaded Macquarie Harbour penal station, lay at anchor in Recherche Bay. Altogether there were 64 people aboard the 24-by-6 metre craft, including a group of 63rd Regiment soldiers under Lieutenant Carew. The *Cyprus* had been storm-bound in the bay for a week during which time the convicts had plotted a mutiny. Carew seemed to have let security slip and four convicts used the opportunity to seize the ship. They unchained their fellow convicts and sent any who did not want to sail with them ashore along with the soldiers, sailors and civilian passengers. Forty-four were cast away on the beach.

At this point one of the mutineers, William Popjoy or Pobjoy, dived off the *Cyrpus* and swam across to join the castaways. He was one of a group who tried to walk through the bush to seek rescue. They managed to swim across the Huon River, but were forced to turn back after being threatened by Aborigines, or so they claimed.

Among the bedraggled castaways on the beach was an ingenious convict named Morgan, who fashioned a crude craft known as a coracle from the few natural materials and personal belongings at hand. Accompanied by Popjoy, he paddled across the sometimes treacherous D'Entrecasteux Channel to alert a sailing ship, the *Orelia*, which rescued the castaways. Back in Hobart, Carew was court-martialled for losing control of the ship, although ultimately acquitted, while Popjoy became a local hero. He was given a pardon and worked his passage to London.

In the meantime, the eighteen convicts aboard the *Cyprus*, led by William Swallow, sailed boldly into the Pacific Ocean in search of freedom. They sailed to New Zealand and then spent six weeks at Niuatoputapu in what is now the island nation of Tonga. They had lost one man overboard and seven of the crew decided to stay on the island. Ten men then put to sea in the *Cyprus* once again.

Despite a dearth of experience as navigators they managed to reach the Chinese city of Canton, now Guangzhou, in February 1830. There, three more went ashore and left the crew. The remaining mutineers decided to scuttle the *Cyprus* and take to the ship's lifeboat, with the aim of pretending they were shipwrecked sailors. The authorities in Canton believed them and the convicts now all came ashore and scattered. While most of the remaining crew elected to remain in Canton, some went to America, never to be heard from again. Swallow and three others sailed aboard a British ship bound for London.

While they were in transit to Europe, news of the mutiny on the *Cyprus* reached Canton and one of the convicts who had remained there confessed to the crime. A fast ship carried the news to England and when Swallow and his accomplices arrived there six days later the authorities were waiting. Swallow managed to escape but was later recaptured. He told convincing lies about how the other convicts had forced him to sail the *Cyprus*, but Popjoy was now in London and prepared to testify against them.

Two of Swallow's accomplices were hanged but he escaped the noose and was sentenced to transportation for life. He again sailed to Van Diemen's Land and arrived at the destination of his original voyage, Macquarie Harbour, two years late. He would die in penal servitude in another notorious prison, Port Arthur.

The sensational story of the mutiny and subsequent voyage of the *Cyprus* inspired convicts to compose admiring ballads. The famous Frank the Poet aka Francis MacNamara composed a well-remembered poem that vividly put across the convict's point of view:

Come all you sons of Freedom, a chorus join with me,
I'll sing a song of heroes, and glorious liberty.
Some lads condemned from England sail'd to Van Diemen's Shore,
Their Country, friends and parents, perhaps never to see more.

When landed in this colony to different Masters went,
For trifling offences, t'Hobart Town gaol were sent,
A second sentence being incurr'd we were order'd for to be
Sent to Macquarie Harbour, that place of tyranny.

The hardships we'd to undergo, are matters of record,
But who believes the convict, or who regards his word?
For starv'd and flogg'd and punish'd, deprived of all redress,
The Bush our only refuge, with death to end distress.

Hundreds of us were shot down, for daring to be free,
Numbers caught and banished, to life-long slavery.
Brave Swallow, Watt and Davis, were in our noble band
Determin'd at the first slant, to quit Van Diemen's Land.

March'd down in chains and guarded, on the *Cyprus* brig
  convey'd
The topsails being hoisted, the anchor being weighed.
The wind it blew Sou'Sou'West and on we went straightaway,
Till we found ourselves wind-bound, in gloomy Recherche Bay.

'Twas August eighteen twenty nine, with thirty one on board,
Lieutenant Carew left the Brig, and soon we passed the word
The Doctor too was absent, the soldiers off their guard,
A better opportunity could never have occur'd.

Confin'd within a dismal hole, we soon contriv'd a plan,
To capture now the *Cyprus*, or perish every man.
But thirteen turn'd faint-hearted and begg'd to go ashore,
So eighteen boys rush'd daring, and took the Brig and store.

We first address'd the soldiers 'for liberty we crave,
Give up your arms this instant, or the sea will be your grave,
By tyranny we've been oppress'd, by your Colonial laws,
But we'll bid adieu to slavery, or die in freedom's cause.'

We next drove off the Skipper, who came to help his crew,
Then gave three cheers for liberty, 'twas answer'd cheerly too.
We brought the sailors from below, and row'd them to the land
Likewise the wife and children of Carew in command.

Supplies of food and water, we gave the vanquish'd crew,
Returning good for evil, as we'd been taught to do.
We mounted guard with Watch and Ward, then haul'd the boat aboard,
We elected William Swallow, and obey'd our Captain's word.

The Morn broke bright the Wind was fair, we headed for the sea
With one more cheer for those on shore and glorious liberty.
For Navigating smartly Bill Swallow was the man,
Who laid a course out neatly to take us to Japan.

Then sound your golden trumpets, play on your tuneful notes,
The *Cyprus* brig is sailing, how proudly now she floats.
May fortune help the Noble lads, and keep them ever free
From Gags, and Cats, and Chains, and Traps, and Cruel Tyranny.

Even as late as the 1960s, an elderly Tasmanian could sing a version of this ballad to a visiting folklorist and it can still occasionally be heard today performed by revival folksingers. It ends with the defiant lines:

> Play on your golden trumpets boys and sound your cheerful notes
> The *Cyprus* Brig's on the ocean boys by justice does she float.

THE GREAT TREK

German Lutherans, many from Prussia, settled the Barossa Valley of South Australia from the 1840s onwards. Generally they did well, despite floods and other natural disasters. But the promise of greener grass and better farming conditions elsewhere in the country always beckoned. In 1852, a group of seven families of mainly Wendish (Slavic–German) background loaded their belongings into eleven brightly painted and canvas-covered wagons and set out for pastures new, beginning a journey over 500 kilometres south to Portland Bay in Victoria. Horses and bullocks drew the wagons. The group of 51 men, women and children herded 52 head of cattle, as well as chaff for the horses, sacks of flour on which they also slept, a 'tucker bin' of food on which they sat and a poultry coop at the back of the wagon.

This wagon train made a great impression on its travels, guided across the country by a bushman and budding scientist named Wilhelm Blandowski. After four weeks slowly creaking south, they arrived at Portland Bay, where the local children ran behind the wagons chanting 'German, German!' The pioneering Henty family (see chapter 1) welcomed the new settlers, partly because many locals had left to seek their fortunes at new gold diggings. Eventually the newcomers were able to buy the large blocks of land available in the area and subdivide them among the families.

A decade or so later, another group of Germans set out from the Barossa Valley to distant horizons, although this time they were pushed by unhappy circumstances rather than drawn by the promise of better ones. The rich yields of the Barossa farming lands had begun to fade. Many of the farms were too small to be economically viable and there was a series of droughts, diseases and poor harvests throughout the 1860s that reduced many to near penury.

There was also a traditional practice that contributed to these problems. It was the custom among the Wendish for the eldest son to leave home at maturity and seek his own fortune and for the younger son to inherit the farm in return for looking after his aged parents. The families in those days were very large, leaving many children with dismal prospects. Quite simply, they needed more land.

At first single families, and then small groups, began to depart. In October 1868, eight families left in covered wagons from the town of Ebenezer in the Barossa Valley, bound for the area that would eventually become Walla Walla in New South Wales, a journey of 1000 kilometres. They sent chaff for their horses and the heavier farm equipment ahead by paddle steamer up the Murray River. They travelled along the Murray to Albury, then north to their destination, arriving after six weeks of rolling across the country, camping out, with regular prayer and worship.

This group was later followed by others leaving the Barossa for the same reasons. Settlements grouped around Lutheran churches grew up along the path of the Great Trek, as this movement became known, and by the 1880s much of the area around Walla Walla was said to be purely German settlements. Despite the many German pioneers in the region, the broader composition of the local population did not foster the same close-knit religious and community contact as had flourished in the Barossa. Nevertheless the German culture lived on in its transplanted home through Lutheran worship, German street names and spoken language.

During World War I the loyalty of the German-speaking population was questioned and four members were interned. Anti-German suspicions were revived during World War II and some Lutheran pastors were monitored by the authorities.

Today in Walla Walla, visitors can see a replica wagon, such as was used on the Great Trek, as well as the grand Zion Lutheran church, built in 1924 with seating for 600 people.

THE LONGEST DROVE

Epic cattle drives across the continent are an important but often overlooked aspect of Australian history. In 1872, some four hundred bullocks were shifted 2500 kilometres from Charters Towers to Palmerston, as Darwin was then known, by D'Arcy Wentworth Uhr. A year later, the man who would become the bushranger Captain Starlight shifted a stolen mob of cattle through tough country between Queensland and South Australia. In the early 1880s, the famous Durack family walked 7500 cattle from south-west Queensland to the Ord River. Often considered the greatest of the drovers, Nat 'Bluey' Buchanan moved some 20,000 head from Queensland to the Victoria Downs Station in the Northern Territory between the late 1870s and the early 1880s.

These were—and remain—celebrated feats of pioneering. But the longest drove of all began in March 1883 when a group of Scottish–Australian families struck out for barely known country almost 6000 kilometres away from where they were living in various parts of New South Wales. Family tradition tells the story like this.

Discoveries of fine pastureland in the remote north-west during the late 1870s attracted the interest of the related MacDonald and McKenzie families. One hundred square miles at the junction of the Margaret and Fitzroy rivers in the Northern Territory was secured for 25 pounds (around $20,000 in today's value). The plan was for the McKenzies to put up the finance and for the MacDonalds to do most of the work overlanding the stock from New South Wales through Queensland to the Gulf of Carpentaria, then across to their lease in the Kimberley.

Preparations for the journey were lengthy and thorough. The women of the families made large amounts of preserved food and an intensive build-up of equipment was supervised by the men.

The food was stored in heavy airtight steel ship lockers, loaded aboard two sturdy bullock wagons, along with almost everything else that might be needed for a journey they calculated would take more than two years.

They set out from Tuena, between Bathurst and Goulburn, bound for their promised land in north-west Australia. The pioneers planned to travel north through Queensland, passing through Charleville, Winton and Burketown to Limmen Bight River on the western coast of the Gulf of Carpentaria. They would turn west across the top end to Katherine then south-west to the station, which was known as Fossil Downs, named for the many ancient bones lying around the area.

The drive included 670 head of cattle and 86 horses, as well as 32 bullocks to haul two wagons and a pack of dogs. The men and stock plodded through Orange to Dubbo, picking up more family members and others to act as assistant drovers as they went. Keeping such a large mob together was a constant problem and there were personality clashes among the strong-willed men in the group. Sometimes they made ten miles a day, following the feed and water available as they went. South of Brewarrina, the Barwon River was running a banker and the whole expedition had to be floated or dragged across.

Furthermore, the whole drove was an expensive business. Terse letters were frequently sent back home with requests for large amounts of money. They were taxed at the Queensland border and as they moved further north local graziers were hostile to the amount of feed the large travelling mob consumed.

At Winton they had to wait for rain in the north. Tensions between the leader Charlie MacDonald and Donald McKenzie reached breaking point. Donald left the drove, wearing out three horses on the almost 2000 kilometre ride back home.

It was not until the rains came in September 1884 that the remaining group could struggle north again. Now, in the wet, the gulf country sucked them into its bogs and the men contracted fevers. Aborigines harassed the cattle, threatening their food resources, and crocodiles feasted on calves. They made it to

Limmen Bight River, down to just one wagon and with the men and stock all badly knocked around.

It was 1886 before they reached the Roper River in what is now the Northern Territory. Here, Charlie McDonald became so ill he had to be taken to Darwin by horse and from there shipped back home via Sydney. Willie and Dan MacDonald, with Charles and George Hall, pushed on to the Ord River in Western Australia's Kimberley region. Here, just three hundred or so kilometres from their goal, Willie MacDonald also had to be sent home with fever. Employee Joe Edmonds was left in charge with riders to 'camp' the cattle until the return of the MacDonalds. Floods held them up and so the restive Edmonds decided to push on to Fossil Downs with the assistance of a local Aboriginal guide.

They left the remaining wagon and most of the supplies in charge of the cook at the Ord River camp. Now much more mobile, they pushed the reduced mob on to their destination at the land grant at the Margaret and Fitzroy Rivers, arriving in July 1886. The MacDonalds, McKenzies and their assistants had travelled more than five and a half thousand kilometres over three years and four months. The rich pastures of Fossil Downs were theirs, together with the 327 cattle and 13 horses that had survived the arduous trip. It was the longest drove in history.

Back home, the MacDonalds and McKenzies were ecstatic at the good news and Joe Edmonds became an instant family hero for accomplishing the almost impossible task. There was feasting and merriment at Tuena and Joe was feted for his pivotal role in pushing the drove on that last difficult leg. But it soon turned out that his real name was not Edmonds and that he was in fact wanted by the authorities. Fortunately his crimes were relatively minor and the McKenzie's managed to use their influence to have the charges quashed.

But paradise had its drawbacks. While the cattle did well on the rich land, it was a long way to take the stock to market. The venture did not turn a profit until the discovery of gold at Kalgoorlie provided a more accessible, if still distant, market for their cattle. The MacDonalds gradually bought out the McKenzie shares. By 1915, Dan MacDonald, one of the original drovers, ended up as the sole owner of Fossil Downs. He later joined with the legendary cattleman Sir Sydney Kidman in a partnership that ended in 1928 when Fossil Downs was auctioned. Donald 'Dan' MacDonald purchased it back and the extensive property remained in the family for many more years.

Epic cattle drives are not just triumphs of the past. In June 2013, the largest single purchase of cattle in Australian history began moving from Western Queensland to the Riverina in New South Wales: 18,000 head were pushed from drought-ridden Winton and Longreach to better pastures in New South Wales. But the drive struck the worst drought year in recent history and, like the MacDonald and McKenzie's before, it had to follow the feed wherever it could be found. Unlike MacDonald and McKenzie, it was not required to pay tax at the Queensland border.

THE LAST RIDE

The man who wrote the poem below blew his brains out on Melbourne's Brighton Beach the day it was published. His name was Adam Lindsay Gordon and it was June 1870.

After an indifferent childhood and youth, the nineteen-year-old Gordon migrated from England to Adelaide in 1853. Although his father secured him an officer's commission in the South Australian mounted police, Gordon enlisted as a trooper, a rank and role that suited his interest in horses. He then became an itinerant horse breaker and established a reputation as a daring horseman. He was elected to the South Australian parliament in 1865 but after two years returned to his main interests of horse racing, speculating and writing verse, providing for his family mainly by winning horse races and other equine activities.

Gordon had expected to inherit his family state in Scotland, but when this did not transpire he became heavily indebted. With no money to pay the printer for his fourth book of verse, *Bush Ballads and Galloping Rhymes*, Gordon succumbed to despair and took his life. His popular reputation and legend grew rapidly after his death and he was accorded the honour of a plaque and statue in Westminster Abbey's Poet's Corner.

Although Gordon is now little known, 'The Sick Stockrider' was one of the first poems to capture the bush tradition that Banjo Paterson and a host of later poets would refine into the famous bush ballad. Its use of Australian place names, situations like running down dingoes and chasing bushrangers, as well as the last resting place beneath the wattles, all became standard images of bush poetry and song.

HOLD hard, Ned! Lift me down once more, and lay me in the
 shade.
Old man, you've had your work cut out to guide
Both horses, and to hold me in the saddle when I sway'd,
All through the hot, slow, sleepy, silent ride.
The dawn at 'Moorabinda' was a mist rack dull and dense,
The sunrise was a sullen, sluggish lamp;
I was dozing in the gateway of Arbuthnot's bound'ry fence,
I was dreaming on the Limestone cattle camp.
We crossed the creek at Carricksford, and sharply through the
 haze,
And suddenly the sun shot flaming forth;
To southward lay 'Katâwa', with the sandpeaks all ablaze,
And the flush'd fields of Glen Lomond lay to north.
Now westward winds the bridle path that leads to Lindisfarm,
And yonder looms the double-headed Bluff;
From the far side of the first hill, when the skies are clear and
 calm,
You can see Sylvester's woolshed fair enough.
Five miles we used to call it from our homestead to the place
Where the big tree spans the roadway like an arch;
'Twas here we ran the dingo down that gave us such a chase
Eight years ago—or was it nine?—last March.

'Twas merry in the glowing morn, among the gleaming grass,
To wander as we've wandered many a mile,

And blow the cool tobacco cloud, and watch the white wreaths
pass,
Sitting loosely in the saddle all the while.
'Twas merry 'mid the blackwoods, when we spied the station
roofs,
To wheel the wild scrub cattle at the yard,
With a running fire of stockwhips and a fiery run of hoofs;
Oh! the hardest day was never then too hard!

Aye! we had a glorious gallop after 'Starlight' and his gang,
When they bolted from Sylvester's on the flat;
How the sun-dried reed-beds crackled, how the flint-strewn
ranges rang
To the strokes of 'Mountaineer' and 'Acrobat'.
Hard behind them in the timber, harder still across the heath,
Close beside them through the tea-tree scrub we dash'd;
And the golden-tinted fern leaves, how they rustled underneath!
And the honeysuckle osiers, how they crash'd!

We led the hunt throughout, Ned, on the chestnut and the grey,
And the troopers were three hundred yards behind,
While we emptied our six-shooters on the bushrangers at bay,
In the creek with stunted box-tree for a blind!
There you grappled with the leader, man to man and horse to
horse,
And you roll'd together when the chestnut rear'd;
He blazed away and missed you in that shallow water-course—
A narrow shave—his powder singed your beard!

In these hours when life is ebbing, how those days when life was
young
Come back to us; how clearly I recall
Even the yarns Jack Hall invented, and the songs Jem Roper sung;
And where are now Jem Roper and Jack Hall?

Aye! nearly all our comrades of the old colonial school,
Our ancient boon companions, Ned, are gone;

Hard livers for the most part, somewhat reckless as a rule,
It seems that you and I are left alone.

There was Hughes, who got in trouble through that business
   with the cards,
It matters little what became of him;
But a steer ripp'd up MacPherson in the Cooraminta yards,
And Sullivan was drown'd at Sink-or-swim.
And Mostyn—poor Frank Mostyn—died at last a fearful wreck,
In 'the horrors', at the Upper Wandinong;
And Carisbrooke, the rider, at the Horsefall broke his neck,
Faith! the wonder was he saved his neck so long!

Ah! those days and nights we squandered at the Logans' in the
   glen—
The Logans, man and wife, have long been dead.
Elsie's tallest girl seems taller than your little Elsie then;
And Ethel is a woman grown and wed.

I've had my share of pastime, and I've done my share of toil,
And life is short—the longest life a span;
I care not now to tarry for the corn or for the oil,
Or for the wine that maketh glad the heart of man.
For good undone and gifts misspent and resolutions vain,
'Tis somewhat late to trouble. This I know—
I should live the same life over, if I had to live again;
And the chances are I go where most men go.

The deep blue skies wax dusky, and the tall green trees grow dim,
The sward beneath me seems to heave and fall;
And sickly, smoky shadows through the sleepy sunlight swim,
And on the very sun's face weave their pall.
Let me slumber in the hollow where the wattle blossoms wave,
With never stone or rail to fence my bed;
Should the sturdy station children pull the bush flowers on my
   grave,
I may chance to hear them romping overhead.

NEW AUSTRALIA BOUND

In the early 1890s a great struggle of shearers, sailors, miners and other workers against what they considered the unjust impositions of capital tore the country apart. This period saw the creation of the modern trade union movement and the birth of what is now the Australian Labor Party. But ultimately the forces of capital, as the strikers called their enemy, were victorious. The bitter disillusionment and despair of some workers, sharpened by the economic depression of the time, led some to take a radical journey. Over two hundred working men and their families sailed away from Australia to build a just new world on the other side of the Pacific Ocean.

Their leader was the labour organiser and writer William Lane, a passionate believer in socialism as a way to a better life for working people. Influenced by the wave of interest in utopian communities, Lane wrote a novel promoting the notion of a working man's paradise and in the same year formed the New Australia Cooperative Settlement Association. Rejecting capitalist Australia as a suitable location for a socialist heaven, Lane and his many followers resolved to establish New Australia in the jungles of Paraguay.

Land was gifted by the Paraguayan government, which was then rebuilding the country's population and infrastructure after a costly war in the late 1860s. They sailed aboard the *Royal Tar* in July 1893, bound for Montevideo via Cape Horn—to 'The Virgin Ground', as the Redgum song catchily put it in 1980. The land where they would build Lane's egalitarian, teetotaller and deeply racist utopia was in the middle of nowhere, 170 kilometres south-east of Asuncion.

The trouble began early. Not unlike many other idealistic visionaries, Lane's dream rapidly became a nightmare. He turned into an autocratic despot, brooking no other opinions. Conflicts between the colonists quickly flared and were only aggravated by Lane's leadership, or lack of it. The first settlement, Cosme, soon split as breakaway groups founded their own communities. There were further schisms, worsened by Lane's absence on a near three-year trip to England between 1896 and 1898. But by the time he left on this journey, disillusionment was already rife among those who had followed him. Ted Channing, previously a Brisbane plumber, wrote from the New Australian Settlement in June 1894:

> Dear Ben,
>
> No doubt you think by this time that I have forgotten you, but needless to say that is not the case. Things have been very much mixed here from the beginning—our leader turned out a complete failure. As a leader he lacked courage and made favourites. You know what that would mean in a thing like this. Unfortunately he had no business tact, and did not pretend to have any. The only good point about him was that he conceived the idea of this Boheme, which I am sure will be a success now; every indication of this, since sentiment and idealist are taking second place to business and common sense, and the people seem to get along better together.
>
> You know, of course, what our troubles have been—first the drink, then Billy Lane's pigheadedness in trying to get the shadow and missing the substance, the retreat of Billy and a few followers (about forty), some of whom have already left him—his best men too. This is one of the finest schemes, and the best country to try it in that I know of. We are gradually dropping into our places.
>
> There are two settlements—the one I am at is called Los Ovejos, the other is Loma Begua. We have about 2000 to 3000 head of cattle, about 50 pigs, 200 horses (very poor samples), about 50 or 60 working bullocks, about 8 or 10 single ploughs, 2 double-furrow ploughs, a mowing machine, a grist mill, a four-wheel trolly just built, 8 or 10 bullock drays. Two blacksmiths are at work fixing up some machinery that Walker bought dirt cheap. There are two blacksmith's shops, one at each settlement, and two lathes, one mine and one the blacksmith's. I am striking for the smith when not employed at my own work (plumbing). We work together.

> There are to be two weddings here next Sunday, and all the fellows at Loma Itegua are coming over. These two will make six marriages that have taken place here, four in Lane's reign, or, as they playfully call it, bondage, and two in freedom. All the single girls are engaged now, so you tell any of the girls that think of making a move in this direction that there are 100 young fellows waiting for wives, and, if they can't offer them much money, they can offer them a home and three meals a day for certain, without fear of the landlord or sheriff's officer poking his nose in, a quarter-acre of ground, and a house which you can furnish which way you like—to make the furniture.
>
> The climate is like Queensland, rather colder in winter of a night when the wind is in the south, generally when rain is about. We have about forty or fifty acres under wheat, and the same under vegetables; in fact, things are beginning to look up beautifully, and you will see very different accounts of us now. Some of the people who went away at the first are applying to come back; three of them were here last week, and seemed highly delighted at the progress we have made, and expressed their sorrow at ever going away. Of course before they can be admitted again they will have to be balloted for. Please remember me to all my old friends, and let them know I shall be glad to reply to any letters they may send me . . .

By the time Ted Channing wrote his letter to *The Queenslander* inviting marriageable women to the venture, a large group of already married women had embarked on the *Royal Tar*'s second voyage to Paraguay. But all did not go smoothly, as reported under the subhead 'Trouble with the Women':

> The excitement caused by Casey had no sooner cooled down than it broke out again in a fresh quarter—this time among the married women. One of these ladies was sick or indisposed, and the doctor ordered her some wine. The result is somewhat startling, especially considering that teetotalism is supposed to be one of the principles of New Australia. The ladies all rose in a body

> and demanded wine. If that woman got wine they must have wine also, for in the tyrannical, squatter-ridden land where they had lived, wine, it appears, was one of the articles of daily consumption, and the loss of this beverage was already commencing to tell on their constitutions. Here was a state of affairs that no one could have provided for, and no one seemed to know exactly how to deal with the trouble. A meeting was called as usual, but that was powerless. Threats of expulsion were of no use, and their sex protected them from violence. Nothing in the rules apparently could be found to solve the problem, and the meeting was finally quelled by a suggestion of the doctor. This was to give them as much wine as they wanted and let them drink it out, for no peace could be expected until it was done. This advice was followed, and peace reigned once more. The Royal Tar entered Monte Video without a spoonful of 'comfort' of any sort, except lime-juice.

By 1896, the Australian press was full of letters and reports from disgruntled New Australia colonists. One of these, originally published in the British press, was gloatingly re-printed in the conservative Australian newspaper, *The Argus*. It was from a man who had joined Lane's experiment two years earlier, when he:

> shook the dust of Australian soil from his feet and set off to create a Communistic Paradise somewhere in the mosquito-tormented forests of Paraguay. He was beckoned thither by dreams, dreams of a new social order, where the police-man was unknown and the capitalist was non-existent; where individualism was to be classed with typhoid as a deadly pestilence, and where, if there was not to be a community of wives there was at least to be a community of almost everything else. This particular member of New Australia, however, now writes to confess that this vision was nothing better than a mirage. The New Arcadia, where 'each was to have not according to his deeds, but according to his needs', and which was to give the signal for a social revolution to wondering mankind, has dwindled down to a little cluster of shabby, half

> savage, and more than half-starved settlements in Paraguay, their chief characteristics being a painful want of clothes and a perpetual ebullition of quarrels.

Anonymous journalists positively howled with delight at the failure of 'the most lunatic social experiments'.

> Socialism, with its dream of equality, its quarrel with individualism, every sane man knows to be pre-doomed to failure. It is in hopeless discord, not only with human nature, but with Nature. Men are diverse in physical and intellectual power, in the range of their wants, and the scale of their faculties; and a social system which proposes to efface these differences or to ignore them would wreck civilisation. But New Australia is the latest and most dramatic demonstration of this rudimentary fact!

The original settlement had by now split into at least five, often competing, groups. Lane's vision was dead. The dreams and hopes of most of his followers were broken. Lane returned to his career in journalism and became a strongly conservative supporter of the British empire. The common property was subdivided into private lots and many of the colonists gradually drifted back to Australia or elsewhere. But some stayed and made lives for themselves and their children and grandchildren.

The poet Dame Mary Gilmore spent her childhood in New Australia, and said late in her life, in 1959, that while it was a communist experiment she did not feel that it had been a total failure.

There are still descendants of the New Australians in Paraguay, some living on the original farms. Although those who stayed often became more Paraguayan than Australian there has been a revival of interest in Oz in recent years. They 'still call Australia home', said one proud Paraguayan Australian on a recent ABC television documentary, though many have migrated to Australia or hope to. Despite their undoubted Australian origins the descendants of William Lane's disaster qualify for no special entry privileges.

A SNOWBALL MARCH

One Sunday morning in October 1915, 3000 people attended a simple religious ceremony in the New South Wales country town of Gilgandra. Then 25 of them began walking to Sydney, over 500 kilometres away. They called themselves the Coo-ees and they planned to march through all the towns along their route gathering volunteers to fight for Australia in World War I.

As they set off they were accompanied by the largest crowd of locals ever seen and followed for a few miles 'by a great cavalcade of horses and vehicles'. Everyone came out, including a guard of honour made up of young horsewomen. After more cheers and a parting volley from the local rifle club, off they went.

The government had taken a long time to approve this novel and unorthodox form of recruiting. But the decline of volunteers after the first flush of enthusiasm in 1914 had them worried and the Gilgandra Coo-ees eventually got the go-ahead. And did they go.

Through the heat and dust they marched on another 100 kilometres to Marthaguy, many of the Gilgandra folk still following them, so high was the excitement. A young woman declared that 'if she had been a boy she would have marched all the way, and gone to the front with the contingent'. She promised to be in Sydney to greet the marchers when they arrived at Martin Place.

As they arrived at each new township the Coo-ees were met by residents cheering and carrying flags, then escorted to prepared camps and fed. Every morning they left with more recruits, flags flying and usually led by crowds of schoolchildren. There were speeches, cheers and enthusiastic renditions of the national anthem.

They reached Eumungerie on the second night. Here again there was music and dancing, speeches and appeals for funds for charity. People could not do enough for the Coo-ees, though most of the marchers, thinking about another day of uncomfortable marching, 'were glad to "sneak" away to their blankets'.

The next day it rained. But that did not stop the marchers or dampen the exuberance of the residents of Mogriguy. In fact, the district had been in drought so the party was even bigger. One of the army officers placed in charge of the Coo-ees had to plead for his men to get a decent night's sleep before tackling the longest stretch of the journey beginning next morning: 'He said that he was beginning to think that the Turk would not kill the men, but that the turkey might, and that before they had gone very far on the road to Sydney.' Despite the festivities, no men joined the marchers at Eumungerie.

After breakfast the next morning, the growing contingent tramped through sticky mud. Nine miles later they reached Brocklehurst for lunch. They 'were then treated to a round of patriotic kissing by a bevy of Brocklehurst girls. The schoolchildren led the march on to the Dubbo road, and the girls escorted the recruits for a mile on their way despite the rain.'

Four miles tramping through the afternoon brought them to Dubbo. Crowds greeted the Coo-ees and a massed band played them through the main street to the town hall where the mayor and 2000 citizens lauded them. After being issued with overcoats at their camp, the marchers returned to the town hall for the formalities.

> The mayor was considerately brief in his speech of welcome, but none the less cordial. After a light repast of tea and cakes, the 'Coo-ees' marched to the drill hall for a wash, and later to the Protestant Hall to a big 'meat tea,' of steak and eggs, bread and butter and jam; a pleasant change of menu after banquets and poultry and such delicacies.

Another four men joined here: 'Thus the snowball army grows as it rolls onward,' wrote the journalist accompanying them.

And so they did. Through Wongarbon where twelve men joined. They got another six in Geurie; 31 in Wellington; one each in Stuart Town and Euchareena; four in Molong; five in Parkes; nineteen in Orange; two in Millthorpe; eleven in Blayney; seventeen in Bathurst; one each in Glanmire and Yetholme; three in Wallerawang; nineteen in Lithgow; two in Blackheath; eleven in Katoomba; one in Leura; ten in Lawson; five in Springwood; four in Penrith; 27 in Parramatta and 22 in Ashfield. Cheered through the streets of country towns and suburbs, the Coo-ees reached the end of their long trek with 263 volunteers to enlist in their ranks.

After more than a month of marching and partying the Coo-ees paraded through the city to the Domain. Here they were supposed to rest but the crowds cheered and prominent men made yet more speeches followed by an official reception at Martin Place. 'Capt. Hitchens, the leader of the band, was accorded a most gratifying reception, and the men were overwhelmed with congratulations and good wishes.'

Then suddenly it was all over. The 263 Coo-ees who had enlisted were taken by train to Liverpool Camp where they learned how to fight. They already knew well how to march.

Their example inspired another nine recruitment marches. Some headed for Sydney, including the Waratahs from Nowra and the Kangaroos from Wagga Wagga. Others marched to their nearest recruitment centres. The Wallabies trekked from Narrabri to Newcastle; the Dungarees from Warwick to Brisbane; the Men from Snowy River from Delegate to Goulburn; the Kurrajongs from Inverell to Narrabri; the Kookaburras from Tooraweenah to Bathurst; the North Coast Boomerangs from Grafton to Maitland and the Central West Boomerangs from Parkes to Bathurst. In total nearly two thousand men joined the snowball recruitment marches of World War I, many never to return.

MAY GIBBS TAKES THE TRANS

After years of surveying, planning, squabbling and labour the Trans-Australian Railway was finally completed and open for business in 1917. World War I was at its height and there was much grim news for Australians to digest. Although it was now possible to travel from the east coast to the west coast in only a few days, and in comfort, the magnitude of the accomplishment was muted in the grief and shock of the past three years of war.

A few months before the fighting in Europe and the Middle East ended, a woman destined for great achievements in writing and illustrating for children took the long ride across the country. Her name was Cecilia May Gibbs, creator of the Gumnut Babies and the Banksia Men.

May Gibbs was then only on the cusp of the great fame she would achieve. At 41 years of age she had already published children's books in England and Australia, as well as occasionally drawing cartoons for the suffragette cause. But she had not yet enjoyed the spectacular success her *Snugglepot and Cuddlepie* series would bring after its publication in 1918.

That year May Gibbs, 'an appalling sailor', gratefully boarded the Trans, as the great railway was already known, to visit family in Perth. On her return to Sydney she described the journey to a journalist, while 'Seated in her gay little studio, before her drawing board, where she is busily at work on her latest creation—the Wattle Babies . . .'

The overland trip did have some drawbacks: 'changing in and out of trains on a journey which lasts four days and five nights isn't all joy', Gibbs complained of the constant need to deal with different railway line gauges and other operational problems. Furthermore, the leg from Perth to Kalgoorlie was made in carriages with no locks on the cabin doors 'and it is rather embarrassing, to say the least of it, when a conductor dashes in with your towels at an awkward moment'.

Gibbs noted that the early train from Perth was known as 'the drunks' train' because it was the only service with a bar. This might have been the best one to catch as from Kalgoorlie there was almost five hundred kilometres of dead straight track across the Nullarbor; 'not a single curve marring its virtuous path', wrote the journalist. Gibbs thought it was 'just like a huge ploughed field with stubble represented by the salt bush, and it is so dried up that the novelty of it is its only charm'.

The food was 'quite decent', Gibbs thought, but the wayside stops were 'not up to much . . . You would have laughed to see some of the quaint little settlements here and there across the desert. Of course, the train was the one event of the day, and the whole township turned up dressed in their best to gaze at us.'

Together with other passengers, Gibbs got out at one stop to take a stroll. But the driver forgot to blow the whistle and the train began pulling out. 'I never ran as fast in my life, and I nearly got left behind. The crowd just laughed, and the last we saw of them was entering their little hessian-covered huts, to await the next arrival.' A favourite railway prank, perhaps?

At another settlement along the line Gibbs was startled when a tall Aboriginal man suddenly popped his head into her compartment. He 'explained that he had just wandered in from the bush to have a squizz'.

The scenery between Port Augusta and Adelaide consisted of fields covered with creamy-looking grass, with hills in the background. Everybody rose at 4 a.m. to view the sunrise, and the sight was evidently an impressive one. 'From Port Augusta to Tarcoola the eye sees nothing but red-soil plains and undulating country . . . it filters in and covers everything with a fine film of dust.'

Gibbs was forthcoming with the fare and costs of her journey: 'The whole trip (single fare) costs £14 odd—a berth being 10/ extra. It is wise to buy 13/6 worth of food tickets for the transcontinental train, and £4 should be allowed for tips and incidentals.' In today's value, Gibbs's ticket cost over $1000 and her tips and incidentals up to $400.

'Oh yes, altogether I enjoyed it, and had a beautifully restful time,' the author concluded.

The following year, Gibbs returned to Perth where she later married. At that time she was described as fairly tall and dark-haired with an artistic face and a refined voice. Photographs of her suggest a slightly impish personality. She continued publishing children's stories and her lovable bush babies and not-so-lovable Banksia Men became established as iconic characters of Australian children's literature and nightmares.

As with so many others, her finances were destroyed by the Depression of the 1930s. Her husband died in 1939 and she lived on at Nutcote, her distinctive home in Neutral Bay, famous but alone apart from her dogs. She published further books for children, though none had the success of *Snugglepot and*

Cuddlepie or her cartoon strip, *Bib and Bub*, all still in print. Her achievements were recognised with the award of a Member of the British Empire and she died in 1969. Her legacy of art and writing is preserved in books and in Nutcote itself, now a museum of her work owned by the North Sydney Council and open to visitors.

A GLIMPSE INTO ETERNITY

Andrew Thomas retired from a 22-year career with the US National Aeronautics and Space Administration (NASA) in 2014. He was the first Australian-born astronaut to journey into space.

Growing up in Adelaide, Andrew was fascinated with space. He finished university with a PhD in mechanical engineering, never thinking that he might one day travel beyond the earth. But after taking American citizenship and years of preparation and training with NASA, he boarded the space shuttle *Endeavour* for its eleventh mission in 1996. He carried with him a piece of wood from Captain James Cook's famous HMS *Endeavour*.

During the voyage, the crew launched two satellites and carried out technical tests and scientific experiments. When the shuttle passed over Adelaide, the city turned on its lights to wink a welcome to its intrepid son as he glided far above them, taking 'a glimpse into eternity' as he later described the experience.

At least one South Australian back on Earth got to share in the moment. On 21 May, Mrs Frances Durdin of Port Elliot waited in the garden with her radio tuned for news of the shuttle. She was hoping for maybe just a glimpse of the orbiting spacecraft through the thick clouds hanging over the region. Just before 6 p.m.:

> 'I looked straight above my head where there was a clear patch of sky and saw the lights of the shuttle quite clearly as it travelled about halfway across the sky before disappearing into cloud to the north west,' she said. 'I was very thrilled to see it—I didn't expect to though because of the overcast conditions. I rang Dr Thomas's father in Hackham to tell him I'd seen the space shuttle and had prayed for his son and the mission. He had not been able

> to see the shuttle despite going to the beach and he was pleased that I had rung.'

Through more than 240 hours *Endeavour* orbited the earth 160 times at a height of 283 kilometres. By the time the shuttle touched down the flight had logged around six and a half million kilometres.

Andrew Thomas made further trips into space and each time took with him a memento of previous great Australian journeys, including a slide rule from Douglas Mawson's Antarctic expedition and the pilot wing insignia of Ross Smith, pilot of the first plane to fly from London to Australia within 30 days. On his 2001 trip he carried a fragment of the propeller of Charles Kingsford Smith's plane *Southern Cross*. In 1928 Kingsford Smith used this three-engined Fokker on the famous flight he made with Charles Ulm in the longest nonstop ocean flight made at that time.

In 1998, Thomas lived aboard the Russian *Mir* space station and in 2001 flew with the eighth shuttle mission. His last space journey was in 2005. Although retired from space travel, he has continued his involvement with space and promotes the possibilities of Australia as a base for space tourism.

Although Andrew Thomas was Australia's first trained astronaut into space, he was not the first Australian to get there. Oceanographer Paul D. Scully-Power flew a shuttle mission as a scientist ten years earlier. These two Australians were travellers at the beginning of humanity's most recent journey—to the stars.

CHAPTER NOTES AND SOURCES

1. ARRIVING

THE FIRST JOURNEY

Estimates of the length of Aboriginal occupation of Australia are controversial. Dates and ranges are continually revised, challenged and debated by researchers. This estimate is based on the most recent evidence and analysis. For a clear discussion of the complexities involved see <http://australianmuseum.net.au/the-spread-of-people-to-australia>.

FIRST ENCOUNTERS

Geoff Wharton, 'The Pennefather River: Place of Australian national heritage', in Royal Geographical Society of Queensland Inc., 'Gulf of Carpentaria Scientific Study Report', p. 35. See also James Henderson, *Sent Forth a Dove: Discovery of the Duyfken*, UWA Publishing, Nedlands, 1998.

A BOY TRANSPORTED

Home Office Convict Transportation Registers, 'Other Fleets and Ships 1791–1868'. Some sources say Tomlinson was aged just seven years. It is possible that Tomlinson was older than ten—perhaps thirteen—and that his age was lowered to elicit sympathy. He received none.

See <http://waves.anmm.gov.au/Immigration-Stories/Stories-from-our-collection/Christopher-Tomlinson.aspx>, accessed June 2016.

ALL HIS JOIFUL CREW

Marnie Bassett, *The Hentys: An Australian colonial tapestry*, Oxford University Press, London, 1954.

ABOUT 600,000 ACRES, MORE OR LESS

John Batman's journal was published in *The Age*, 28 October 1882, Melbourne, p. 1S.

GYPSY JOURNEYS

'The women stick to the old dress': *The Argus*, 26 May 1866, p. 4; from the *Orange Guardian*; 'The Greek people of Melbourne': *Advocate*, 15 October 1898, Melbourne, p. 16; James Jupp (ed.), *The Australian People*, Cambridge University Press, Melbourne, 2001, pp. 63–4.

TO AUSTRALIA BY SUBMARINE

'it is divided into eight compartments': Thomas Michael Jones, *Watchdogs of the Deep: Life in a submarine during the Great War*, Angus & Robertson, Sydney, 1935, pp. 7–8; Michael D. White, *Australian Submarines: A history*, AGPS, Canberra, 1992; *Mercury*, 19 January 1921, Hobart, p. 4; *Mercury*, 24 January 1921, Hobart, p. 4.

2. SURVIVING

WITHIN A FEW HOURS OF ETERNITY

'None can read the above account': *The Sydney Gazette and New South Wales Advertiser*, 28 June 1803, p. 4; David Levell, *Tour to Hell: Convict Australia's great escape myths*, University of Queensland Press, St Lucia, 2007; Anne-Maree Whitaker, *Unfinished Revolution: United Irishmen in New South Wales, 1800–1810*, Crossing Press, 1994.

UP, UP AND AWAY!

'I hailed the crowd in Hyde Park': *The Maitland Mercury* and *Hunter River General Advertiser*, 22 January 1859, Maitland, p. 3.

AFTER BURKE AND WILLS

Ian D. Clark and Fred Cahir (eds), *The Aboriginal Story of Burke and Wills: Lost narratives*, CSIRO Publishing, Canberra, 2013; Welch's journal is held by the State Library of New South Wales and his field book by the State Library of Victoria. In 2002 the National Library of Australia included some of Edwin Welch's collections in an exhibition titled 'From Melbourne to Myth', curated by historian Tim Bonyhady.

A DANGEROUS VISIT

'The dress of his Royal Highness was removed': *The Sydney Morning Herald*, 13 March 1868, Sydney, p. 5.

HARRY STOCKDALE'S LONG RIDE

'came suddenly upon a camp of natives': Harry Stockdale's journal of exploration in the far north-west of Australia, 1884–85, document no. A 1580, State Library of New South Wales, <http://acms.sl.nsw.gov.au/_transcript/2013/D21617/a8202.pdf> accessed May 2015.

ACROSS THE ICE

Mawson's account is in his *Home of the Blizzard*, first published in 1915 and reprinted in many editions since. There is an excellent recreation of his hut at the Mawson's Huts Replica Museum in Hobart, including archival material and artefacts. In 2015–16 archaeologists conducted excavations at Mawson's surprisingly well-preserved hut at Cape Denison, Commonwealth Bay, in Antarctica.

LIFEBOAT NO. 7

'Soon Britannia's forward hold filled': Ian McIntosh's account at <www.australiansatwar.gov.au/stories/stories_war=W2_id=248.html> accessed May 2015.

DUNERA BOYS

Ken Inglis, 'From Berlin to the Bush', *The Monthly*, August 2010; a 1985 TV mini-series popularised the collective name 'Dunera Boys'. The 75th anniversary of the event was celebrated with a number of commemorative activities in 2015.

3. DANGEROUS JOURNEYS

VOYAGE TO FREEDOM

'The Natives came down': Tim Causer (ed.), *Memorandoms of James Martin*, The Bentham Project, University College London Library Special Collections, London, 2014.

NED KELLY'S POOR DRIVING

'I did not bail up at first': *The Argus*, 12 December 1878, Melbourne, pp. 4, 5.

THE CAMELEER FACTOR

'we travelled to Ngoaaddapa': J.G. Hill (comp.) *The Calvert Scientific Exploring Expedition*, George Philip & Son, London and Liverpool, 1905; *'Anyone who has read the plain'*: *News*, 25 May 1933, Adelaide, p. 8.

WHEELS ACROSS THE WILDERNESS

'I have been a wanderer': *Australian Town and Country Journal*, 20 December 1906; *'Oh . . . I fancy the trip'*: *The West Australian*, 10 January 1907, p. 8; *'I have made my second attempt'*: *The Sydney*

Morning Herald, 6 March 1907, Sydney, p. 12; *'as one of the most important'*: *The Sydney Morning Herald*, 9 May 1907, Sydney, p. 3. Though he had changed bicycles and was now riding a Davies Franklin fitted with gears.

MRS BELL'S OLDSMOBILE

'Hundreds of stark naked natives': *Mirror*, 24 April 1926, Perth, p. 7; *'It speaks highly for Mrs Bell's'*: *News*, 2 March 1926, Adelaide, p. 9; *'Smartly clad in riding breeches'*: *The West Australian*, 8 April 1926, Perth, p. 10; Georgine Clarsen, *Eat My Dust: Early women motorists*, John Hopkins University Press, Baltimore, 2011.

THE SECRET ORDER OF THE DOUBLE SUNRISE

'It is an enormous flight non-stop': *The Sydney Morning Herald*, 5 August 1944, Sydney, p. 4; *It is said that the Double Sunrise Cats*: *ABC News*, 22 May 2015, <www.abc.net.au/news/2015-05-22/restored-flying-boat-takes-pride-of-place-at-qantas-museum/6488426> accessed September 2015.

THE REAL GREAT ESCAPE

Some sources say 54 men escaped; *'While we all hoped for the future'*: Paul Brickhill, *The Great Escape*, Faber & Faber, London, 1950; Paul Royle, interview, 2 December 2003, Imperial War Museum, London, catalogue no. 26605, <www.iwm.org.uk/collections/item/object/80024171> accessed May 2016.

A JENOLAN JOURNEY

'Of all the gambles': *The Sun-Herald*, 10 October 1954, Sydney, p. 31.

MANHUNT

The Citation (the newsletter of the Northern Territory Police Historical Society), vol. 3, no. 13, September 1998, pp. 7–8; Rosa Ellen, 'Incredible Feat of Tracking . . .', *ABC News*, 23 October 2015, <www.abc.net.au/news/2015-10-23/tracker-ted-finally-recognised-with-nt-police-valour-medal/6878610> accessed May 2016; Megan Dillon, 'Billy Benn's Journey from Hunted Outlaw to Celebrated Artist', *NT News*, 8 January 2014, <www.heraldsun.com.au/news/law-order/billy-benns-journey-from-hunted-outlaw-to-celebrated-artist/story-fni0fee2-1226796715886> accessed May 2016.

4. MYSTERIOUS JOURNEYS

LEICHHARDT'S RIFLE

'Some time around 1900': This is commonly referred to as 'Leichhardt's rifle', though it may have been a pistol. The National Museum of

Australia usually refers to the object on which the plate was reportedly found as a 'firearm'; *'There was also a story'*: Glenville Pike, 'Where Did Leichhardt Wander? A Theory of His Probable Route and Fate', paper presented to the Historical Society of Queensland, 25 August 1949, <http://espace.library.uq.edu.au/view/UQ:212573/s18378366_1949_4_2_271.pdf> accessed August 2015; there have been at least another eleven attempts to find Leichhardt since the first search parties went out, <www.nma.gov.au/audio/transcripts/leichhardt/NMA_panel_20070615.html>; according to the *Australian Dictionary of Biography* entry on the bushman Walter Smith, Joe Harding was involved in stealing horses, cattle and camels, sometimes known as 'tea and sugar bushranging'.

NAMING THE DESERT

'I said, "Well, can you shoe?"': Ernest Giles, *Australia Twice Traversed: The romance of exploration: Being a narrative compiled from the journals of five exploring expeditions into and through central South Australia, and Western Australia from 1872 to 1876*, S. Low, Marston, Searle & Rivington, London, 1889.

LASSETER'S FIRST FIND

Billy Marshall-Stoneking, *Lasseter: The making of a legend*, Allen & Unwin, Sydney, 1985; Fred Blakely, *Dream Millions: New light on Lasseter's lost reef*, Angus & Robertson, Sydney, 1972.

THE WARATAH MYSTERY

'I first noticed something peculiar': Board of Trade wreck report for 'Waratah', 1909; *In 1915, an Irish soldier*: *The Argus*, 19 August 1915, Melbourne, p. 9.

THE DIAMOND FLIGHT

Tony Barass, 'Captain Smirnoff and the $20m Diamond', *The Australian*, 3 March 2012, <www.theaustralian.com.au/news/nation/captain-smirnoff-and-the-20m-diamond-dogs-of-war/story-e6frg6nf-1226287780757> accessed October 2015; the author's personal correspondence. It is usually said that the same Zero returned to bomb the survivors. However, as these planes only carried two bombs, it must have been another Zero that attacked the second time.

TAMAN SHUD

Derek Abbott, 'On the Trail of the Somerton Man', *The Huffington Post*, 6 June 2015, <www.huffingtonpost.com/derek-abbott/on-the-trail-of-the-somer_b_7310672.html?ir=Australia> accessed October 2015; the most comprehensive set of sources is that compiled by

Professor Derek Abbott, Adelaide University at <www.eleceng.adelaide.edu.au/personal/dabbott/wiki/index.php/Primary_source_material_on_the_Taman_Shud_Case> accessed October 2015; see also G.M. Feltus, *The Unknown Man: A suspicious death at Somerton beach*, privately published, Greenacres, South Australia, 2010. Feltus investigated the case as a police officer and subsequently as a private investigator.

ROAMING GNOMES

Museum of Hoaxes <http://hoaxes.org/weblog/categories/category/Gnomes>; Graham Seal, *Great Australian Urban Myths*, 2nd edn., HarperCollins, Sydney, 2001, pp. 142–3; for more gnome journeys see <www.gardengnomesale.com/Gnome_Pranks>.

TIGGA'S TRAVELS

One of many treatments of the tale can be found at <www.bbc.co.uk/programmes/p02v3p16>; see also <www.facebook.com/armaghcatsprotection/timeline/>.

5. COMING AND GOING

PLATYPUS DREAMING

'The bark of some of the Eucalypti': Charles Darwin's New South Wales notebook, January 1836, p. 526, at <http://darwin-online.org.uk>.

MARCH TO NEW GOLD MOUNTAIN

Paul Jones, *Chinese Australian Journeys: Records on travel, migration and settlement, 1860–1975*, National Archives of Australia, Canberra, 2005, p. 14; 'The Walk from Robe', SBS (from the Golden Dragon Museum, Bendigo) <www.sbs.com.au/gold/story.php?storyid=57>; *The South Australian Register*, 31 January 1852, Adelaide, p. 3.

SPIDER WOMAN

'The full perfection of her frame': State Library of New South Wales <www.sl.nsw.gov.au/discover_collections/history_nation/gold/miners_life/montez/> accessed May 2016; Michael Cannon, 'Montez, Lola (1818–1861)', *Australian Dictionary of Biography*, National Centre of Biography, Australian National University, <http://adb.anu.edu.au/biography/montez-lola-4226/text6815>; *'There are few leaders of the newspaper'*: *New York Times*, 21 January 1861, New York City at <www.nytimes.com/1861/01/21/news/obituary-death-of-lola-montez.html?pagewanted=all> accessed August 2015.

BLACK LORDS OF SUMMER

'considered to be one of the hundred defining': 'Defining moments in Australian history', National Museum of Australia <www.nma.gov.au/online_features/defining_moments> accessed May 2016; *'After a game played at the Oval'*: *The Bendigo Advertiser*, 19 August 1868, Bendigo, p. 3; Ashley Mallet, *The Black Lords of Summer*, University of Queensland, St Lucia, 2002.

STEAMSHIP TO MELBOURNE

'We went below to see our future home': 'Journeys to Australia' Museum of Victoria <http://museumvictoria.com.au/discoverycentre/websites-mini/journeys-australia/> accessed May 2016; *Geelong Advertiser*, 17 November 1874, Geelong, p. 2; *The Argus*, 17 November 1874, Melbourne, p. 4.

THE MOST BEAUTIFUL LIES

Mark Twain, *Following the Equator* (also published as *More Tramps Abroad*), American Publishing Company, Hartford, 1897.

SONS OF EMPIRE

As Harry Leigh Pink, the Canadian writer of boys' own yarns, recollected in 1959, 'frontiersmen have always been found in the most unlikely places' <https://frontiersmenhistorian.wordpress.com/2015/06/22/> accessed May 2016; *'The younger son he's earned his bread'*: 'Stray Papers by a Private', *The Canadian Scottish*, Rosemount Press, Aberdeen, 1915, p. 34; Robert H. MacDonald, *The Language of Empire: Myths and metaphors of popular imperialism, 1880–1918*, Manchester University Press, Manchester, 1994.

THE GREAT WHITE FLEET

'Our allies, friends and brothers': *Freeman's Journal*, 6 August 1908, Sydney, p. 17.

THE MIGRANT LORD

The Advertiser, 26 May 1925, Adelaide, p. 17; Michael Roe, *Australia, Britain and Migration, 1915–1940: A study of desperate hopes*, Cambridge University Press, Cambridge, 2002; Lord and Lady Apsley, *The Amateur Settlers*, Hodder & Stoughton, London, 1926.

6. JOURNEYS OF THE HEART

THE LADY ON THE SAND

'I felt that its correct place': Louis de Freycinet, *Voyage Historique*, vol. I, p. 449; *'The de Vlamingh plate they retrieved'*: Marc Serge Rivière (trans. and ed.), *A Woman of Courage: The journal of Rose*

de Freycinet on her voyage around the world, 1817–1820, National Library of Australia, Canberra, 1996, pp. 51–2.

PLEADING THE BELLY

The Times, 18 October 1791, London, p. 3.

MY HEART IS STILL UNCHANGED

The Life and Adventures of John Nicol, Mariner, 1822, <https://archive.org/details/cihm_41947> accessed August 2015; Sarah was in fact transported for stealing a very large amount of clothing and material, probably from a shop. See Michael C. Flynn, *The Second Fleet: Britain's grim convict armada of 1790*, Library of Australian History, Sydney, 1993, p. 610.

FOOTSTEPS OF THE SAINT

Mary was a great letter writer and her writings are considered an important aspect of her life and legacy. They can be accessed through the official St Mary MacKillop website <www.marymackillop.org.au/>.

AN AUSTRALIAN LADY TRAVELS

Australian Town and Country Journal, 19 March 1892, Sydney, p. 35.

LES DARCY'S GIRL

'Darcy is always smiling': *Referee*, 7 February 1917, San Francisco, p. 8; '*Way down in the USA*': *'No, he would have been a farmer'*: Ruth Park, 'In Search of Les Darcy in America', part 1, at <www.darcy-niland.com.au/LesDarcy.html> accessed May 2015. See also *Sydney Sportsman*, 11 July 1917, Sydney, p. 7.

CAB ACROSS THE NULLARBOR

'The lady was large, very vocal': *The Cumberland Argus*, 14 September 1955, Parramatta, p. 1; *'Primarily I undertook the trip to collect'*: *Sunday Times*, 23 January 1955, Perth, pp. 1, 3.

A CRUSH OF CRABS

Watch the event on video at <https://vimeo.com/75370696>.

ON THE HIPPIE TRAIL

For an extended account of an Australian on the hippie trail in 1974 see 'A brief history of the hippie trail', <www.richardgregory.org.uk/history/hippie-trail.htm> accessed May 2016; Andrew Anthony, 'On the trail of the serpent: The fatal charm of Charles Sobhraj', *GQ* magazine, 11 April 2014, at <www.gq-magazine.co.uk/article/charles-sobhraj-serial-killer-interview> accessed May 2016.

DOING THE DOUGHNUT

<http://thegreynomads.com/>.

7. THE TRACK

THE ROAD WEST

'A Narrative of Proceedings of William Cox, Esq., of Clarendon . . . in the Years 1814 & 1815'. *Windsor and Richmond Gazette*, 31 July 1931, Windsor, p. 12.

ROADS TO RUIN

'Well we chucked our blooming swags': quoted in a story by A.B. Paterson, 'In No Man's Land', *The Chronicle*, 10 March 1900, Adelaide pp 35–6; *'I'm a broken-hearted shearer'*: *The Queenslander*, 13 October 1894, Brisbane, p. 692.

BY TRAIN TO HOBART TOWN

Launceston Examiner, 10 February 1876, Launceston, p. 4.

TRUDGING THROUGH PURGATORY

Henry Lawson, *While the Billy Boils*, Angus & Robertson, Sydney, 1896.

THE STARS FOR A LANTERN

'TRIPOS' (Jennacubbine) *Western Mail*, 13 May 1937, Perth, p. 10.

HARDSHIPS OF THE TRACK

The Braidwood Dispatch and *Mining Journal*, 21 April 1933, Braidwood, p. 1.

BACK OF THE MILKY WAY

North Queensland Register, 15 February 1926, p. 90, in 'On the Track' section.

KIANDRA TO KOSCIUSZKO

The Sydney Morning Herald, 31 January 1934, Sydney, p. 14.

A FORGOTTEN WAY

John Blay, *On Track: Searching out the Bundian Way*, NewSouth Publishing, Sydney, 2015. The Bundian Way was given New South Wales heritage listing in 2013.

8. WORKING WAYS

HURDY-GURDY GIRLS

'Those ubiquitous German girls with cracked voices': *Empire*, 19 November 1860, Sydney, p. 2; *'Tens of thousands of miners'*: *The Sydney Mail* and *New South Wales Advertiser*, 23 December 1893, Sydney, p. 1.

COBB & CO TO MELBOURNE

'Such a journey, on a 'Cobbs' coach': Douglas Sellick (ed.), *Venus in Transit: Australia's woman travellers 1788–1930*, Fremantle Arts Centre Press, Fremantle, 2003; Kurt Gänzl, 'Soldene, Emily (1838?–1912)', *Oxford Dictionary of National Biography*, Oxford University Press, Oxford, 2004.

ACROSS THE BORDER

Bendigo Advertiser, 5 November 1881, Bendigo, p. 1S.

WAY OF THE CHARLATAN

The La Trobe Journal, no. 28, October 1981, Melbourne, pp. 95–6.

RAZING THE RODNEY

'At the same moment his fireman': *Truth*, 2 September 1894, Sydney, p. 3; *The arsonists gave three cheers*: Dennis O'Keeffe, *Waltzing Matilda: The secret history of Australia's favourite song*, Allen & Unwin, Sydney, 2012.

THE MAGIC LANTERN MAN

Warren Fahey, Joe Watson: traditional singer, Australian Folklore Unit, Paddington, 1975.

TRAVELLING TEACHERS

Janet Campbell, '1901: The first year of Queensland's itinerant teaching service', *Memoirs of the Queensland Museum, Cultural Heritage Series*, vol. 2, part 2, 2002, p. 240; *Morning Bulletin*, 16 November 1936, Rockhampton, p. 5.

THE ROAD URCHIN

'I painted it up brightly': 'The Saw Doctor's Wagon', video recording, Culture Victoria <http://www.cv.vic.gov.au/stories/a-diverse-state/but-thats-another-story/the-saw-doctor-s-wagon/>; *'like a bowerbird's nest on wheels'*: Barking Spider Visual Theatre group, <http://barkingspidertheatre.com.au/big-objects-on-show>; 'Saw Doctor's Wagon', National Museum of Australia <www.nma.gov.au/exhibitions/hall/saw_doctors_wagon> accessed May 2016.

JUMPING THE RATTLERS

'He was a young Australian': *Daily Mercury*, 2 April 1932, Mackay, p. 2; *'came a terrible gutzer'*: *Daily Mercury*, 22 April 1925, Mackay, p. 2; *'What have you been doing'*: *The Newcastle Sun*, 27 August 1930, Newcastle, p. 8.

SYDNEY TO DARWIN ON A NINE-BOB PONY

Glen Innes Examiner, 12 July 1938, Glen Innes, p. 6; *'Miss Howard has had a variety'*: *Maryborough Chronicle*, 14 April 1939, Maryborough, Vic., p. 8; *'she went to Darwin and thence'*: *The Daily News*, 26 August 1940, Perth, p. 14.

FOREIGN FABLES

Graham Seal, *The Cane-Toad High: Great Australian urban myths*, HarperCollins, Sydney, 2001.

9. LEAVING

BY JUSTICE DOES SHE FLOAT

John Mulvaney, *The Axe Had Never Sounded: Place, people and heritage of Recherche Bay*, Tasmania, ANU Press, Canberra, 2007.

THE GREAT TREK

Grapevine, vol. 13, no. 3, September 2013; Noris Ioannou, *Barossa Journeys: Into a valley of tradition*, Paringa Press, Kent Town, South Australia, 1997.

THE LONGEST DROVE

Keith McKenzie, 'They Paved the Way: Australian pioneering stories', *Mudgee Guardian*, Mudgee, 1980.

THE LAST RIDE

Adam Lindsay Gordon, *Bush Ballads and Galloping Rhymes*, Clarson, Massina & Co, Melbourne, 1870.

NEW AUSTRALIA BOUND

'No doubt you think by this time': *The Queenslander*, 13 October 1894, Brisbane, p. 712; *'The excitement caused by Casey'*: *Brisbane Courier*, 9 July 1894, Brisbane, p. 3; *'shook the dust of Australian soil'*: *The Argus*, 25 January 1896, Melbourne, p. 6; *there are still descendants of the New Australians*: Laurence Blair, 'Nueva Londres: where Paraguay, Australia and Great Britain converge', *The Guardian*, 7 July 2015, <www.theguardian.com/world/2015/jul/06/nueva-londres-paraguay-australia-great-britain> accessed May 2016.

A SNOWBALL MARCH

The Farmer and Settler from October 1915 ran a regular feature reported by one of their journalists who travelled with the marchers under the title 'Coo-ees Column', <http://nla.gov.au/nla.news-title451> accessed August 2015.

MAY GIBBS TAKES THE TRANS

Birregurra Times, 27 August 1918, Birregurra, Vic., p. 2 (reprinted from the Sydney *Sun*), <http://nla.gov.au/nla.news-title760> accessed June 2016.

A GLIMPSE INTO ETERNITY

Times, 24 May 1996, Victor Harbour, South Australia, p. 11.

ACKNOWLEDGMENTS

Many people assisted with the making of this book. Thanks to Maureen Seal, Rob Willis, Olya Willis, Mark Gregory, Warren Fahey, and the friendly staff at Allen & Unwin.

PHOTO CREDITS

Page xiv: The Dutch trader *Duyfken*.

Page 22: Sir Douglas Mawson on the *Aurora*, circa 1911, courtesy of the State Library of Victoria

Page 50: Francis Birtles with his bicycle, Sydney, courtesy of the National Library of Australia

Page 80: The 1930 `CAGE' expedition led by Lasseter through Central Australian, courtesy the State Library of New South Wales

Page 104: A portrait of Lola Montez, courtesy of Getty Images

Page 123: Bea Miles on one of her taxi trips, by Harry Martin, courtesy of Fairfax Photos

Page 162: A swagman with his pack, Yass region, New South Wales, 1910, courtesy of the National Library of Australia

Page 188: The tinker, Harold Wright, and his daughter, Narrandera, New South Wales, 1953 by Jeff Carter, courtesy of the Estate of Jeff Carter and the National Library of Australia

Page 220: The commencement of a Coo-ees route march to Sydney, courtesy of the Australian War Memorial